Advances in Evidence-Based Policing

**Edited by Johannes Knutsson
and Lisa Tompson**

Routledge
Taylor & Francis Group

LONDON AND NEW YORK

First published 2017 by Routledge

2 Park Square, Milton Park, Abingdon, Oxfordshire OX14 4RN
52 Vanderbilt Avenue, New York, NY 10017

Routledge is an imprint of the Taylor & Francis Group, an informa business

First issued in paperback 2019

British Library Cataloguing-in-Publication Data
A catalogue record for this book is available from the British Library

Library of Congress Cataloging-in-Publication Data
Names: Knutsson, Johannes, 1947– editor. | Tompson, Lisa, editor.
Title: Advances in evidence based policing / edited by Johannes Knutsson and Lisa Tompson.
Description: Abingdon, Oxon ; New York, NY : Routledge, 2017. |
    Series: Crime science series ; 19 | Includes bibliographical references and index.
Identifiers: LCCN 2016052920 | ISBN 9781138698734 (hardback) |
    ISBN 9781315518299 (ebook)
Subjects: LCSH: Police. | Police administration.
Classification: LCC HV7921 .A425 2017 | DDC 363.2/3—dc23
LC record available at https://lccn.loc.gov/2016052920

ISBN: 978-1-138-69873-4 (hbk)
ISBN: 978-0-367-22665-7 (pbk)

Typeset in Times New Roman
by Apex CoVantage, LLC

Advances in Evidence-Based Policing

The evidence-based policing (EBP) movement has intensified in many countries around the world in recent years, resulting in a proliferation of policies and infrastructure to support such a transformation. This movement has come to be associated with particular methods of evaluation and systematic review, which have been drawn from what is assumed to prevail in medicine.

Given the credibility EBP is currently enjoying with both practitioners and government, it is timely to subject its underpinning logic to thoughtful scrutiny. This involves deliberating upon the meaning of evidence and what different models of knowledge accumulation and research methods have to offer in realising the aims of EBP. The communication and presentation of evidence to practitioner audiences is another important aspect of EBP, as are collaborative efforts to 'co-produce' new knowledge on police practice.

This is the first book that takes a kaleidoscopic approach to depict what EBP presently is and how it could develop. The chapters individually and collectively challenge the underlying logic to the mainstream EBP position, and the book concludes with an agenda for a more inclusive conceptualisation of evidence and EBP for the future. It is aimed at students and academics who are interested in being part of this movement, as well as policymakers and practitioners interested in integrating EBP principles into their practices.

Johannes Knutsson is Professor of Police Research at the Norwegian Police University College. He has been employed at the Swedish National Police Academy and the Swedish National Police Board. He has conducted studies with and for the police for 40 years. Among other publications he has co-edited several books on different aspects of policing – *Putting Theory to Work: Implementing situational prevention and problem-oriented policing* (with Ron Clarke), *Evaluating Crime Reduction Initiatives* (with Nick Tilley), *Police Use of Force: A global perspective* (with Joseph Kuhns), *Preventing Crowd Violence* (with Tamara Madensen) and *Applied Police Research: Challenges and opportunities* (with Ella Cockbain).

Lisa Tompson is a Lecturer at the UCL Department of Security and Crime Science. As a former police crime intelligence analyst, her work focuses on research which has immediate relevance and benefit to police and crime reduction agencies. She has recently worked on research that underpins the UK's What Works Centre for Crime Reduction, for which she and the team won a Chief Constable's commendation in 2015.

Crime Science Series
Edited by Richard Wortley, UCL

For a full list of titles in this series, please visit www.routledge.com

Crime science is a new way of thinking about and responding to the problem of crime in society. The distinctive nature of crime science is captured in the name.

First, crime science is about crime. Instead of the usual focus in criminology on the characteristics of the criminal offender, crime science is concerned with the characteristics of the criminal event. The analysis shifts from the distant causes of criminality – biological makeup, upbringing, social disadvantage and the like – to the near causes of crime. Crime scientists are interested in why, where, when and how particular crimes occur. They examine trends and patterns in crime in order to devise immediate and practical strategies to disrupt these patterns.

Second, crime science is about science. Many traditional responses to crime control are unsystematic, reactive and populist, too often based on untested assumptions about what works. In contrast crime science advocates an evidence-based, problem-solving approach to crime control. Adopting the scientific method, crime scientists collect data on crime, generate hypotheses about observed crime trends, devise interventions to respond to crime problems and test the adequacy of those interventions.

Crime science is utilitarian in its orientation and multidisciplinary in its foundations. Crime scientists actively engage with frontline criminal justice practitioners to reduce crime by making it more difficult for individuals to offend and making it more likely that they will be detected if they do offend. To achieve these objectives, crime science draws on disciplines from both the social and physical sciences, including criminology, sociology, psychology, geography, economics, architecture, industrial design, epidemiology, computer science, mathematics, engineering and biology.

Contents

Figures

Tables

Contributors

Dr Jyoti Belur qualified in Economics at the University of Mumbai where she worked as a lecturer before joining the Indian Police Service as a senior police officer. Currently she is Lecturer at the UCL Department of Security and Crime Science and is the programme director for the Masters in Policing. She has undertaken research for the UK Home Office, College of Policing, ESRC and the Metropolitan Police. Her research interests include countering terrorism, violence against women and children, crime prevention and police related topics such as ethics and misconduct, police deviance, use of force and investigations.

Kate Bowers is a Professor in Crime Science at the UCL Department of Security and Crime Science. She has worked in the field of crime science for over 20 years and has published 100 papers, books and book chapters in environmental criminology and crime science. Her most recent research has focused on developing advanced methods for crime analysis and prediction, improving the evidence base for crime prevention and using innovative data sets to answer crime and security questions.

Karen Bullock is Professor of Criminology in the Department of Sociology at the University of Surrey, Guildford, UK. She received her PhD from University College London in 2007. Karen's research interests are in the field of policing and crime prevention theory and practice, and she has published widely in these areas. Her most recent book, *Citizens, Community and Crime Control*, was published by Palgrave in 2014.

Jeffrey A. Butts is Director of the Research and Evaluation Center at John Jay College. His work focuses on policies and programs for at-risk and disconnected youth, especially those involved with the justice system. Previously, he was a research fellow with Chapin Hall at the University of Chicago and director of the Program on Youth Justice at the Urban Institute in Washington, DC. Jeff is a graduate of the University of Oregon and he earned his PhD from the University of Michigan.

Adam Crawford is Professor of Criminology and Criminal Justice at the University of Leeds, where he is Director of the Leeds Social Sciences Institute. He is Director of the N8 Policing Research Partnership, a collaboration between eight universities and twelve policing partners in the north of England (funded by Higher Education Funding Council for England [HEFCE]). Together with Joanna Shapland (University of Sheffield) he is researching the use of restorative policing funded by the College of Policing's Police Knowledge Fund. His research has focused on policing, community safety partnerships, restorative justice, youth crime and victims. Recent publications include *Legitimacy and Compliance in Criminal Justice* (Routledge 2013).

John E. Eck is Professor of Criminal Justice at the University of Cincinnati. His research focuses on high-crime places and what to do about them, as well as police crime control effectiveness. Eck is generally skeptical of all methodological enthusiasms. He spends much of his time in Maine, so he knows how to get to Mt. Katadin and would never confuse it with Meddybemps.

Elizabeth Eggins is a Research Fellow at the University of Queensland School of Social Science and Associate Fellow with the Australian Research Council Centre of Excellence for Children and Families over the Life Course. Her research interests focus on advancing evidence-based practice through robust quantitative research methodology specifically, and crime prevention more generally. She is co-author of a number of systematic reviews, is a co-developer of the Global Policing Database (GPD) and also manages the GPD compilation process.

Latifa T. Fletcher is pursuing her PhD in Human Development Psychology at City University of New York Graduate Center. Her research focuses on racial and ethnic identity development among Black individuals in the northeast region and how family cultural socialization shapes adult identity within communities of color. Latifa completed her BA in Psychology at Hobart and William Smith Colleges and her MA in Forensic Psychology at John Jay College. Previously she held research positions with the NYU Child Study Center and Doctors of the World-USA. Latifa was a Graduate Research Fellow with Evidence Generation from 2012–2014.

Angela Higginson is a Lecturer in the School of Justice, Faculty of Law, Queensland University of Technology. She holds a PhD in Criminology, a BA (Hons) in Psychology and a Graduate Certificate in Research Commercialisation. She previously worked as the Principal Advisor in the Department of Emergency Services. Angela's recent work focuses on policing and community processes for crime control, with a particular interest in the evaluation of policing practice through systematic reviews and meta-analysis. Much of her work is situated in a comparative framework and examines the contextual differences between the Global North and South.

Yuchen Hou is a doctoral student in Criminal Justice at John Jay College of Criminal Justice/ Graduate Center, City University of New York. Hou earned his master's degree in Procedural Law at People's Public Security University of China, after receiving his bachelor of laws in Criminal Investigation at National Police University of China in July 2012. Hou's research interests include comparative policing; multi- and mixed-method research design; and Asian Americans' involvement in the American criminal justice system as offenders, victims and criminal justice professionals.

Mike Hough is Professor of Criminal Policy in the School of Law, Birkbeck, University of London, and Associate Director of the Institute from Criminal Policy Research, which he set up in the 1990s.

Gillian Hunter is a Senior Research Fellow at the Institute for Criminal Policy Research, Birkbeck College. She is a lead researcher on the independent evaluation of the What Works Centre for Crime Reduction, hosted by the UK College of Policing. She has over 15 years' experience of conducting criminal policy research, including research on criminal justice interventions, such as arrest and court diversion schemes for vulnerable populations and community services for women offenders. More recently her research interests have focused on lay understanding of the criminal justice process and on victims', witnesses' and defendants' experiences of the criminal courts.

Shane D. Johnson is a Professor at the UCL Department of Security and Crime Science, University College London, England. He has a PhD and an MA in psychology and a BSc in computer science. Shane has published over 120 articles and book chapters and has particular interests in the spatial and temporal distribution of crime, complexity science and evaluation methods.

Johannes Knutsson is Professor of Police Research at the Norwegian Police University College. He has been employed at the Swedish National Police Academy and the Swedish National Police Board. He has conducted studies with and for the police for 40 years. Among other publications he has co-edited several books on different aspects of policing – *Putting Theory to Work. Implementing situational prevention and problem-oriented policing* (with Ron Clarke), *Evaluating Crime Reduction Initiatives* (with Nick Tilley), *Police Use of Force: A global perspective* (with Joseph Kuhns), *Preventing Crowd Violence* (with Tamara Madensen) and *Applied Police Research. Challenges and opportunities* (with Ella Cockbain).

Gloria Laycock has a BSc and PhD in Psychology from UCL. She established and headed the Police Research Group in the UK Home Office and was founding Director of the UCL Jill Dando Institute. She has carried out research and development in prisons, policing and crime prevention and has acted as a consultant and trainer on policing matters around the world. She is currently UCL Professor of Crime Science and is Director of research supporting the What Works Centre for Crime Reduction. She was awarded an Order of the British Empire (OBE) in the Queen's Birthday Honours 2008 for services to crime policy.

Mike Maxfield is Professor of Criminal Justice at John Jay College. He is the author of articles and books on a variety of topics – victimization, policing, homicide, community corrections, auto theft and long-term consequences of child abuse and neglect. He is the co-author (with Earl Babbie) of the textbook *Research Methods for Criminal Justice and Criminology*, now in its seventh edition. He served as editor of the *Journal of Research in Crime and Delinquency* from 2008–2016.

Tiggey May is a Senior Research Fellow at the Institute for Criminal Policy Research at Birkbeck, University of London. Throughout Tiggey's career she has focused on various aspects of policing; in her early career this involved examining the policing of sex and drug markets, pimps and young people. More recently, the policing of organised crime groups involved in fraud, community policing models across Europe, senior officer misconduct and the use of evidence-based policing among operational and senior officers. Tiggey's research interests include police legitimacy, police culture and the changing nature of policing in the twenty-first century.

Lorraine Mazerolle is an Australian Research Council Laureate Fellow (2010–2015) and a Professor in the School of Social Science at the University of Queensland. She is the Editor-in-Chief of the *Journal of Experimental Criminology*, past Chair of the American Society of Criminology's (ASC) Division of Experimental Criminology (2014–2015), an elected Fellow and past president of the Academy of Experimental Criminology (AEC) and elected fellow of the Academy of the Social Sciences, Australia. Professor Mazerolle is the winner of the 2013 AEC Joan McCord Award and the 2010 ASC Division of International Criminology Freda Adler Distinguished Scholar Award.

Julia Morris is the What Works Standards Manager at the College of Policing, currently leading on the development of evidence-based guidance and practice standards. Julia has been working in policing research for the last 13 years and prior roles include leading the research programme for the National Policing Improvement Agency, as well as various research roles in the Home Office, including co-investigator on the evaluation of the UK's National Reassurance Policing Programme. Julia has a background in organisational psychology and began her career working as a human factors consultant in the oil and gas industry.

Ken Pease is a Chartered Forensic Psychologist. He has held chairs at Manchester University and the University of Saskatchewan. His research interests remain diverse, from repeat crime victimisation to child pedestrian behaviour.

Bryce Peterson is a Research Associate in the Urban Institute's Justice Policy Center. He leads several projects funded by the National Institute of Justice, the National Institute of Corrections and the Bureau of Justice Assistance. His work focuses on research and evaluation of law enforcement and correctional interventions, including contraband and interdiction modalities in prisons and jails, children of incarcerated parents and treatment programs. He received his PhD in Criminal Justice from John Jay College/The Graduate Center, City University of New York. He was a Graduate Research Fellow with Evidence Generation from 2012–2013.

Jennifer M. Pipitone is a doctoral candidate in Environmental Psychology at the Graduate Center of the City University of New York and a Visiting Instructor at Pratt Institute in Brooklyn. Her research explores the human–environment relationship through experiential education, focusing on faculty-led study abroad programs. In 2015, Jennifer co-founded Narrating NYC (narrating-nyc.org), a community-based participatory action research project that aims to foster urban youth's sense of agency and ownership over the communities to which they belong through photography and storytelling. Jennifer was a Graduate Research Fellow with Evidence Generation from 2012–2014.

Jason Roach is a Reader in Psychology, Crime and Policing and the Associate Director for the Applied Criminology Centre, University of Huddersfield, which undertakes a broad range of criminological and psychological research for UK police forces. His research interests are in criminological and forensic psychology, where he has published work on topics such as evolutionary psychology and crime, criminal investigative practice, police decision-making, behavioural analysis, terrorism, violence, homicide and child murder. His latest book, *Self-Selection Policing: Research, Theory and Practice*, is co-authored with Ken Pease.

Michael S. Scott is Clinical Professor at Arizona State University's School of Criminology & Criminal Justice and director of the Center for Problem-Oriented Policing. He was a clinical professor, University of Wisconsin Law School; chief of police, Lauderhill, Florida; special assistant to the police chief, St. Louis, Missouri Metropolitan Police Department; director of administration, Fort Pierce, Florida Police Department; senior researcher, Police Executive Research Forum, Washington, DC; legal assistant to the police commissioner; New York City Police Department; and police officer, Madison, Wisconsin Police Department. In 1996, he received Police Executive Research Forum's (PERF's) Gary P. Hayes Award for innovation and leadership in policing.

Aiden Sidebottom is a Senior Lecturer in the Department of Security and Crime Science at University College London. His research interests are situational crime prevention, problem-oriented policing and programme evaluation. Recent research has focused on methods of synthesising research evidence to support crime prevention policy and practice, undertaken in collaboration with the UK College of Policing. He is the co-editor of the Routledge *Handbook of Crime Prevention and Community Safety* (2017).

Betsy Stanko, OBE, is the former (retired) Head of Evidence and Insight, Mayor's Office for Policing and Crime in London; an emeritus professor at Royal Holloway; a Fellow of the Royal Society of the Arts; a Visiting Professor in the Department of Crime Science and Security at UCL; and a Visiting Professor in the Sociology Department, City University. She has been awarded a number of lifetime academic achievement awards, notably the American Society of Criminology's Vollmer Award (1996), recognising outstanding influence on criminal justice practice.

Nick Tilley is a Professor in the UCL Department of Security and Crime Science, Emeritus Professor of Sociology at Nottingham Trent University and an adjunct Professor at the Griffith Criminology Institute in Brisbane. He has long-term interests in theoretically informed applied social science. Recent research projects have focused on the international crime drop, the use of evidence to inform policing and crime prevention and sexual violence and abuse.

Lisa Tompson is a Lecturer at the UCL Department of Security and Crime Science. As a former police crime intelligence analyst, her work focuses on research which has immediate relevance and benefit to the police and crime reduction agencies. She has recently worked on research that underpins the What Works Centre for Crime Reduction, for which she and the team won a Chief Constable's commendation in 2015.

Rachel Tuffin previously led research teams in the Home Office. She has published studies on issues ranging from neighbourhood policing and leadership, to race hate and flexible working. Rachel has been seconded to several national police reviews and was sent to Macedonia to co-ordinate evacuation of refugees from Kosovo. Before starting work as a researcher in a university in 1995, she worked in France as a trainer, interpreter and course director. Her OBE was awarded in 2013 for championing evidence-based policing.

Series editor's foreword

This latest book in the Crime Science series is very much a logical follow-on to Ella Cockbain and Johannes Knutsson's 2015 *Applied Police Research: Challenges and opportunities*. That book guided researchers through the process of building productive relationships with police forces in order to position themselves to carry out research that is ultimately useful to police. This current book, *Advances in Evidence-Based Policing* by Johannes Knutsson and Lisa Tompson, examines the fundamental question of just what is 'useful' police research and how it can be used to inform policy and practice.

At first blush, the proposal to base police policy and practice on accumulated research evidence seems so self-evidently sensible as to be beyond serious dispute. Who – least of all those aspiring to the title of scientist – could possibly question the crucial role that research evidence should have in police decision-making? But as this book shows, evidence-based policing is a much more complex and contentious concept than it first appears. The devil is in the detail.

This book, then, does not present an uncritical eulogy to evidence-based policing; rather, it puts the concept under the microscope. Knutsson and Tompson have brought together an outstanding international cast of policing scholars who examine the adequacy of evidence-based policing from various theoretical and practical perspectives. Fundamental questions are raised about the validity of applying an evidence-based model developed in medicine to social problems such as those encountered by police. At the heart of this critique is the issue of the generalizability of police research findings: that is to say, to what extent can evidence gathered in one policing circumstance be effectively applied in another?

Although the book offers challenges to the concept of evidence-based policing, it is also constructive in its approach and optimistic in tone. The chapters take us through ways of thinking about the use of evidence that go beyond the mechanistic replication of policing strategies across disparate policing contexts. There are lessons in this book not just for police and policing scholars, but for all those with an interest in crime prevention who are grappling with the issue of translating research into practice.

Richard Wortley
Crime Science Series Editor
UCL Jill Dando Institute of Security and Crime Science
London, October 2016

Foreword

It appears that policing is at a critical juncture in history. Across Europe, Australasia and parts of North (and South) America, the evidence-based policing (EBP) movement is gaining purchase. As with all new philosophies, it is important that EBP not be accepted uncritically, but that its conceptualisation and underlying assumptions be carefully deliberated. To encourage the further advancement of EBP, we invited a group of leading experts to contribute their expertise on specific topics to this book. In May 2016, we hosted a conference at the Police Center for Training and Practice in Kongsvinger, Norway. Here, our contributors presented their papers to their peers for in-depth discussions and debate. We thank all participants for their insightful and constructive comments on each other's drafts. We are delighted to present the revised and refined final papers in the chapters that follow.[1] We are extremely grateful to Gloria Laycock and Nick Tilley, both of whom have made invaluable inputs throughout the entire process of producing this book. We would also like to express our gratitude to the staff at the center who made everyone's stay so enjoyable. Finally, we are indebted to Director Nina Skarpenes at the Norwegian Police University College for wholeheartedly supporting the project from the inception of this book to its completion.

Johannes Knutsson
Norwegian Police University College
Lisa Tompson
University College London

Note

1 This publication was co-funded by the Norwegian Police University College, the UK College of Policing and the Economic and Social Research Council (ESRC); Grant title: 'University Consortium for Evidence-Based Crime Reduction'. Grant Ref: ES/ L007223/1.

1   Introduction

Johannes Knutsson and Lisa Tompson

The momentum of the *evidence-based policing* (EBP) movement has intensified in many countries around the world in recent years, resulting in a proliferation of policies and infrastructure to support such a sea change. So what is it about this moment in policing history that makes EBP such an attractive guiding philosophy? And second, to what extent does EBP actually bring novel and practically useful insights in support of more effective policing?

Given the credibility EBP is currently enjoying with both practitioners and government, it is timely to subject its underpinning logic to thoughtful scrutiny. This involves deliberating upon the meaning of evidence and what different models of knowledge accumulation and research methods have to offer in realising the aims of EBP. The communication and presentation of evidence to practitioner audiences are also important aspects of EBP, as are collaborative efforts to 'co-produce' new knowledge on police practice. This is the first book that takes a kaleidoscopic approach to depict what EBP is now and how it could develop. It is aimed at students and academics who are interested in being part of this movement, as well as policymakers and practitioners interested in integrating EBP principles into their practices.

Presently the stars have aligned to support the transition to EBP, encouraged by actors across many different fields of interest, including, but not limited to, scholars, policymakers, governments and practitioners (Sherman, 2013). A critical mass of voices in support of the notion that policing practices need to be rooted in an evidence base has thus been reached.

The forces leading to this tipping point come from several directions. A recurrent theme is a political fixation on the efficiency and effectiveness of public services, which becomes especially acute in times of austerity. Evidence-based practice has percolated from other fields and policy areas, where it has been used to justify public spending decisions and to reassure funders that their returns on investment are being maximised. Hence EBP is part of a wider movement in what might be dubbed the 'era of evidence'.

Contemporaneously, the context in which the police operate has changed rapidly in the twenty-first century (Mawby and Wright, 2008). Revolutions in technology and communication have transformed social interaction and, as a natural consequence, offending and victimisation. In many places communities have become more diverse and, accordingly, the needs of the public, and their expectations of the police, have become more personalised and nuanced. Both social life and crime have thus become more multifaceted.

The complexity of modern problems, such as counterterrorism, human trafficking, child sex abuse and cybercrime, places a heavy demand on the police (Loader and Mulcahy, 2003). In times of drastically reduced public spending, overtime budgets cannot be depended on to produce the resources needed to deal with such demands. Instead, responding to these crime types requires staff with specialist skills who are able to use their knowledge judiciously. Such personnel are presently in short supply in many police services.

Other aspects of policing are similarly ill equipped to deal with this contemporary reality. For example, command-and-control structures have served policing sufficiently in the twentieth century, but are no longer up to navigating the complexity of social problems that generate crime, and are suboptimal for the organisational flexibility that is required to deal with them (Herrington and Colvin, 2015). Traditional hierarchical police management styles have led to a system where accountability for decisions falls upon senior managers, whereas frontline staff are expected to comply with procedures rather than think. In part, this explains why the training of frontline staff has, until recently, emphasised procedural knowledge over critical thinking skills and codified evidence.

Relatedly, in response to high-profile scandals and mistakes involving police officer decision-making, government-led reforms in democratic countries have sought to standardise police procedure both within and between agencies over recent decades. Such prescriptive processes have removed the scope for police discretion and may have contributed to the 'deskilling' of officers (Heslop, 2011) and promoted a culture of risk aversion (Flanagan, 2008).

In brief, then, expectations on the roles and responsibilities of the police service have been escalating at the same time that fiscal constraints have severely restricted the resources that are available to adequately respond to these demands. New and more imaginative ways of working are thus sorely needed (Laycock, 2014). For many, professionalisation is the solution to these issues,[1] with the ambition of transforming police officers and staff into reflective and enquiring practitioners who can be trusted to make discretionary decisions and spend public money wisely.

Although the police may be a service that often acts professionally, it is not, presently, a professional service (Neyroud, 2011). Amongst others, Kennedy (2015) has lucidly argued that policing bears none of the hallmarks of a profession. That is, the police service does not currently have the means of educating practitioners to think systematically about police practices. It similarly does not expect or support continual professional development that relates to research evidence. And, crucially, it does not assess performance against standards established or supported by research.

So what is required to induce such a transformation to a police profession? Reviewing the traditional professions – medicine and law – reveals a number of defining features. Both require extensive training to enter, both have a codified set of research evidence from which all professional practice and knowledge is drawn, both are regulated by codes of ethics and national professional bodies (in the UK at least) and both expect members to actively develop the evidence base on which their profession is founded. In recent decades a number of occupations, such as dentistry, nursing, engineering, architecture and accountancy, have gained the status of professions in some countries by adopting these defining features.

Evidence and knowledge are tightly bound into notions of being a profession. Autonomous practitioners making discretionary decisions need to be well versed in what is known about multiple practice areas and what action is best to take in varying circumstances. Different role specialisations require different sorts of knowledge, at different levels within an organisation, for tactical and strategic decision-making. Arguably, transforming policing into a profession would increase the 'appetite' or 'demand' for evidence and thus be the necessary precursor to police officers welcoming research evidence into their decision-making (Kennedy, 2015).

The professionalisation of police education has been part of a general trend in Europe and other parts of the world for some time, albeit with varying results. This has involved developing closer ties with universities, as well as developments in police education organisations, such as the Police University Colleges in Norway and Finland, and the Police University in Germany. In the UK, to bring the police service in line with other public service professions, graduate entry is to be phased in. The situation in the United States is more complex given its fragmented policing systems.

The movement in support of EBP has been supported and partly shaped by practitioners at the grassroots level. Since 2010 dedicated professional societies have been established, largely by police officers, in the UK, the United States, Canada, Australia and New Zealand. Centres supporting collaborations between practitioners and academics have been created in universities and research institutions across many westernised democracies. Funding streams have opened up to nurture the development of personal and professional networks that straddle both the supply and demand of research evidence.

From all of this it would seem that we are currently living within a unique era of policing – where the early adopters of a new philosophy are proliferating and collectively are aiming for a paradigm shift towards a new style of policing (Sherman, 2015). This is why it is timely to look carefully at what EBP is and might become so that the movement takes directions that most benefit the police service and the public served by the police.

Reflections on the journey so far

Although the term EBP was coined in the late 1990s, the idea that police should utilise research evidence when conducting their business, and that research should be a cooperative effort by researchers and police, has a long history. Early studies like the *Kansas City Preventive Patrol Experiment* (Kelling et al., 1974) and the *Newark Foot Patrol Experiment* (Police Foundation, 1981) nowadays have an iconic status, although their influence has perhaps shaped debates on how the police *should* operate, rather than on actual policing itself. As the titles indicate, both were experiments, although they did not include randomised allocation to experimental and control groups. Instead they followed quasi-experimental designs. The combined message, if taken on its face value, is to decrease random preventive car patrol and to increase targeted foot patrol. Even if there has been a repeated strong political demand for this to happen, often with references to these studies, police organisations find it difficult to act on the evidence provided by the studies (see e.g. Mclean and Hillier, 2011; Holgersson and Knutsson, 2012).

These studies were published by the US Police Foundation, established in 1970. Its mission was – and still is – to support policing through research, often in the form of social experiments. In the organisation's own words:

> its leadership has insisted that the organization's work have a practical impact on policing, that the knowledge gained through empirical investigation be such that it could be applied outside the "laboratory," with the end result being improvement in the way that police do their work.
>
> (www.policefoundation.org/about)

Partly by using some of these early studies to support his arguments, in the late 1970s, Herman Goldstein formulated an evidence-based policing model (Goldstein, 1979). In this, he drew on research evidence to challenge the efficacy of three core functions of the dominant 'professional' policing model[2] – preventive patrol, rapid response and solving crimes to catch offenders (Kelling et al., 1974; Greenwood and Petersilia, 1975; Pate et al., 1976). In essence Goldstein's (1979) proposed philosophy of problem-oriented policing offered a roadmap for the police to leave a reactive mode of policing and enter a proactive preventive mode.

It was not just in United States that practical police research began to be conducted in the 1970s. It was also supported in UK, for example, by various groups in the British Home Office (the Home Office Research Unit, the Crime Prevention Unit and later the Police Research Group) and in Sweden by the Swedish National Council for Crime Prevention where evaluation studies were included among their work programmes (see e.g. for the UK Forrester, Chatterton and Pease, 1988, and for Sweden Kühlhorn, 1978 and Knutsson, 1984).

Thus, the idea that applied police research – research for and with the police (Cockbain and Knutsson, 2015) – should provide evidence for the police is nothing new. The novelty of the first incarnation of EBP was the proposed standard of what was to be judged useful and reliable evidence, how it should be generated and how it should be systematised and made available to the police.

It was with this in mind that the term EBP first appeared in a report from the Police Foundation (Sherman, 1998). This drew heavily upon experience in medical science and argued that the research designs commonly used in medicine should be used as the quality yardstick for policing research. Central to this is the notion that randomised controlled trials (RCTs) generate the strongest evidence for forming an evidence base on policing. This idea has later been forcefully championed by other proponents of EBP (e.g. Weisburd and Neyroud, 2011).

The parallel organisation to the Cochrane Collaboration for medicine – the Campbell Collaboration – was founded with the express purpose of producing systematic reviews in social policy, thereby developing an evidence base for practice. The reviews emanating from this organisation commonly aspire to the conventions of the Cochrane collaboration, that is, to (ideally) meta-analyse RCTs to arrive at reliable judgements of the effectiveness of different interventions or policing practices. The overarching intent is to synthesise and summarise the evidence base on a topic so that it is readily available to inform decision-making in policy and practice. The Campbell Collaboration systematic reviews on police issues are, to a large extent, populated by quantitative studies of effectiveness, albeit only those fulfilling the inclusion criterions: RCTs or quasi-experimental designs with controls.

However, just as in medicine (Greenhalgh, 2014), the popularity of RCTs as a gold standard is waning in several scholarly communities. Sampson (2010) rejects the gold standard notion and argues that observational studies can produce strong evidence in the service of policy decisions. Tilley (2006, 2009) questions the feasibility, suitability and utility of RCTs to determine 'what works'. Another line of criticism deals with the differences between the medical and policing professions (Kennedy, 2015), and that it is inappropriate that policing should aspire to ape the medical model – as Bradley and Nixon (2009) evocatively state, 'arrests are not like aspirins'. Among other things Sparrow (2011) argues that police, when making reforms and introducing new practices, usefully draw on other sources of knowledge.

An example supporting Sparrow's argument is white papers or committee reports that might come in the wake of major police failures and that stimulate reforms of policing. For example, following failure to take charge of riots or to police them in an acceptable manner, politically appointed committees might investigate the event aiming to establish in what ways police failed and propose reforms to overcome flaws in practice. The reports include retrospective studies and analyses of the occurrences and recommendations of how improvements can come about (see SOU, 2002 or HMIC, 2009, 2011). This process can be looked upon as an evidence-based mechanism to induce enhancements of policing, but is not recognised within the archetypal EBP framework.

The fundamental problem with the original EBP proclamation is that it has become synonymous with experimental research designs to the exclusion of all others (Sparrow, 2016). RCTs can be extremely useful designs for generating evidence, but, like all methods, they are not infallible (see Tilley, 2016). As prominent policing scholars note, many activities that are central to the police function are simply not amenable to strict experimental design evaluations (Laycock, 2012; Greene, 2014). Furthermore, evidence syntheses, which are popular with evidence-hungry – but busy – policymakers and practitioners, use strict inclusion criteria, which serve as 'filters' for what counts as reliable evidence. Such criteria typically render nonexperimental studies as ineligible for synthesis, which devalues and excludes a large portion of valuable systematised knowledge on core police practice. Given this, the evidence base on which practitioners are currently supposed to draw from has some significant gaps.

A case in point is the Campbell Collaboration study of problem-oriented policing. After a wide search, producing more than 5,000 possible studies, the screening process produced 406 records that related to problem-oriented policing. Of these, just ten fulfilled the inclusion criterion; four were RCTs and six were quasi-experiments (Weisburd et al., 2010). This attrition rate implies there is a wider body of evidence that does not make it through the 'quality' filter, but that might contain valuable insights into how problem-oriented policing operates on the ground.

In brief, the original EBP concept has come to be identified with a restricted view of what research designs are capable of producing evidence strong enough for the police to act on. The central thrust of this book is that by broadening this view, EBP will be able to service the police more effectively with research-based evidence, ultimately for the improvement of policing. We thus wish to liberate EBP from the 'tyranny of method' (Bernstein, 1983: xi) that has characterised EBP to date and believe that, to borrow from Herrington (2016: 14), the 'conscious uncoupling' of RCTs from evidence can advance how we understand the evidence needs of practitioners and how best to serve them. Hence the title of the book – *Advances in Evidence-Based Policing*. Our hope is that this book will propel EBP into the next phase of its evolution by deliberating different understandings of what constitutes evidence and modes of conducting EBP.

Most contributors to the book have long-standing records of conducting applied police research. Several have, in various positions, been employees of police organisations. Their rich experiences wash through the following contributions.

The chapters in the book are grouped according to theme. Following Chapter 1 – the introduction – Chapters 2, 3 and 4 introduce EBP and appraise its underlying philosophy and logic. This involves an incisive discussion on questions such as: What is accepted as evidence and how is it generated? What are the similarities and differences between two dominant approaches that speak to EBP? How can research evidence be useful and generalizable to other settings than where produced?

The second theme (Chapters 5, 6, 7 and 8) concerns evidence generation and dissemination. Chapters 5 and 6 propose alternative research methods to elicit practice-based knowledge from practitioners and to systematise it into evidence. Chapters 7 and 8 describe sources of evidence that are available to practitioners, with a particular emphasis on evidence warehouses. Chapter 7 is prospective, in that it focuses on how evidence syntheses can be made more useful for practitioners in the future by emphasising different aspects of interventions. In contrast, Chapter 8 is more retrospective, examining the existing evidence base in policing using conventional EBP definitions of evidence quality.

The next set (Chapters 9 and 10) discuss the difficulties encountered when trying to inject evidence into police practice. These collectively expose the distance between the optimism of the early adopters of EBP and what the reality is at the coalface of policing.

The penultimate theme (covered in Chapters 11 and 12) illustrates collaborative enterprises between the police and academia. These expose the barriers to working in partnership and provide direction for increasing and sustaining coalitions across both communities, resulting in a mutually constructive relationship, with the ultimate aim of generating useful knowledge that they have actively contributed to producing.

The last chapter (Chapter 13) draws conclusions from the contributions and makes a case for a new realist EBP agenda.

Notes

1 For example, see the Chair of the UK College of Policing's press release: www.college. police.uk/News/College-news/Pages/College-of-Policing-chair.aspx
2 The 'professional' model was introduced during the 1930s and 1940s and has become a dominant model in many countries. It focuses on 'crime fighting' with strong reliance on preventive patrol and rapid response to achieve the outcome: crime control (see e.g. Kelling and Moore, 1988).

References

Bernstein, R.J. (1983). *Beyond Objectivism and Relativism: Science, Hermeneutics, and Praxis*, Philadelphia: University of Pennsylvania Press.

Bradley, D. and Nixon, C. (2009). 'Ending the "dialogue of the deaf": Evidence and policing policies and practices. An Australian case study', *Police Practice and Research*, 10(5/6): 423–35.

Cockbain, E. and Knutsson, J. (2015). 'Introduction', in E. Cockbain and J. Knutsson (eds) *Applied Police Research*, Abingdon, Oxon: Routledge.

Flanagan, R. (2008). *The Review of Policing: Final Report*, London: HMIC.

Forrester, D., Chatterton, M. and Pease, K. (1988). *The Kirkholt Burglary Prevention Project, Rochdale*, Crime Prevention Unit: Paper 13, London: Home Office.

Goldstein, H. (1979). 'Improving policing: A problem-oriented approach', *Crime & Delinquency*, 25(2): 236–58.

Greene, J.R. (2014). 'The upside and downside of the 'police science' epistemic community', *Policing*, (8)4: 379–92.

Greenhalgh, T. (2014). 'Evidence based medicine: A movement in crisis?', *BMJ*, 348: g3725, doi: 10.1136/bmj.g3725 (Published 13 June 2014).

Greenwood, P.W. and Petersilia, J.R. (1975). *The Criminal Investigation Process. Volume I: Summary and Policy Implications*, Santa Monica, CA: Rand Corporation.

Herrington, V. (2016). 'The importance of evidence based policing for the thinking professional police officer', *POLICE SCIENCE, Australia & New Zealand Journal of Evidence based Policing*, 1(1): 13–18.

Herrington, V. and Colvin, A. (2015). 'Police leadership for complex times', *Policing*, 10(1): 7–16.

Heslop, R. (2011). 'The British police service: Professionalization or 'McDonaldization?', *International Journal of Police Science & Management*, 13(4): 312–21.

HMIC. (2009). *Adapting to Protest: Nurturing the British Model of Policing*, London: Her Majesty's Chief Inspector of Constabulary. Retrieved from www.hmic.gov.uk/Site CollectionDocuments/Individually%20Referenced/PPR_20091125.pdf (accessed 30 June 2010).

HMIC. (2011). *Policing Public Order*, London: Her Majesty's Chief Inspector of Constabulary.

Holgersson, S. and Knutsson, J. (2012). *Hva gjør egentlig politiet?* [What do the police actually do?], PHS-Forskning 2012:4, Oslo: Politihøgskolen.

Kelling, G. and Moore, M.H. (1988). *The Evolving Strategy of Policing*, Perspectives on Policing, no. 4, U.S. National Institute of Justice, John F. Kennedy School of Government, Cambridge, MA: Harvard University.

Kelling, G., Pate, A., Dieckman, D. and Brown, C.E. (1974). *The Kansas City Preventive Patrol Experiment*, Washington, DC: Police Foundation.

Kennedy, D. (2015). 'Working in the Field: Police Research in Theory and in Practice', in E. Cockbain and J. Knutsson (eds) *Applied Police Research: Challenges and Opportunities*, pp. 9–20, London: Routledge.

Knutsson, J. (1984). *Operation Identification – a Way to Prevent Burglaries?* The National Swedish Council for Crime Prevention, Stockholm: Liber förlag.

Kühlhorn, E. (1978). *Deprivation of Freedom and the Police – an Evaluation of the Temporary Custody Act*, National Swedish Council for Crime Prevention, Stockholm: Liber förlag.

Laycock, G. (2012). 'Happy Birthday?', *Policing*, 6(2): 101–7.

Laycock, G. (2014). 'Crime science and policing: Lessons of translation', *Policing*, 8(4), 393–401. Retrieved from http://doi.org/10.1093/police/pau028

Loader, I. and Mulcahy, A. (2003). *Policing and the Condition of England: Memory, Politics and Culture*, Oxford: Oxford University Press.

Mawby, R.C. and Wright, A. (2008). 'The Police Organisation', in T. Newburn (ed) *Handbook of Policing*, 2nd edition, pp. 224–52, Uffculme: Willan.

Mclean, F. and Hillier, J. (2011). *An Observational Study of Response and Neighbourhood Officers*, National Policing Improvement Agency. Retrieved from www.npia.police.uk/en/18155.htm

Neyroud, P. (2011). *Review of Police Leadership and Training*, London: HMSO.

Pate, A. (1981). *Newark Foot Patrol Experiment*, Washington, DC: Police Foundation.

Pate, T., Ferrara, A., Bowers, R.A. and Lorence, J. (1976). *Police Response Time: Its Determinants and Effects*, Washington, DC: Police Foundation.

Sampson, R.J. (2010). 'Gold standard myths: Observations on the experimental turn in quantitative criminology', *Journal of Quantitative Criminology*, 25, 489–500.

Sherman, L.W. (1998). *Evidence Based Policing*, Washington, DC: Police Foundation.

Sherman, L.W. (2013). 'The rise of evidence-based policing: Targeting, testing, and tracking', *Crime and Justice*, 42(1): 377–451.

Sherman, L.W. (2015). 'A tipping point for "totally evidenced policing"', *International Criminal Justice Review*, 25(1): 11–29.

SOU. (2002). *Göteborg 2001. Betänkande från Göteborgskommittén*, [Gothenburg 2001. Report from the Gothenburg committee], Statens offentliga utredningar, 2002:122, Stockholm: Fritzes förlag.

Sparrow, M. (2011). *Governing Science*, Paper of the Harvard Executive Session on Policing and Public Safety 2010, Washington, DC: National Institute of Justice.

Sparrow, M. (2016). *Handcuffed: What Holds Policing Back, and the Keys to Reform*, Washington, DC: Brookings Institution Press.

Tilley, N. (2006). 'Knowing and Doing: Guidance and Good Practice in Crime Prevention', in J. Knutsson and R.V. Clarke (eds) *Putting Theory to Work: Implementing Situational Prevention and Problem-Oriented Policing*, Crime Prevention Studies, vol. 20, pp. 217–252, Monsey, NY: Criminal Justice Press.

Tilley, N. (2009). 'Sherman vs Sherman: Realism vs rhetoric', *Criminology & Criminal Justice*, 9(2): 135–44.

Tilley, N. (2016). 'EMMIE and engineering: What works as evidence to improve decisions?', *Evaluation*, 22(3): 304–22.

Weisburd, D. and Neyroud, P. (2011). *Police Science: Toward a New Paradigm*, Paper of the Harvard Executive Session on Policing and Public Safety 2010, Washington, DC: National Institute of Justice.

Weisburd, D., Telep, C.W., Hinkle, J.C. and Eck, J.E. (2010). *The Effects of Problem-Oriented Policing on Crime and Disorder*, Crime Prevention Research Review, no. 4, Washington, DC: US Department of Justice, Office of Community Oriented Policing Services.

2 The why, what, when and how of evidence-based policing

Nick Tilley and Gloria Laycock

In this chapter we consider the why, what, when and how of 'evidence-based policing'. We draw parallels with other fields where the use of evidence has been crucial to their success, most notably medicine and engineering. In the first section we review why we need to make more use of evidence in policing. In the second section we outline several differing kinds of evidence that have a role to play, making the point that the evidence which is now being emphasised is not 'injected' into an evidence vacuum. In the third section we go on to discuss when and how evidence of different kinds can be most usefully injected into policing, and we conclude with a section summarising the arguments of the paper.

Why should we adopt evidence-based policing?

The rationale for evidence-based policing is similar to that for evidence-based medicine or evidence-based education. The main hope in each case is that policy and practice decisions informed by evidence will lead to better service to the public. As set out later, evidence can improve policing in seven separate ways. As we go through these, examples of evidence-based policing and crime prevention are given, but these tend to be relatively rare and sporadic compared to the normality of evidence use in other professions.

We need a good understanding of problems to develop effective solutions to them

The first reason for evidence-based policing relates to the need to understand the problems the police are attempting to address. If a problem is misconstrued, then finding an evidence-based solution to it will be difficult. The clinical counterpart in medicine is diagnosis. The physician needs to recognise the nature of the condition to determine which treatment fits it, and that can be tricky. In order to pick a treatment for which there is some evidence of potential effectiveness, that is, 'what (potentially) works' in relation to the condition, the physician needs to know enough about how the body works, what might go wrong and what signs can be used to estimate what's wrong. The same goes for public health. Semmelweis's research on the causes of childbed fever in the Viennese hospital in the nineteenth century involved the collection and analysis of data to give a good enough fix on what was causing the problem before an effective pre-emptive measure (thorough handwashing) could be selected (Semmelweis, 1861). Likewise John Snow's celebrated success in tracking down the origin of a cholera epidemic to a water pump in London's Broad Street involved the careful collection and analysis of evidence on the distribution of the disease (Snow, 1855). John Snow is often referred to as the father of epidemiology because of this work. It was a triumph of evidence-based public health. In engineering, the Wright brothers identified the problem of repeated failures of fixed-wing aeroplanes and the fatalities that often accompanied these failures (Wright, 1954). Prior to their successes they devoted much of their time to assembling evidence that allowed them to understand what had gone wrong as a prelude to developing a successful strategy, rooted in a much improved understanding of the forces involved in failed flight, which was forged through a variety of experiments.

Problem-oriented policing (POP) stresses the importance of identifying and understanding the recurrent problems the police are expected to deal with before launching in with a response. The acronym SARA, referring to iterative processes of Scanning, Analysis, Response and Assessment, describes what is involved in POP. The initial identification and analysis of the problem is crucial. Errors at these stages lead to errors in response decisions. Failures in the outcome of interventions reflect errors in analysis. This is as true in health as in policing. In health care a Plan, Do, Study, Act (PDSA) process closely resembles POP's SARA. PDSA, like SARA, is a cyclical process that can start at any point.

We need to check that the theories we use are not false

All action intended to achieve an outcome, be it by police officers or anyone else, is undertaken in terms of a 'theory', in the sense that it assumes there is a causal relationship between what is done and the expected consequences. The theory may or may not be explicit. Much of the time the theories we use are implicit, given that they serve us well enough.

If a senior officer issues an instruction to a subordinate, it is done on the assumption that the instruction will be understood as intended by the person to whom it is issued, that it will be followed and that following it will achieve the results the senior officer has in mind. The senior officer has a theory about the organisation in which they work and a theory about the causal effects of the conduct following acquiescence to their instructions, but they do not necessarily articulate that theory. The theory may or may not be false. It is false if either the instruction is not followed or if it is followed and the consequences are not as expected. The theory may be false for a variety of different reasons: because there was ambiguity in the instruction, because the subordinate was unable to understand the instruction, because the subordinate forgot what they were supposed to do, because events overtook the conduct required by the instruction which became redundant or unworkable, because the subordinate went off sick, because the organisation was not one where subordinates automatically follow instructions or because (again for any of a variety of reasons) the instructed action was unable to bring about its expected consequences. This is a trivial example used here simply to show that working theories are endemic.

Theories that inform standard ways of working and/or that inform strategies are what matter. These may again be explicit or implicit. They may or may not be false. Where implicit and taken for granted they are apt to be reproduced uncritically. It is very easy to miss disconfirming evidence and cognitive biases in favour of our own theories. Moreover, it appears that we are apt to find it difficult to attend to evidence that refutes our theories. Yet it is important to assemble evidence that will test taken-for-granted theories as well as the theories informing new measures.

Prevailing theories that evidence has found wanting as they relate to crime include the following. 'Once someone has suffered a crime they are at reduced risk of further victimisation they have had their turn and should not worry about future risk': We now know that becoming a victim of crime increases future risks. 'There is a fixed volume of crime that if thwarted in one way will manifest itself in another to which it is displaced': We now know that measures thwarting particular crimes rarely lead to complete displacement and more often lead to a diffusion of benefits, with reductions in crime beyond the operational range of the measures introduced. 'Randomised police patrols reduce crime': There is now ample evidence that although targeted police patrols can reduce crime, random patrols do not do so.

The role of evidence in exposing false theories that have prevailed and have misinformed practice has been important in driving progress in health and aeronautical engineering. In health there has been a radical shift from witchcraft to science-based health, where assumptions about how the body works and what can change it have been shown to be false. Likewise, the false theories that lay behind many failed efforts at human fixed-wing flight prior to the Wright brothers' achievements were exposed in part by the Wright brothers themselves in the run-up to their own achievements. They devised and used better theories than those of their failed predecessors.

We need to avoid interventions that produce more harm than good

The third and classic reason for evidence-based policing turns on the fact that good intentions are not sufficient to produce good outcomes. Interventions have been found inadvertently to backfire, leading to more harms than benefits. Even well-established practices can turn out not to work as expected. In regard to this, one of the clearest examples of the benefits of evidence-based policy comes from childcare. Babies seem to sleep better and to be more comfortable if put to bed on their fronts. Moreover, if the child vomits and the baby is on its front, it had been assumed that they are less likely to choke than if they are on their back. However, it turns out that babies are less at risk of cot death if they are put to sleep on their backs. That is now the standard evidence-based advice to carers, and it has saved the lives of many children. Common sense and concern for the child's welfare had in this case been putting babies at risk. The evidence has made a difference (Gilbert et al., 2005).

Another example from health concerns surgery for women suffering from breast cancer. Over the course of about a century surgery became more and more radical to try to prevent metastases. This surgery caused enormous pain and disfigurement to women who underwent the treatment before trials were undertaken showing that it was often ineffective (Mukherjee, 2011). A third example relates to thalidomide. This was initially hailed as a wonder drug, but had tragic consequences that might have been averted with initial testing that focused on its side effects on foetal development if taken by women at the crucial stage of an expectant mother's pregnancy (Brynner and Stephens, 2001).

Engineering errors have led to inadvertent harms aplenty. Buildings collapse, aeroplanes crash and brakes on cars fail from time to time due to flaws in engineering. Evidence has then been collected to understand those flaws, and improvements in engineering design have followed (Petroski, 1982, 2006). The result has been a reduction in those harms. Perhaps the most striking example comes from air travel, where partly as a consequence of careful evidence collection following tragedies air travel has gone from being a rather risky to a very safe experience.

With respect to policing and crime prevention, several studies have likewise shown that well-intentioned interventions have made matters worse rather than better. Scared Straight is one example (Petrosino et al., 2004). Past experiments taking adolescents on the fringes of delinquency to prisons to see what might befall them if they become involved in crime have, unfortunately, been found on balance to increase rather than decrease the probability of later criminal activity. Similar results have been found for Drug Abuse Resistance Education (DARE), which attempts to build young people's capacity to resist invitations to take illicit drugs by offering a police-led course in schools. On balance DARE has been found to backfire (Rosenbaum and Hanson, 1998). Again, some delinquency treatment programmes have been found to cause more harm than good, most famously the Cambridge Somerville Study where counsellors advised and befriended young people. What it was about that experiment which caused its iatrogenic effects, however, remains uncertain (Zane et al., 2016).

A key principle often conveyed to physicians is, 'First, do no harm' (frequently misattributed to the Hippocratic oath). This reflects recognition that harm can be created inadvertently and that doctors should try to avoid causing it at all costs. Evidence is deemed a key resource for doctors trying to adhere to the principle. In policing and crime prevention a similar principle might be advanced, and it is a powerful reason for collecting the best evidence we can about the unintended as well as intended consequences of what is done (Braga, 2016; Zane et al., 2016).

Resources are always limited and we need to use them to maximise utilities

A fourth reason for evidence-based policing refers to the disposition of limited resources that can be put to alternative uses. Even if a new policy or practice is producing no harms and is instead producing benefits, that alone is an insufficient rationale for it (Manning et al., 2016). Limitations in resources are ubiquitous, even if more obvious in periods of austerity or retrenchment. Custodians of public resources, in particular, have a responsibility to make sure that their use of those resources is producing as much good as possible. Public servants make decisions about how to allocate resources available to them. In the absence of evidence, that disposition of resources is liable to reflect self-interest, ideology, social pressure, horse trading or the prejudices of the powerful. Evidence-based guidance is issued to medical practitioners that is attentive to the returns that are achieved on the basis of resources that can be put to alternative uses, where all those uses produce benefits but where it is not possible to afford all of them. Engineers' briefs are always constrained by the limited resources that are available. Engineers have to design (and test) within the limits of the resources that are made available, which could be put to alternative uses (Petroski, 1996; Collins and Pinch, 1998).

Evidence-based policing and crime prevention aspire to put informed estimates of likely consequences at the heart of decision-making so that most benefits can be yielded from the limited resources that are available. Evidence-based policing also contributes to transparency in that the empirical grounds for decisions can be presented and the adequacy of the evidence then becomes open to challenge. It is not clear that resource allocation decisions in policing, be they at the level of central government, force, sector or beat level, are currently made on the basis of any systematic, evidence-based estimate of costs and expected benefits to the community.

There is always room for us to improve

In health care there is a strong improvement movement, which turns on experimentation and measurements of outcomes (Batalden and Davidoff, 2007). Clinical care has certainly improved as a result of continuous research efforts involving empirical research and the evidence that has been collected as part of that. Progressive, science-based fields of endeavour have led to better health care and better health outcomes. The same goes for engineering where enormous achievements are delivered for less and less in bridge building, aeronautics, automobile design and computing. Both health care and engineering have at their core research, trials and systematic evidence collection.

Karl Popper was amongst the first to articulate arguments in favour of gradual social reform, making use of evidence collected from modest experiments (Popper, 1957). He suggested that progress could be made in harm reduction through what he called piecemeal social engineering. This involves tinkering to try to make improvements but checking that the tinkering is producing the intended outcome, without accidentally causing harm, before applying measures more widely. Just as physical engineering draws on (and feeds into) the natural sciences, so, too, he saw piecemeal social engineering drawing on (and feeding into) the social sciences. Donald Campbell, who has probably done more than any other single individual to promote and devise robust methods for evidence-based policy and practice, drew extensively on Popper's work in his writings on experimental methods in social programmes as vehicles for informing reforms (see the essays collected in Campbell and Russo, 1999).

Research into situational crime prevention has proceeded in this way and over a period of around 30 years an evidence-based framework of interventions has emerged from a sustained programme of research that has identified five main mechanisms through which prevention is achieved: increasing effort, increasing risk, reducing reward, removing excuses and removing provocations (Tilley, 2009). Likewise the sustained programme of research specifically on repeat victimisation has produced compelling evidence that the tendency towards revictimisation of the same or a closely related target is ubiquitous and provides a strong basis for the allocation of limited policing and preventive resources (Laycock, 2001; Laycock and Farrell, 2003). Both the evidence related to situational crime prevention and that related to repeat victimisation and its prevention have led to improvements of preventive responses to specific crime harms.

We need to know what our present and likely future problems are

The Internet has provided a host of new problems, some new kinds of crime and some new means of committing old crimes. It presents the police (and others with crime prevention responsibilities) with new challenges. Moreover the Internet is itself changing as cyberspace evolves, creating new challenges for potential victims, potential offenders and potential guardians. There are both known unknowns (for example, the volume of crimes of different types that are enabled by or are associated with the Internet) and unknown unknowns, including future inventions within the cyber world. The priorities for police also change. The domestic sphere provides an example, where the police are expected to focus more attention now on abuses of different kinds than was the case 50 years ago, regardless of whether there have been increases in the rate or level of the activities of concern.

The adaptability of the offending community and periods of rapid technological innovation require the police to be nimble in identifying problems for preventive intervention. This adds urgency to identifying the size and trajectory of the problems to be addressed, including significant gaps in current understanding that need to be filled. One successful example at a local level relates to predictive policing, where techniques have been developed to anticipate where and when crimes are most likely to occur to inform the allocation of resources in an effort to pre-empt them (Bowers et al., 2004). This research is an extension of previous work on repeat victimisation, which showed the elevated short-term risks faced by victims of crime that are often committed by prolific offenders. This evidence can inform both efforts to prevent successor crime events from taking place by protecting the target and, failing this, it can be used to inform proactive efforts at detection.

Evidence can have the power to persuade

A final reason for evidence-based policing specifically with respect to crime prevention, which may not be so important in other professions, has to do with the power of good quality information itself to change situations (Scott, 2005). Even when 'everybody knows' about a problem, those who need to act on it (and in the prevention of crime, it is usually not the police themselves) can resist pressure more easily if there is no solid evidence supporting the need for change. In health, this issue arose in relation to the link between smoking and lung cancer. Until the evidence became overwhelming, tobacco companies resisted the findings. Likewise, solid evidence linking the association of car theft with vehicle insecurity was needed to persuade manufacturers to build security into their products (Laycock, 2004).

Local data can be assembled and analysed to provide evidence that can be used to alert those who are unknowingly host to a crime problem about which they may be able to do something. A good example comes from Sidebottom et al. (2012), who discuss theft from shopping trollies and an effort to reduce it with a redesigned trolley. Here the supermarket in question did not realise that there was a problem of bag thefts from trollies in their store and responded co-operatively when told and when offered help in working out a way of reducing it.

The case for making systematic use of evidence in delivering better policing to the public, as outlined here, is compelling, easily made and easily understood. There is, however, devil in the practical detail. We move next to discuss what evidence is needed before moving on to points at which it would be most useful to inject it.

What kinds of evidence are needed in policing?

The choice of which evidence to use in evidence-based policing is complex and controversial. At one extreme are those who argue that there is a hierarchy of evidence and we should not use any that falls below a minimum standard. At the other extreme are those who would argue that anything goes, provided it is of use in effecting improvements.

One issue of evidence choice relates to data on levels of crime. Recorded crime data are notoriously prone to weaknesses in reporting and recording. High rates of attrition from offences committed to persons charged and convicted mean that impressions of crime levels, and of offenders, risk being artefacts of the processes through which events are reported, recorded and processed rather than any underlying reality. This has led some to want to disregard recorded crime and to depend instead on victimisation surveys that ask a large randomly selected cross-section of the population about their crime experiences over a prior reference period, most often twelve months. Such well-designed victimisation surveys are generally recognised as yielding more accurate counts and estimates of rates of crime. However, they have their own shortcomings: they ask only about certain types of crime (and can be slow to adapt when new ones emerge); they tend to omit certain important victim populations, including the very young, the homeless and institutional victims of various kinds, such as those in residential homes, public-sector organisations and businesses; they have reducing response rates; they tend to cap levels of repeat victimization, giving misleading impressions of incidence rates; and they are rarely of much use at very local levels, being large-scale and expensive national initiatives that fail to provide the level of local detail necessary to understand problems as they are manifested within specific communities.

Another issue of evidence quality relates to research design. Again one view has it that there is an established hierarchy with some study designs being unreliable. This was the strategy used in the famous review by Sherman et al. (1997) of what works in crime prevention, which proposed a five-point Maryland Scale to weigh the evidence from different studies in favour of or against certain interventions. At the pinnacle are randomised controlled trials (RCTs), which score five points and try to mimic the methods used in clinical trials to test the effectiveness of drug treatments. At the other end of the scale, with only one point, we find simple before/after studies, often with no matched comparison group or no comparison group at all.

At the other extreme is a view that any and all types of evidence are admissible provided a) that they are relevant to the question being posed and b) are approached critically to consider specific biases or distortions that may have crept in. Although we might hope for victimisation survey data on our problem and wish that randomised controlled trials could be used to test the measure or suite of measures we are contemplating to reduce our problem, they will rarely be available or feasible. Instead, decision-makers have to deal with what they have got or can easily collect. We thus propose that any and all evidence should be considered, providing it is relevant to the question at issue. In the fast-moving environment in which we are all working it is often not practical to depend only on the very best evidence. This is in part because some decisions cannot be postponed to the point at which such evidence is available and in part because for some issues the ideal evidence is unlikely ever to be available. A pragmatic approach involves accepting that the evidence we use is fallible but trying to assemble sufficient for the purpose at hand, taking account of specific weaknesses of which we are aware. This orientation to evidence should be familiar to police officers. It is the one that has to be taken in investigating crimes. Although perfect, conclusive evidence may be highly desirable, it is seldom available, and the police service works with what it has and can collect in practice. A very wide range of evidence is potentially available, although much of it will be of dubious probative value. Pieces of evidence are assembled to reduce doubt over who committed or did not commit the crime. Even where no individual element clinches the case, enough independent elements pointing in the same direction may be sufficient for prosecution, and the evidence is then tested in court. If the case is important enough greater lengths are gone to in order to collect more and stronger evidence. Less important cases warrant less effort. In all instances good investigators will try to guard against cognitive biases that lead them to try to build a case against a suspect, paying insufficient attention to alternative possibilities. So it goes for evidence-based policing more broadly.

It is important to remember that all types of evidence are fallible. Single pieces of evidence are rarely sufficient to warrant conclusions on patterns, explanations or interventions. Evidence always needs to be interpreted. Several types of evidence pointing in the same direction are preferable to single sources. There are the same risks of the cognitive biases that jeopardise police investigations and lead to selective collection and use of evidence as in research aiming to inform police practice. There is nothing new in these comments on the use of evidence in science. Karl Popper was a major philosopher of science who showed that all scientific propositions are fallible and that the role of scientific research is to winnow out error by subjecting theories to efforts to falsify them. Those that are used enjoy their credibility (at least for a time) because they have survived efforts to find fault in them. Finding fault stimulates efforts to develop better theories (Popper, 1959). Popper noted similarities between courts of law in assessing evidence and the work of the scientific community in assessing scientific work (Popper, 1959; Tilley, 1993). Judges and juries come to their conclusions only after the cases put before them have been subjected to searching critical scrutiny aiming to find fault in them. Another philosopher of science, Paul Feyerabend, used the slogan, 'Anything goes' to capture the diversity of methods and evidence types that had contributed to scientific progress (Feyerabend, 1975). A sociologist of science, Harry Collins, has noted that it is never possible in advance to know what is crucial evidence. It only becomes clear once a consensus has emerged following critical discussion of the types of evidence that have emerged from scientific practice (Collins, 2004). A whole slew of cognitive psychologists have shown how habits of thought incorporate cognitive biases, including Daniel Kahneman, Amos Tversky and Philip Johnson-Laird (Tversky and Kahneman, 1974; Johnson-Laird, 2009; Kahneman, 2011). Hence the fallibility of evidence, the need for diverse types of evidence, the shortage of strictly conclusive evidence, the challenge of sorting and sifting strong from weak evidence, the risks of cognitive biases, the ever-open possibility of error and the need for critical third parties to make case-by-case judgements about the validity and relevance of evidence are common to police 'conventional' use of evidence in the proper investigation of crimes and in the proper use of evidence in 'evidence-based policing'.

In the applied sciences, notably medicine and engineering, evidence of diverse kinds is also used to inform judgements. Physicians diagnose patients using diverse indicators of their underlying conditions in deciding what is wrong and what might be done to put it right. Engineers draw on diverse types of evidence in designing new bridges, high-rise buildings, aeroplanes, airports and motor vehicles.

What is now referred to formally as 'evidence-based policing' is not therefore bringing research evidence to an evidence desert. Rather, police officers are already in many ways evidence savvy, as reflected in their systematic collection, interpretation, analysis and use of various types of evidence, both in the investigation of crimes and in improving their practice. That skill needs to be remembered and built on in furthering the current vogue for evidence-based policing. No methods are infallible, and many types of research evidence can play a role in correcting errors and improving practice. Police officers need to develop those habits of scepticism and openness to the various forms of evidence that mark scientific work more generally.

When and how should we incorporate evidence into policing?

This chapter has argued so far that there are many ways in which greater use of research evidence can contribute to improvements in policing. It has also argued that that evidence can take many forms. Specifications of exclusive gold standards for sources of evidence and designs of studies are liable to rule out the useful and stultify progress. Here we turn to a discussion of when and how increased attention to research evidence might best be effected. As with the previous sections, we draw attention to parallels with medicine and aeronautical engineering. Following the discussion so far we briefly suggest eight key points at which research evidence might be injected.

Education and training

Doctors and engineers learn first about how the biological and the physical worlds work. They learn basic science using systematic observation and theory testing before they are allowed to put people at risk from their interventions and designs. Although the social sciences may be less well developed than their physical and biological counterparts, much is known about human behaviour, including that defined as criminal. This would mark a substantial change, where police officers currently seem to learn how they should police and how to apply the law before learning what is known of what they are to police. In medicine and engineering it is the other way round, and this is a model that police education and training might usefully follow.

Innovation and experimentation

It is clear that as a practice policing has a great deal to learn, as there continues to be much to learn in medicine and engineering. There is thus a lot to be said for innovation and experimentation in the interests of better achieving policing objectives. The division of labour between practitioner and researcher in medicine and engineering is often quite fuzzy. Practitioners and researchers work together in innovation, research and development where theory and practice are bridged. There are some exemplars of this in policing that are also worth emulating. Prominent amongst these are the projects that targeted repeat victimisation in the UK (e.g. Forrester et al., 1988) and projects targeting youth gang-related shootings in the United States (e.g. Braga et al., 2001). These projects have drawn on developed and tested theory; they have also used diverse research methods and various data sources, and the work has been useful in informing further initiatives. Changing crime patterns underline the importance of innovative projects to address new problems, for example, those to do with cyberattacks, with new forms of terrorism and with transnational organised crime. Likewise, new technologies may offer new opportunities for creative developments in policing, a recent example being the use of body-worn cameras.

Setting default practices

There are some evidence-based practices that apply almost everywhere. Thorough handwashing before touching a patient provides a medical example. In policing a comparable example may have to do with the bagging of physical evidence at a crime scene. These are helpful habits that produce net benefits. We refer to them here as 'defaults' rather than 'standards' or 'doctrine' on the grounds that professionals may encounter situations where their informed understanding of the specific situation means that they decide to set the default aside. While preparing this paper one of us talked to a hospital consultant in emergency medicine about the changed rules for placing babies on their backs rather than fronts, to be given examples where in the hospital they would decide that it was in a particular baby's best interests to be placed on his or her front rather than back. Informed professional judgement set the default good practice aside.

Reflexive practice

Most professional occupations that root their practices in evidence require both continuous professional development to keep practitioners up to date with new evidence and also that neophytes spend a period under supervision while they learn to interpret the conditions they encounter so that they recognise which pieces of evidence are relevant to specific cases. In science itself this is seen in the process of supervising doctoral students and in the postdoctoral training that frequently follows. The 'tacit dimension' is learned as would-be scientists pick up the craft of research. What goes for scientists themselves goes for others at the early stages of their evidence: attentive practice. They need the advice and encouragement of senior practitioners with whom to discuss cases and the use of relevant evidence in decision-making. The policing equivalent might be the probationer constable who is tutored by an experienced sergeant. But the current emphasis is on experience rather than on the tutor's known expertise in the interpretation and application of evidence.

Organised scepticism

Taken-for-granted policies and practices, which are simply reproduced with no authority other than tradition or ideology, need to be tested empirically. As indicated earlier, established practice is no guarantee of effectiveness. Indeed, counterproductive practices can survive in the absence of empirical test. Science itself is marked by organised scepticism, which means that scientists are perpetually open to doubt, to the possibility that they are mistaken. Even though in practical terms this might risk paralysis from uncertainty, it provides a healthy corrective to complacency. In a disciplined organisation in which there is a strong can-do attitude, such as the police, it may be especially difficult to make routine that critical sceptical attitude which is the hallmark of science and which can be crucial to the early identification of weaknesses in working theories. Yet there are senior police officers who do, indeed, encourage their staff to raise doubts about standard working practices.

Routine monitoring and horizon scanning

The problems the police are expected to deal with change for a variety of reasons. Scanning the environment for evidence of upcoming issues so as to implement current good practice expediently or, where necessary, to develop pre-emptive preventive strategies clearly makes sense. This aligns with the point earlier relating to the need for innovative and experimental initiatives. In the very short term the intelligence used to identify embryonic terrorist and organised crime groups with a view to their disruption comprises one example. On a longer timeframe and at a more macro scale, collecting evidence of new problem patterns consequent on technological and political changes is important in equipping the police to look to ways of intervening early. In relation to health, Ginsberg et al. (2009) suggest that early detection of disease activity enabling rapid response, for example, in relation to influenza, is possible by analysing online search queries. There is much to be said for efforts to develop early warning systems akin to this for problems that might increasingly be coming to the attention of the police.

Identification and rigorous analysis of failures

Errors are made in both health and engineering from time to time: doctors make false diagnoses and prescribe courses of treatment that may cause more harm than good. The history of medicine is littered with errors and with treatments that backfired, however well intentioned. Examples mentioned earlier include the use of thalidomide to treat morning sickness and the radical surgery that became commonplace for breast cancer. Likewise, there have been spectacular engineering failures, for example, where planes have crashed and bridges collapsed. What has been important to advances in medicine and engineering are the lessons learned from failure and the ways in which potential disasters can be averted by focusing on and learning from error.

It is worth dwelling on the crucial role of evidence relating to error across the pure and applied sciences and in criminal investigation. Popper had a famous way of putting this in relation to science. However many white swans we see, he tells us, one bona-fide black swan is sufficient to falsify the theory that all swans are white. As another example, however many times we see the sun rising, it does not mean that the sun is actually moving relative to us. In medicine, no matter how many women may have had their morning sickness remedied through thalidomide, it does not mean that there are no unintended negative effects that outweigh those benefits. In engineering, however many flights of a given type of plane take off and land safely from their respective airports, one crash is sufficient to indicate that something is seriously amiss and this needs to be understood with a view to taking remedial action. Similarly in policing, however many people may have had cases against them supported by the use of forensic evidence, the more powerful use of it has been to show that convicted individuals are not in fact guilty. This has perhaps been one of the major achievements of DNA evidence as used in the Innocence Project (www.innocenceproject.org).

Popper believed that the exposure of hypotheses to critical examination, including empirical test, operates in similar ways in biological evolution, scientific development, technological progress and successful social problem-solving (Popper, 1999). He devised a couple of related formulae to describe the use of evidence that cuts across all these disciplines and approaches. The formulae are very simple, as shown in Figure 2.1.

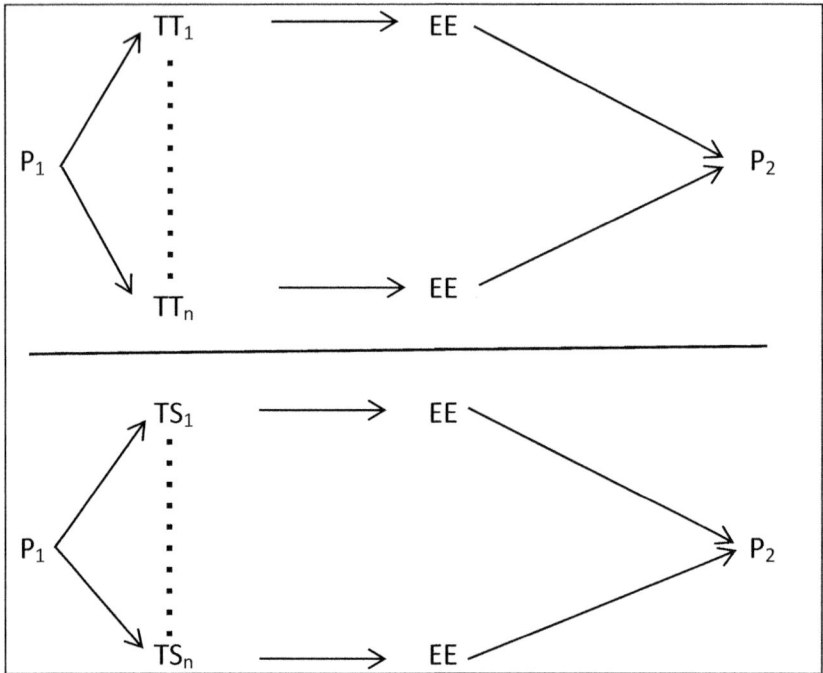

Figure 2.1 A generic model of error elimination in problem-solving (see Popper, 1972)

In science or practical social problem-solving, we start with a problem (P_1), then move to tentative theories ($TT_1 \ldots TT_n$, in science) or tentative solution ($TS_1 \ldots TS_n$, in practical problem-solving), then test them to eliminate errors (EE) as rigorously as we are able using the best evidence we can find. The tentative theory or tentative solution that survives error elimination processes (at least for a while), then presents a new situation within which different problems will arise (P_2), and the process of theory/solution proposal and error elimination starts again. In biological evolution, mutations embody hypotheses that are tested for their survival value. If they fail, they perish. Popper talked about 'errors dying in our stead' where as human beings we test hypotheses in a limited way before putting our lives at stake by acting as if they were true (Popper, 1957; Tilley, 1982). Only fit hypotheses survive if put to rigorous test. For applied sciences, the trials undertaken in medicine and engineering in advance of the widespread adoption of practices are cases in point. The enquiries following failure where the preliminary testing has failed to eliminate crucial errors, especially where there are catastrophes, reflect efforts to unpick what went wrong in order to avoid repeat disasters (see Petroski, 2006). Research in forensic science is currently trying to understand how miscarriages of justice have occurred or could occur due to failures in assumptions in forensic science. For example James French et al. (2014) have shown how gunshot residues can be transmitted from person A to person B, rather than necessarily indicating that person B had in fact handled the weapon in question.

Cumulative problem-solving and intervention design

The fields of engineering and medicine are marked by successive, sometimes small-scale improvements through problem solving, and also by acknowledgement of what is possible and not possible and what is known and not known. Knowing what is known and not known means knowing what can be built on with some confidence in practice. Knowing what is not known (but could be known) sets a research agenda.

Medicine and engineering are both heavily imbued with theory that has been tested using the methods of error elimination described earlier. Theories about the body, its normal functioning and abnormal functioning, have been devised, tested and refined over the past two millennia. Engineering likewise has a long history of theory development and use. Medical and engineering students learn this theory and apply it. Physicians and engineers are educated in universities, where they develop habits of attention to research. As we have said, there are still errors. Moreover new theories, new treatments and new materials are under constant development, involving extensive testing and refinement. Practitioners of medicine and engineering work closely with academics, and many professionals are engaged in practice as they undertake research. There is much to be said for similar close working relationships between those engaged in research supporting police problem-solving and those doing policing, just as the development of researcher-practitioners in policing comprises a step in the direction of bringing an understanding of tested theory to police practice and the conduct of development work that refines the application.

Conclusion

It is clear from what we have argued in this chapter that increased collection and analysis of information – that is, evidence – has a crucial role to play in informing improvements in policing and that it can do so in a variety of ways. It should also be clear that it would be counterproductive to confine one's sources of evidence to any specific form or to that collected using any specific method. Finally, we have suggested that there is scope for greater use of evidence at diverse points in the education and training of police officers, in the conduct of their work, in original research and in reviewing and learning from failures. What we are suggesting is a very broad-based agenda for the injection of research-based evidence into policing and its further development within the profession.

Throughout this chapter we have drawn parallels between the use of evidence in health care and engineering and that which could enhance policing. Our conclusions relating to the uses of evidence in the interests of improvement, on the diverse types of evidence used and on the multiple points at which evidence needs to be heard in decision-making are rooted in comparisons with medicine and engineering. It is in emulating this that policing may properly professionalise, by being undertaken by those with a thorough grasp of tested theory, whose work involves sensitivity to research, an ability to understand it, an enquiring mind and a willingness to contribute to studies that help build the evidence base.

Although the title of our chapter refers to 'evidence-based policing' and we acknowledge the catchiness of the term, we remain worried by the baggage it attracts, which seems to include for many an emphasis on randomised controlled trials and an assumption that the main role of evidence is to sort out what does and doesn't work. We have set out a much broader agenda for evidence in the improvement of policing. Moreover, we doubt whether the craft aspects of policing can or should be entirely abandoned. There are lively debates on just this in medicine (for example, Goitein and James, 2016). It would seem to us premature to conclude in policing in particular that well-established and hard-won craft skills be entirely abandoned in favour of mechanically following directives deriving from trials. In the complex and changing world of policing, judgment will be unavoidable, which is best *informed* by evidence but not hamstrung by it.

References

Batalden, P. and Davidoff, F. (2007). 'What is "quality improvement" and how can it transform healthcare?', *Quality and Safety in Healthcare*, 16: 2–3.

Bowers, K.J., Johnson, S.D. and Pease, K. (2004). 'Prospective hot-spotting: The future of crime mapping?', *British Journal of Criminology*, 44(5): 641–58, doi: 10.1093/bjc/azh036

Braga, A.A. (2016). 'The continued importance of measuring potentially harmful impacts of crime prevention programs: The academy of experimental criminology 2014 Joan McCord lecture', *Journal of Experimental Criminology*, 12(2): 1–20, doi: 10.1007/s11292-016-9252-4

Braga, A.A., Kennedy, D.M., Waring, E.J. and Piehl, A.M. (2001). 'Problem-oriented policing, deterrence, and youth violence: An evaluation of Boston's operation ceasefire', *Journal of Research in Crime and Delinquency*, 38, 195–225.

Brynner, R. and Stephens, T. (2001). *Dark Remedy: The Impact of Thalidomide and Its Revival as a Vital Medicine*, New York: Basic Books.

Campbell, D. and Russo, M. (1999). *Social Experimentation*, Thousand Oaks, CA: Sage.

Clarke, R. and Newman, G. (2006). *Outsmarting the Terrorists*, Westport, CT: Praeger.

Collins, H. (2004). *Gravity's Shadow*, Chicago: University of Chicago Press.

Collins, H. and Pinch, T. (1998). *The Golem at Large*, Cambridge: Cambridge University Press.

Feyerabend, P. (1975). *Against Method*, London: New Left Books.

Forrester, D., Chatterton, M. and Pease, K. with the assistance of Robin Brown. (1988). *The Kirkholt Burglary Prevention Project, Rochdale*, Crime Prevention Unit Paper 13, London: Home Office.

French, J., Morgan, R. and Davy, J. (2014). 'The secondary transfer of gunshot residue: An experimental investigation carried out with SEM-EDX analysis', *Spectometry*, 43(1): 56–61.

Gilbert, R., Salanti, G., Harden, M. and See, S. (2005). 'Infant sleeping position and the sudden infant death syndrome: Systematic review of observational studies and historical review of recommendations from 1940 to 2002', *International Journal of Epidemiology*, 34: 874–87.

Ginsberg, J., Mohebb, M., Patel, R., Brammer, L., Smolonski, M. and Brilliant, L. (2009). 'Detecting influenza epidemics using search engine query data', *Nature*, 457, doi: 10.1038/nature07637

Goitein, L. and James, B. (2016). 'Standardised best practices and individual craft-based medicine: A conversation about quality', *JAMA Internal Medicine*, 176(6): 835–8.

Johnson-Laird, P. (2009). *How we Reason*, Oxford: Oxford University Press.

Kahneman, D. (2011). *Thinking Fast and Slow*, London: Allen Lane.

Laycock, G. (2001). 'Hypothesis based research: The repeat victimization story', *Criminal Justice: The International Journal of Policy and Practice*, 1(1): 59–82.

Laycock, G. (2004). 'The UK Car Theft Index: An Example of Government Leverage', in M. Maxfield and R.V. Clarke (eds) *Understanding and Preventing Car Theft*, Crime Prevention Studies, vol. 17, Monsey, NY: Criminal Justice Press.

Laycock, G. and Farrell, G. (2003). 'Repeat Victimization: Lessons for Implementing Problem-Oriented Policing', in J. Knutsson (ed) *Problem-Oriented Policing: From Innovation to Mainstream*, Crime Prevention Studies, vol. 15, pp. 213–37, Monsay: Criminal Justice Press.

Manning, M., Johnson, S., Tilley, N., Wong, G. and Vorsina, M. (2016). *Economic Analysis and Efficiency in Policing, Criminal Justice and Crime Reduction: What Works?* Basingstoke: Palgrave Macmillan.

Mukherjee, S. (2011). *The Emperor of all Maladies: A Biography of Cancer*, London: Fourth Estate.

Petrosino, A., Turpin-Petrosino, C. and Buehler, J. (2004). *"Scared Straight" and other Juvenile Awareness Programs for Preventing Juvenile Delinquency*, Campbell Systematic Reviews, Oslo: Campbell Collaboration.

Petroski, H. (1982). *To Engineer Is Human: The Role of Failure in Successful Design*, New York: Random House.

Petroski, H. (1996). *Invention by Design: How Engineers get from Thought to Thing*, Cambridge, MA: Harvard University Press.

Petroski, H. (2006). *Success through Failure: The Paradox of Design*, Princeton: Princeton University Press.

Popper, K. (1957). *The Poverty of Historicism*, London: Routledge.

Popper, K. (1959). *The Logic of Scientific Discovery*, London: Hutchinson.

Popper, K. (1972). *Objective Knowledge*, Oxford: Clarendon Press.

Popper, K. (1999). *All Life Is Problem-Solving*, London: Routledge.

Rosenbaum, D. and Hanson, G. (1998). 'Assessing the effects of school-based drug education: A six-year mutli-level analysis of project D.A.R.E.', *Journal of Research in Crime and Delinquency*, 35(4): 381–412.

Scott, M. (2005). 'Shifting and Sharing Responsibility to Address Public Safety Problems', in N. Tilley (ed) *Handbook of Crime Prevention and Community Safety*, pp. 385–409, London: Routledge.

Semmelweis, I. (1861, trans 1983). *The Etiology, Concept, and Prophylaxis of Childbed Fever*, Madison: University of Wisconsin Press.

Sherman, L.W., Gottfredson, D., MacKenzie, D., Eck, J., Reuter, P. and Bushway, S. (1997). *Preventing Crime: What Works, What Doesn't and What's Promising*, Washington, DC: US Department of Justice, Office of Justice Programs.

Sidebottom, A., Guillaume, P. and Archer, T. (2012). 'Findings from the First Trial of a Design-Based Intervention to Reduce Bag Theft from Supermarket Trolleys', in

P. Ekblom (ed) *Design against Crime: Crime Proofing Everyday Products*, Crime Prevention Studies, vol. 27, pp. 201–28, Boulder, CO: Lynne Rienner.

Snow, J. (1855). *On the Mode of Communication of Cholera*, London: Churchill.

Tilley, N. (1982). 'Popper, historicism and emergence', *Philosophy of the Social Sciences*, 12: 59–67.

Tilley, N. (1993). 'Popper and prescriptive methodology', *Metaphilosophy*, 24(1/2): 155–66.

Tilley, N. (2009). *Crime Prevention*, London: Routledge.

Tversky, A. and Kahneman, D. (1974). 'Judgment under uncertainty: Heuristics and biases', *Science*, 185(4157): 1124–31.

Wright, O. (1954). *How We Invented the Airplane*, New York: Dover Publication.

Zane, S., Welsh, B. and Zimmerman, G. (2016). 'Examining the iatrogenic effects of the Cambridge-Somerville youth study: Existing explanations and new appraisals', *British Journal of Criminology*, 56(1): 141–60.

3 Reconciling problem-oriented policing and evidence-based policing

Michael S. Scott

Once, there was just 'policing'. At least through the early 1970s, before scholars got deeply interested in how the police understood and carried out their function, most police officers and administrators took for granted that the basic police function and methods were firmly established and not much up for debate. Whether police understood their function as 'maintaining order', 'fighting crime', or 'enforcing the law', all variations could be distilled to a common understanding that police would use their authority to enforce the criminal law as the primary mechanism for keeping society orderly and criminals under control. Whatever minor disagreements existed over this common understanding, no need was felt to clarify the meaning of 'policing' with adjectives: nouns and verbs sufficed. But modern policing is different: it is replete with adjectives that seek to further explain policing and to distinguish one approach to policing from others. With no pretense to being comprehensive, modern policing includes community policing, evidence-based policing, hot-spots policing, intelligence-led policing, order-maintenance policing (i.e., broken windows policing), predictive policing, problem-oriented policing, pulling-levers policing, reassurance policing, and third-party policing. Whatever confusion adjectival policing engenders for police practitioners and others, it has, on the whole, been beneficial insofar as it acknowledges that the policing function and its methods are complex and that there are important policy choices to be made as to how policing will be organized and carried out.

Much has been written about each of these policing approaches and the relationships among them (Scott, 2000: 97–107; Weisburd and Braga, 2006; Ratcliffe, 2008: 65–83). This chapter examines the relationship between evidence-based policing (hereafter, EBP) and problem-oriented policing (hereafter, POP), two approaches that are similar and distinct in detail as between them, but also both of them distinct in kind from most other approaches. As the chapter title suggests, I set out to 'reconcile' EBP and POP, aware that 'reconcile' can variously mean a) to cause to become amicable, b) to settle a dispute, c) to make compatible or consistent, or d) to cause to be resigned to something not desired. Readers can decide for themselves what has been achieved by my effort.

So that all readers start with the same frame of reference, the following are succinct definitions of POP and EBP by their principal proponents, Herman Goldstein and Lawrence Sherman, respectively.

Problem-oriented policing

PROBLEM-ORIENTED POLICING (POP) is an approach to policing in which **(1) DISCRETE PIECES OF POLICE BUSINESS** (each consisting of a cluster of similar incidents, whether crimes or acts of disorder, that the police are expected to handle) are subject to **(2) MICROSCOPIC EXAMINATION** (drawing on the especially honed skills of crime analysts and the accumulated experience of operating field personnel) in hopes that what is freshly learned about each problem will lead to discovering a **(3) NEW AND MORE EFFECTIVE STRATEGY** for dealing with it. POP places a high value on new responses that are **(4) PREVENTIVE** in nature, that are **(5) NOT DEPENDENT ON THE USE OF THE CRIMINAL JUSTICE SYSTEM**, and that **(6) ENGAGE OTHER PUBLIC AGENCIES, THE COMMUNITY AND THE PRIVATE SECTOR** when their involvement has the potential for significantly contributing to the reduction of the problem. POP carries a commitment to **(7) IMPLEMENTING THE NEW STRATEGY, (8) RIGOROUSLY EVALUATING ITS EFFECTIVENESS**, and, subsequently, **(9) REPORTING THE RESULTS** in ways that will benefit other police agencies and that will ultimately contribute to **(10) BUILDING A BODY OF KNOWLEDGE** that supports the further professionalization of the police.

(Goldstein, 2001)

Evidence-based policing

Evidence-based policing is the use of the best available research on the outcomes of police work to implement guidelines and evaluate agencies, units, and officers. Put more simply, evidence-based policing uses research to guide practice and evaluate practitioners. It uses the best evidence to shape the best practice. It is a systematic effort to parse out and codify unsystematic "experience" as the basis for police work, refining it by ongoing systematic testing of hypotheses.

Evidence-based policing is about two very different kinds of research: basic research on what works best when implemented properly under controlled conditions, and ongoing outcomes research about the results each unit is actually achieving by applying (or ignoring) basic research in practice.

(Sherman, 1998: 3–4)

The earliest articulation of a problem-oriented approach to policing (Goldstein, 1979) predates the more recent articulation of an evidence-based approach to policing (Sherman, 1998) by nearly two decades, although, as Sherman notes, August Vollmer was advocating an evidence-based policing approach in the early twentieth century (Carte and Carte, 1975, as cited in Sherman, 1998).

Because Goldstein proposed his approach first, Sherman had the opportunity to compare and contrast his approach to POP when he first articulated it. Sherman (1998: 5–6) explicitly credited POP with being the major source for EBP, but he distinguished his approach principally by asserting that POP did not explicitly call for using scientifically derived evidence to determine what strategies and tactics police ought to employ in addressing specific policing problems, nor in evaluating the results of those strategies, once implemented.

In turn, Goldstein has credited EBP as being compatible with POP, citing Sherman's and others' experimental studies of the effects of various policing strategies on domestic violence as exemplifying POP (Goldstein, 2003: 21). Other scholars have likewise taken note of the fundamental compatibility of POP and EBP, even going so far as to decree POP a form of evidence-based practice (Bullock and Tilley, 2006: 167–89).

At a minimum, it is easy to see that Vollmer's, Goldstein's, and Sherman's ideas are all part of a larger historical movement whose common feature is the belief that policing can and should be improved through the application of scientific principles and methods, a movement that has more recently been joined by the development of crime science (as distinct from criminology) (Laycock, 2005).

Each of these thinkers and their ideas emphasized various aspects of science in the context of policing. Vollmer had in mind applying scientific principles to all aspects of policing, including police administration and criminal investigation, as well as to preventing and responding to the substantive behavioral problems that comprise the business of policing (Vollmer, 1930, 1933). Goldstein's POP has emphasized using social science principles and methods to enhance the capacity of the police, as an institution, to achieve its objectives effectively and fairly. Sherman's EBP has emphasized using science to improve our understanding of which policing methods are effective and which are not and under what conditions. Laycock's crime science has emphasized using science to improve our understanding of crime and disorder (as distinct from understanding criminals) for the purpose of better preventing them, but does not emphasize the particular role police play in this endeavor.

The compatibility of problem-oriented policing and evidence-based policing

Problem-oriented policing and EBP are alike in one major respect that distinguishes them in kind from many other policing approaches: POP and EBP are organizational theories about how police should decide what to do in response to the demands of their business – very broadly and loosely defined as crime and disorder, and the fear thereof. They are not criminological theories, nor are they based on them, as are policing approaches such as hot-spots policing, order-maintenance policing, pulling-levers policing, reassurance policing, and third-party policing.[1] In other words, they are prescriptions for figuring out what to do, not prescriptions for what to do. This is important because determining whether POP and EBP are viable policing approaches depends not on whether their application reduces crime and disorder directly, but on whether they enable police to figure out how to handle their business effectively and fairly better than do other approaches.[2]

In addition to sharing the feature of being organizational theories rather than criminological theories, POP and EBP share the common feature of being principally aimed at improving substantive policing outcomes and not merely policing processes or administrative practices, even though both approaches could also be employed for the latter purposes. This substantive focus is hugely important because it is a corrective to what Goldstein referred to as the 'means-over-ends syndrome', by which police become preoccupied with the running of their organizations to the neglect of examining what effects their organizations are having on substantive outcomes. Having the adherents of another policing approach also working to correct this serious imbalance is to the good of police and society. In practice, EBP has tended toward a somewhat different way of thinking about policing practices than has POP, a distinction about which I will elaborate next, but the overall commonality of having a focus on substantive policing outcomes remains.

Distinctions between problem-oriented policing and evidence-based policing

Against the background of the two primary common elements of POP and EBP described earlier, there are several important distinctions between them, some theoretical and some practical.

Core objective

The core objective of POP is to improve the police institution by improving its capacity to achieve its policing objectives effectively and fairly. It is a means to the ultimate goal of developing a police institution that is integral and vital to democratic governance in free and open societies and not a threat to it. The core objective of EBP, by contrast, is to build a robust and reliable body of research-based evidence on which police can rely in deciding how to police.

Type of research involved

Problem-oriented policing calls for an eclectic and flexible form of action research in which researchers (either internal crime analysts or external scholars) work closely with police practitioners to identify and analyze local policing problems, develop and implement responses to them, and assess the impact of those responses on the problems. Goldstein analogized it to 'product research' (1979: 256) and characterized it as being 'practical and concrete' (1979: 257). By contrast, EBP calls principally for so-called 'basic research' (Sherman, 1998: 4) to determine 'what works best [. . .] under controlled conditions', employing experimental research methods, although Sherman also envisioned a second form of 'ongoing outcomes research' that closely parallels Goldstein's problem-oriented inquiries and draws from the principles of total quality management in the business sector (Sherman, 1998: 6).

Standards of proof

Whereas EBP strives for a 'gold-standard' level of scientific proof (typically derived from a series of randomized controlled experiments) to determine what is and is not effective in reducing crime and disorder, POP is, in both theory and practice, far more accepting of lesser standards of proof for justifying the employment of particular policing activities and for assessing the extent to which they were effective in controlling the problem at hand. Because EBP has as its primary objective building a body of scientifically valid evidence on the basis of which prescriptions can be made as to what strategies and tactics police should and should not employ, it makes sense that such prescriptions be based on highly reliable and generalizable research findings. By comparison, because POP has as its primary objective developing and implementing new responses to local policing problems, responses that are, at a minimum, an improvement over what was previously being done to address that problem, it makes sense that it not insist upon the most rigorous standards of scientific research in judging the merit of new responses.

Sources of knowledge

Problem-oriented policing explicitly values the knowledge that police practitioners, including and perhaps especially, line-level officers, can bring to bear on the development of new responses to problems, knowledge that is rooted heavily in their practical experiences dealing with the problem at hand and in their knowledge of local conditions and factors. Problem-oriented policing seeks then to marry this practitioner knowledge with existing research (ideally, perhaps, EBP research) as to what is generally known to be effective and a careful data-based analysis of the local problem in determining what new strategies and tactics ought to be adopted. By contrast, EBP explicitly seeks to privilege research-based knowledge over practitioner experience – indeed to replace it as the primary basis for deciding what policing action to take. Although neither Sherman nor Goldstein put it this way, POP assumes that local practitioners' experience is likely to be at least somewhat correct, and therefore valuable, whereas EBP assumes the opposite: that local practitioners' experience is likely to be at least somewhat incorrect, and therefore a distraction from the pursuit of a more effective response to the problem at hand.

Unit of analysis

As implied in the phrase itself, problem-oriented policing chooses the 'problem' as its basic unit of analysis, and by 'problem' is meant a localized pattern of behavior in the community that compels police to intervene. Depending upon localized judgment on the matter, these problems could be defined in very narrow terms, perhaps down to the behavior occurring at one location or even by one person, or they could be defined in wider terms, encompassing behavioral patterns manifesting across a larger segment of the community. In POP, the local context of each problem matters greatly (Welsh, 2006: 306). Moreover, in developing new strategies and tactics to employ in addressing problems, POP emphasizes employing a combination of responses tailored to local conditions. In practice, POP practitioners commonly employ a combination of a half-dozen or more discrete responses to address one local problem (Scott and Clarke, 2000: 216; Rojek, 2003). But seldom does POP seek to develop within any one initiative knowledge that is likely to lead to prescriptive responses to all problems of a particular behavioral type in all places. By contrast, such is precisely the goal of EBP: to gain knowledge sufficient to justify recommending that police, in all places, employ or do not employ a particular strategy or tactic, or, as Sherman (1998: 7) put it: to create 'industrial quality improvement'. One important implication of this objective is that EBP prefers testing one strategy or tactic at a time so as to minimize the confounding effects of multiple independent variables.[3]

Role of normative judgments in decision-making

At the heart of EBP is the idea that police decision-making about strategies and tactics ought to be removed from the realm of political and personal preferences and based in the realm of scientific evidence as far as possible, while acknowledging that some qualitative judgment is inevitable (Sherman, 1998: 13) and perhaps even beneficial (Sherman, 2013: 418–19). In rather sharp contrast, POP, although strongly promoting the use of research findings in crafting policing strategies and tactics, explicitly encourages police decision-makers to take account of local community norms, values, preferences, and priorities, as well as professional ethics, in deciding, ultimately, which strategies and tactics from among those being considered will actually be adopted (Goldstein, 1990: 143). Whereas EBP exhorts police to focus on effectiveness (the impact of the action on the problem at hand), POP also exhorts police to concern themselves with whether their actions are perceived as being fair (Goldstein, 1990: 145–7; Engel and Eck, 2015).[4]

Interest in the generalizability of findings

Evidence-based policing is directly interested in the generalizability of its research findings; POP is less interested in generalizability, and then only indirectly so. One implication is that EBP is likely to prefer conducting its experimental studies under conditions that are not unique or rare. Because POP has as its core purpose addressing local problems, it is not concerned about the distinctive features of the problem environment. As an illustration, one notable POP initiative involved reducing harm from alcohol intoxication in a remote Alaskan community (North Slope Borough Department of Public Safety, 1995). The social, cultural, political, and environmental conditions of this community were so distinctive that the prospects of generalizing the project's findings and results to other communities would be remote indeed.

Principal actor

Problem-oriented policing is a police-practitioner–driven approach; EBP is a researcher-driven approach. Both explicitly involve collaborations between practitioners and researchers, but given their respective core objectives and interests at stake, they necessarily differ in terms of who must make final determinations about the conduct of the inquiry. Problem-oriented policing was developed mainly as a means of encouraging police to become more reflective and analytical about the nature of their work and how they seek to achieve their objectives. In so doing, Goldstein was mindful that police officials were unlikely to be receptive to having important decision-making taken out of their hands. Indeed, POP is often distinguished from community policing in this same regard: whereas community policing explicitly cedes some police decision-making to the community, POP pointedly reserves most final decision-making to the police, even while encouraging police to take community preferences into account. This reluctance to intrude too sharply on police authority is not merely for the pragmatic purpose of not putting police off to the concept, but also because the concept highly values police judgments about the nature of local policing problems and how they ought to be addressed. Because EBP strives for high scientific standards, it cannot afford to cede important final decisions about experimental design to police practitioners even though police retain ultimate authority over their operations, regardless of the consequences for the experiment. It would be better that EBP experiments be abandoned if experimental conditions could not be maintained adequately.

Accountability mechanisms

Both POP and EBP are keenly interested in holding police accountable for their selection of policing strategies and tactics. Sherman emphasizes holding police accountable to the emerging body of EBP knowledge, proposing such accountability mechanisms as national rankings of police agencies according to their fidelity to EBP practices, nationally mandated police data systems that would store and facilitate the analysis of data on which policing practices could be studied, and the employment of trained researchers in police agencies to serve as 'evidence cops'. Goldstein, too, seeks to hold the police more accountable for their choices of policing strategies and tactics, choices that he hopes will be more strongly informed by available research and local analysis, but the accountability for which would be mediated through local political processes and not solely through a body of scientific knowledge. Because POP is rooted in concerns about democratic governance, it emphasizes police considering and choosing alternatives for addressing local problems that best meet the community's and local government's needs and expectations. Although he doesn't say so explicitly, Goldstein implies that political accountability would and should, in the end, trump scientific accountability.

Reconciling theory and practice in problem-oriented policing and evidence-based policing

Much of what I have written thus far in this chapter is based on the theoretical constructs for Goldstein's POP and Sherman's EBP and the ideal application of their models that they envision and articulate, respectively. But theory and practice seldom match perfectly. Theories are revised – by better theories and by the experience of practice – but they are also distorted, misunderstood, or applied imperfectly. And there are innumerable practical obstacles that compel some infidelity to the original theory or vision. Both POP and EBP have probably suffered in the translation from theory to practice, although both may have benefited some as well. Neither concept has been applied entirely as its chief proponent has hoped (Goldstein, 2003; Sherman, 2015).

Problem-oriented policing

Measured against Goldstein's (1979) original vision for POP, the concept has diverged or fallen short in several key respects. If it has not been put into practice in an ideal form anywhere – as it surely has not – it has been put into practice in some form in many places around the world, to the point that 'problem-solving' has become part of the modern police lexicon, with at least some of its use being generally faithful to Goldstein's concept. The concept has an institutional home in the Center for Problem-Oriented Policing, which serves as one base from which the concept is promoted and its practice disseminated. Although there is no reliable count, the number of POP case studies, project narratives, and research studies must be in the tens of thousands.[5] Through conferences, guidebooks, case studies, and other publications and educational tools, a large, rich, and comprehensible body of information – organized and crafted to comport with the police perspective on their work – has been made readily available to police worldwide to help them improve the effectiveness and fairness of their responses to local policing problems.

In Goldstein's original vision, POP would be undertaken at the higher levels of police administration, with trained in-house or external analysts working closely with senior police executives in examining the current police response to large-scale problems and developing and implementing improved responses to them. Some of this sort of work has been undertaken, to be sure, but there has also emerged a street-level form of problem-solving, which was unanticipated, but welcomed for the infusion of locally knowledgeable and committed police officers in the business of improving policing (Eck and Spelman, 1987). Street-level problem-solving would likely never be as methodologically sophisticated as administrative-level, problem-oriented inquiries, but it would greatly and quickly expand the sheer number and range of problems for which police would take a fresh and preventive look and for which police would try new approaches.

Although David Weisburd et al. (2010: 140) found some reliable studies demonstrating that the application of POP principles yielded significant crime reductions, they concluded that '. . . the evidence base . . . is deficient given the strong investment in POP . . .'. In short, they did not find as many POP initiatives with strong evaluation designs and outcomes as they believe would be desirable. They did, however, report that the less rigorous POP studies they reviewed were more numerous and '. . . the results . . . indicate an overwhelmingly positive impact from POP' (Weisburd et al., 2010: 140). Other scholars have likewise concluded that much of the analytical and evaluative work undertaken under the banner of

POP has been rather deficient, at least as of the time these assessments were made, which might no longer reflect the current state of affairs (Clarke, 1997; Scott, 2000; Cordner and Biebel, 2005; Bullock, Erol and Tilley, 2006). None of these critiques, however, are of the theory, but of the practice to date. All of the previously cited reviewers are advocates of POP and express hope for improving the rigor of both the analysis of policing problems and the evaluation of outcomes.

Evidence-based policing

Similarly, measured against Sherman's (1998) original vision, EBP has thus far fallen short of its ideal. Although Sherman's EBP concept has only been in circulation just less than two decades and some important high-quality policing research has been undertaken under its auspices during that time, Sherman counts just 100 'tests of police practice' in existence through 2015, few of which appear to have had much impact on actual police practice across the profession (Sherman, 2015: 1). Like POP, EBP is enduring similar challenges in gaining traction, first conceptually, and then in its routine practice.

The sheer scope of work required in an ideal, totally EBP approach illustrates a major challenge confronting the approach. If Goldstein is correct that policing constitutes dealing with a set of specific behavioral problems, each sufficiently different that tailored responses to each of them are indicated, then we need some idea how many discrete policing problems exist that require controlled, high-quality experimentation to determine what works best in addressing them. Although there is not, and never will be, a definitive and fixed number of policing problems, my own list of common, contemporary policing problems runs to nearly 250 discrete problems (Scott, 2015: 47–64; see also Eck and Clarke, 2003). And if it is true that effective responses to policing problems often entail the application of a combination of discrete responses (I count about 35 common police responses to problems, some with multiple subcategories, and POP initiatives report an average of a half-dozen tactics employed per problem), the experimentation necessary to disentangle the effects of particular responses becomes that much more extensive and complex. And if it is true that even the most rigorously designed and implemented studies call for at least several replications in other settings to establish the generalizability of findings, the research task expands by yet another order of magnitude (Tilley, 2009). By this logic, there could be need for tens of thousands of clinical trials to amass a comprehensive body of EBP knowledge. At the current pace that Sherman reports, it would take several thousand years to build this body of knowledge. Accelerating the pace at which clinical trials are funded and completed would help, but the scope of work remains enormous.

As Sherman and others acknowledge, an ideal adoption of EBP is not solely a matter of securing the funding and research capacity to conduct all these clinical trials; it also requires a deeper commitment from police executives (and, ultimately, their line personnel) and political leaders to routinely conduct police operations under experimental conditions (Weisburd and Neyroud, 2011; Sherman, 2015). Because maintaining the integrity of experimental conditions requires police to hold in abeyance some of their ordinary discretion and requires police executives and their political leaders to tolerate the political risks that invariably accompany experimentation involving people's safety and security, the challenge to full adoption of EBP becomes greater yet.

Sherman's vision of holding police agencies accountable for employing EBP practices through professional police regulatory authorities and the placement of 'evidence cops' within police agencies remains a distant one. Although police regulatory authorities exist in all U.S. states and in the UK national government, none as yet are holding police agencies accountable for their policing methods. And although the U.S. national government is increasingly insinuating itself in the business of telling local police agencies how to operate,[6] it has yet to dictate that police use EBP methods. The focus has remained on policing processes rather than on the substance of policing. And although many police agencies now employ crime analysts (a growing number of whom hold social science doctorates) and/or have routine communications with local university researchers and a few have had 'embedded criminologists' working for them on a temporary basis, the police field as a whole remains a long way from having criminological advice readily available to all police decision-makers in the way Sherman envisions (Braga, 2013).

Choosing between problem-oriented policing and evidence-based policing

The schism between POP and EBP, to the extent one exists, is at once trivial and important. It is trivial in that much of the disagreement seems to turn on what constitutes reliable evidence on which police should base their decisions as to how to address policing problems. If the choice were between no scientific basis whatsoever (the historically dominant basis) and some scientific basis, POP and EBP proponents alike would uniformly endorse the latter. But the schism in perspective becomes highly important if the choice is between a standard such as 'the best scientific basis practically available that is feasible and politically acceptable at the time of the decision' and a standard such as 'the highest degree of scientific certainty'.

Given the highly discretionary nature of policing – at all organizational levels – each police official can decide where on this decision-making spectrum it is most sensible to ground real-world policing decisions. And given, at least in the United States, the highly decentralized system of police accountability, each mayor, city council, or other entity with supervisory authority over police can decide where on this spectrum they are comfortable ratifying policing decisions.

Police scholars other than Goldstein and Sherman have also weighed in on the relative merits of a problem-oriented versus an evidence-based approach to policing. Moore (2006), Sparrow (2011), and Tilley (2009) have expressed a preference for a more moderate standard than is proposed under EBP, not merely for practical reasons, but because they reject the premise that scientific experimentation is the only, or necessarily the best, method for ascertaining the truth or for making what are ultimately political decisions.[7] Perhaps in reaction to such critiques, EBP proponents have subtly scaled back some of the ambitious vision in which science would dictate police policy and practice (Bueermann, 2012; Sherman, 2015), making EBP rhetoric increasingly echo POP rhetoric.[8]

Police officials, government overseers, and policing scholars are, of course, free to adopt or advocate whichever policing framework makes most sense to them, whether it's POP, EBP, or any of the myriad other conceptual approaches that have been or will be proposed. But even if governments or the scholastic academy had the authority to impose one approach to policing by edict, it likely wouldn't work anyway. Given the highly variable and complex nature of the police function and the discretionary decision-making inherent in carrying it out, the delivery of police services will likely always be based on some blend of concepts, whether explicitly or implicitly. Notwithstanding this reality about the melding and muddling of policing concepts, to the extent police, government officials, and scholars seek to choose between POP and EBP, there ought to be some principled basis for doing so.

Unsurprisingly, given my long-standing association with POP, I favor POP over EBP as the framework best fit for policing, at least for the present time. I will enumerate my inter-related reasons next.

The scope of policing rationale

By design, POP is a framework for the entirety of policing, and that entirety is truly quite large. As multifaceted and complex as is the enterprise of preventing, reducing, and controlling crime, all that work comprises but a portion of police work. Police also address social problems that don't neatly fit into the crime category (e.g., resolving conflicts and disputes, attending to suicide attempts, controlling dangerous animals, safeguarding people who cannot care for themselves, responding to disasters, and regulating traffic and crowds). Problem-oriented policing provides police a framework for developing ever-better methods of addressing all the particular pressing problems within their community, in whatever locally specific form those problems are manifested. Because every type of policing problem can vary in important ways from community to community, police are seldom able to perfectly replicate what was proved to work elsewhere or under other conditions: usually they must adapt their response to a highly particular local context.

The complexity of policing rationale

Police objectives with regard to any of the hundreds of social problems with which they contend are seldom one-dimensional. For example, in the context of sexual assault, although main police objectives are to apprehend perpetrators and to reduce the incidence of sexual assault, they also seek to ensure that victims are properly cared for, suspects are fairly treated, and the public is fearful of sexual assault only to the degree appropriate to its actual risk in that time and place.

Accordingly, determining 'what works' in policing, as EBP aspires to do, is not merely a large undertaking, as noted earlier, but is one that begs further clarification of what is meant by 'works'. A scientific experiment might establish that a particular policing strategy effectively reduces the incidence of a type of sexual assault, but if that strategy has the side effects of leaving victims poorly treated, suspects mistreated, or the public scared well out of proportion to actual risk, one might be hard-pressed to claim that that strategy 'worked' in a comprehensive sense. And because police often must make trade-offs in reconciling their multiple, and sometimes competing, objectives, they might deliberately have to sacrifice some degree of effectiveness to achieve other important objectives. Broadly speaking, the public is entitled to expect of its police not only that they be effective, but that they also be fair and efficient. A police response that can be said to have 'worked' in a comprehensive sense would be one that might have to be determined by several measures of effectiveness, several measures of fairness, and several measures of efficiency (Sweeten, 2015).

There are seldom perfect outcomes to policing. Usually, the best that can be achieved are optimal outcomes, and determining optimality is hard to do through experimental methods. This helps explain why such policing strategies as random preventive patrols and teaching drug abuse resistance to schoolchildren (e.g., the DARE program) remain in common practice, strong research evidence of their ineffectiveness notwithstanding. Police who advocate DARE often claim, perhaps rightly, that even if the program fails to achieve its primary objective of preventing future drug use, it achieves the secondary objectives of establishing good relationships between police and schoolchildren and, by extension, their parents. Police who continue to employ random preventive patrols, as most do, might acknowledge its limited crime and fear reduction effects, as demonstrated by experimental studies, and yet still defend its practice on grounds that their public constituents still expect it and that it remains a reasonable model for positioning police officers to respond to emergency situations.[9] Of course, EBP studies would be useful to test such alternative-objective claims, but the fact that many policing strategies and tactics plausibly help police achieve multiple objectives further adds to the scope of research required to build a comprehensive understanding of 'what works' in policing.

The 'fit for purpose' rationale

Policing is fundamentally about responding, relatively quickly, to a wide array of social problems that threaten people's safety and security. Given the constant stream of demands for police service, some of them immediate and urgent, policing is action oriented rather than research oriented. Both POP and EBP encourage police to introduce some measure of a research orientation into the enterprise to improve the quality of police service, but POP urges that the research orientation be action based in several senses. It urges that those doing the research be part of the action; that they work closely with the police officers most directly involved in dealing with the problem at hand so as to promote an exchange of expertise deemed important to understanding problems and developing and implementing new responses to them. Police officers help researchers better understand problems on the basis of their experience dealing with them and design and implement new practical responses. In turn, researchers help police officers better understand problems on the basis of data analysis and existing research and design new responses that are more likely to be effective because they are based on an understanding of the causal mechanisms of problems. Responsibility for thinking and doing is shared between police and researchers. It is also action oriented in that it recognizes that police seldom have the option of doing nothing about problems for which no scientifically tested responses exist. Even in the face of uncertainty, police are usually expected to do something. This research–practice model is better suited to the pace and complexity of the policing environment than is the more academic EBP model. Although POP calls for a more deliberative pace than police are accustomed to in a reactive, incident-oriented approach to policing, in practice it tends to eschew the decidedly slower pace associated with scholarly experimentation and publication, which is almost always measured in years, rather than weeks or months.

The 'flexible standards of proof' rationale

As noted earlier, POP is more tolerant of lesser standards of proof in deeming whether a policing initiative 'worked' than is EBP which aspires to high social science research standards of proof, although many POP evaluations could and should be more rigorous than they are (Knutsson, 2009). Problem-oriented policing welcomes the opportunities that might arise to evaluate policing interventions on a more rigorous scientific basis, but recognizing that such opportunities are likely to be rare and not always appropriate, settles for so-called 'good enough' evaluation (Eck, 2002a).

The strength of evidence required depends heavily on what questions one wants answered and what are the costs of being wrong (Eck, 2002b). For many relatively small-scale policing problems, the police only want to know whether their efforts to control the problem did so; they are less concerned with determining with certainty which of their particular actions caused the result. Such a lack of practical interest in causation obviates the need for rigorous scientific methodology (Bullock, Erol and Tilley, 2006: 132). And even if there is interest in understanding what specifically caused the result, it is often the case that the cost of being wrong in one's conclusion is small. Interventions that are not expensive to implement and which cause little or no unintended harm probably don't require rigorous proof to justify their use again in the future.

The context of legal standards of proof is analogous. The criminal law has progressively higher standards of proof depending upon the severity of the consequences of official action (in U.S. legalese, 'reasonable suspicion' for police to detain a suspect; 'probable cause' for police to arrest a suspect; and 'proof beyond a reasonable doubt' for a court to convict a defendant), and criminal law standards of proof tend to be more stringent than those in civil law (where a 'preponderance of the evidence' suffices). Problem-oriented policing aspires to higher evidentiary standards in determining whether a policing strategy worked when the consequences of being wrong and the interest in replicating the strategy are both high, but is content with lesser evidentiary standards otherwise.

The 'walk-before-you-run' rationale

Finally, POP seems a better approach than EBP at this stage in police history. If the long-term goal is to move police officials and their government overseers from a) not asking any questions whatsoever about known effectiveness prior to implementing a strategy, to b) asking what reasons exist to think a strategy might work locally, to c) asking what scientific evidence exists that the strategy works, to d) asking what is the strength of the evidence on the scientific methods scale that the strategy will work under local conditions, the police institution is, in the main, still moving from a) to b), and getting to d) seems a long way into the future, even if it is a desirable destination. Just getting police in the habit of routinely asking whether there are any data to support their experiential suppositions about the nature of policing problems, their causes and contributing conditions, and the effectiveness of alternative responses will be a major step forward, as will be getting police to recognize the full range of alternative strategies and tactics available to them in dealing with problems and be willing to try some of them. Engaging many police officers in an even rudimentary research orientation today should pave the way toward an increasingly sophisticated understanding of research methods and their application to policing in the future. Fully and properly understood, evaluating the effects of policing in accordance with rigorous scientific standards is very challenging even for the most skilled researchers because it entails controlling for multiple dependent and independent variables that exist and interact in highly dynamic social contexts and interpreting research findings that are rarely overwhelmingly clear and consistent. Obtaining a confluence of conditions necessary to carry out a fully controlled experiment of a policing practice is extraordinarily difficult and rare, even for the most capable researchers.

Conclusion

It would seem desirable that the efforts being expended under the banner of POP and those being expended under the banner of EBP be simultaneously encouraged, but better integrated. Just as no proponent of POP should ever desire that experimental research of policing be halted, no proponent of EBP should ever desire that police suspend all of their problem-solving because it isn't sufficiently scientific. Each approach has much to offer toward improving police effectiveness and fairness, though their methods and particular value differ. Ideally, police executives, political leaders, and police researchers would all encourage and support continual efforts to improve responses to local policing problems through pragmatic and eclectic forms of inquiry, while simultaneously being alert for the right opportunities and circumstances for subjecting selected policing practices to scientifically rigorous experimentation that has the potential to improve not just local conditions, but policing practice across the entire profession (EBP). The kinds of knowledge and wisdom that the two approaches offer differ, but both are valuable. They can and should challenge or validate one another. At least where human behavior is involved, no single method of inquiry and discovery enjoys a monopoly on truth. This being said, POP seems the approach best suited for the complex realities of policing, allowing room to incorporate EBP research findings without the constraints imposed by rigid scientific methods and standards, and embracing the human judgments that often differentiate between good and bad policing.

Notes

1 To some degree, intelligence-led policing and community policing are also organizational theories, although community policing is less about figuring out what police should do about crime and disorder than it is about how police should relate to the community in going about it. Intelligence-led policing, at least in practice, has become more about concentrating police attention and resources on offenders and offender networks to identify them and disrupt their activities through law enforcement methods.
2 Perhaps ironically, the EBP movement, through the Campbell Collaboration, published a systematic review to determine whether POP 'works' to reduce crime. It determined that there is evidence it does (Weisburd et al., 2010). But if POP and EBP are both organizational theories rather than criminological theories, would it make as much sense for the EBP movement to conduct a systematic review to determine whether EBP 'works' to reduce crime? The notion seems preposterous on its face and a product of circular logic (Scott, 2010: 136–7; Tilley, 2010: 192).
3 In some respects, the differences in the unit of analysis between POP and EBP are reflected in the distinction between the principal focus of the Center for Problem-Oriented Policing's publication output and that of the Campbell Collaboration (which is based on an evidence-based approach to crime control and other social problems). The bulk of the research-and-practice reviews published by the Center for Problem-Oriented Policing is found in its *Problem-Specific Guides*, which has thus far published on six dozen discrete policing problems, with at least as many more discrete problems that could be covered. By contrast, most, although not all, of the *Crime Prevention Research Reviews* published by the Campbell Collaboration concern themselves with determining whether a particular strategy or tactic 'works'. These include reviews of such strategies and tactics as Scared Straight programs, drug courts, formal system processing of juveniles, pulling levers strategies, boot camps, and neighborhood watch. Although employing a different research methodology, the Center for Problem-Oriented Policing's *Response Guides* cover such strategies and tactics as assigning police officers to schools, asset forfeiture, street lighting, sting operations, crime prevention publicity campaigns, video surveillance of public places, street closings, and police crackdowns, thereby demonstrating some commonality of interests between POP and EBP.
4 Sherman (2013: 380, 383) has more recently acknowledged the need for EBP studies to simultaneously examine effects of police practices on public perceptions of fairness.
5 The Campbell Collaboration systematic review of POP reviewed over 5,500 reports and studies; the Center for Problem-Oriented Policing has approximately 1,500 reports and collections of many more project summaries in its files; and there are uncounted numbers of POP project reports in police agency files, and many more projects for which no final narrative was ever written, but on which work was completed.
6 This is being done principally through the authority granted to the U.S. Department of Justice to bring 'pattern-and-practice' lawsuits against local police agencies, which usually are resolved by giving the federal government substantial authority to mandate that

the local agency adopt various administrative and operational practices to remedy its unconstitutional policing practices.

7 In other fields involving human decision-making and behavior, such as psychiatry, public health, and economics, skepticism persists over whether effective interventions can be determined through randomized clinical trials alone (Sampson, 2010).

8 For example, Sherman's (2013) recent articulation of a 'Triple Ts' (targeting, testing, and tracking) strategy parallels the 'scanning', 'assessment', and 'response' phases of the SARA model developed under the auspices of POP.

9 See Sherman (2013: 396–416) for an extensive discussion of the contrast between available research findings and what police do in practice.

References

Braga, A.A. (2013). *Embedded Criminologists in Police Departments*, Ideas in American Policing series, no. 17, Washington, DC: Police Foundation.

Bueermann, J. (2012). 'Being smart on crime with evidence-based policing', *NIJ Journal*, (March), 269: 12–15.

Bullock, K., Erol, R. and Tilley, N. (2006). *Problem-Oriented Policing and Partnerships: Implementing an Evidence-based Approach to Crime Reduction*, Devon: Willan Publishing.

Carte, G. and Carte, E. (1975). *Police Reform in the United States: The Era of August Vollmer*, Berkeley: University of California Press.

Clarke, R.V. (1997). *Problem-Oriented Policing and the Potential Contribution of Criminology*, Unpublished Report to the National Institute of Justice.

Cordner, G. and Biebel, E. (2005). 'Problem-oriented policing in practice', *Criminology & Public Policy*, 4(2): 155–80.

Eck, J.E. (2002a). 'Learning from Experience in Problem-Oriented Policing and Situational Prevention: The Positive Functions of Weak Evaluations and the Negative Functions of Strong Ones', in N. Tilley (ed) *Evaluation for Crime Prevention*, pp. 93–117, Crime Prevention Studies, vol. 14, Monsey, NY: Criminal Justice Press.

Eck, J.E. (2002b). *Assessing Responses to Problems: An Introductory Guide for Police Problem-Solvers*, Problem-Oriented Guides for Police. Problem-Solving Tools Series No. 1. Washington, DC: US Department of Justice, Office of Community Oriented Policing Services.

Eck, J.E. and Clarke, R.V. (2003). 'Classifying Common Police Problems: A Routine Activity Approach', in M.J. Smith and D.B. Cornish (eds) *Theory for Practice in Situational Crime Prevention*, pp. 7–39, Crime Prevention Studies, vol. 16, Monsey, NY: Criminal Justice Press.

Eck, J.E. and Spelman, W. (1987). *Problem-Solving: Problem-Oriented Policing in Newport News*, Washington, DC: Police Executive Research Forum.

Engel, R.S. and Eck, J.E. (2015). *Effectiveness vs. Equity in Policing: Is a Tradeoff Inevitable?* Ideas in American Policing, No. 18, Washington, DC: Police Foundation.

Goldstein, H. (1979). 'Improving policing: A problem-oriented approach', *Crime & Delinquency*, 25(2): 236–58.

Goldstein, H. (1990) *Problem-Oriented Policing*, New York: McGraw-Hill.

Goldstein, H. (2001). 'Problem-Oriented Policing in a Nutshell', presentation at the International Problem-oriented Policing Conference, San Diego, CA.

Goldstein, H. (2003). 'On Further Developing Problem-Oriented Policing: The most Critical Need, the Major Impediments, and a Proposal', in J. Knutsson (ed) *Problem-Oriented Policing: From Innovation to Mainstream*, pp. 13–47, Monsey, NY: Criminal Justice Press.

Knutsson, J. (2009). 'Standards of Evaluation in Problem-Oriented Policing Projects: Good Enough?', in J. Knutsson and N. Tilley (eds) *Evaluating Crime Reduction Initiatives*, pp. 7–28, Crime Prevention Studies, vol. 24, Monsey, NY: Criminal Justice Press.

Laycock, G. (2005). 'Defining crime science', in M.J. Smith and N. Tilley (eds) *Crime Science: New Approaches to Preventing and Detecting Crime*, pp. 3–24, Devon: Willan Publishing.

Moore, M.H. (2006). 'Improving Policing through Expertise, Experience, and Experiments', in D. Weisburd and A.A. Braga (eds) *Police Innovation: Contrasting Perspectives*, pp. 322–338, Cambridge: Cambridge University Press.

North Slope Borough Department of Public Safety. (1995). 'The Barrow Temperance Project: Reducing Alcohol-Related Crime and Disorder with Prohibition in an Alaskan Community', *Submission to the Herman Goldstein Award for Excellence in Problem-oriented Policing*. Retrieved from www.popcenter.org/library/awards/goldstein/1995/95-56(W).pdf (accessed 17 March 2016).

Ratcliffe, J. (2008). *Intelligence-led Policing*, Devon: Willan Publishing.

Rojek, J. (2003). 'A decade of excellence in problem-oriented policing: Characteristics of the Goldstein award winners', *Police Quarterly*, 6(4): 492–515.

Sampson, R.J. (2010). 'Gold standard myths: Observations on the experimental turn in quantitative criminology', *Journal of Quantitative Criminology*, 26: 489–500.

Scott, M.S. (2000). *Problem-Oriented Policing: Reflections on the First 20 Years*, Washington, DC: US Department of Justice, Office of Community Oriented Policing Services.

Scott, M.S. (2010). 'Evaluating the effectiveness of problem-oriented policing', Editorial introduction, *Criminology & Public Policy*, 9(1): 135–7.

Scott, M.S. (2015). *Identifying and Defining Policing Problems*, Problem-Oriented Guides for Police. Problem-Solving Tools Series No. 13, Washington, DC: US Department of Justice, Office of Community Oriented Policing Services.

Scott, M.S. and Clarke, R.V. (2000). 'A Review of Submissions for the Herman Goldstein Award for Excellence in Problem-Oriented Policing', in C. Solé Brito and E.E. Gratto (eds) *Problem-Oriented Policing: Crime-Specific Problems*, pp. 213–230, Critical Issues and Making POP Work, vol. 3, Washington, DC: Police Executive Research Forum.

Sherman, L.W. (1998). *Evidence-Based Policing*, Ideas in American Policing series, Washington, DC: Police Foundation.

Sherman, L.W. (2013). 'The rise of evidence-based policing: Targeting, testing, and tracking', *Crime & Justice*, 42(1): 377–451.

Sherman, L.W. (2015). 'A tipping point for "totally evidenced policing": Ten ideas for building an evidence-based police agency', *International Criminal Justice Review*, 25(1): 11–29.

Sparrow, M. (2011). *Governing Science*, New Perspectives in Policing, Cambridge, MA: Harvard Kennedy School of Government.

Sweeten, G. (2015). 'What works, what doesn't, what's Constitutional?', *Criminology & Public Policy*, 15(1): 67–73.

Tilley, N. (2009). 'What's the "What" in "What Works?" Health, Policing and Crime Prevention', in J. Knutsson and N. Tilley (eds) *Evaluating Crime Reduction Initiatives*, pp. 121–145, Crime Prevention Studies, vol. 24, Monsey, NY: Criminal Justice Press.

Tilley, N. (2010). 'Whither problem-oriented policing', Policy essay, *Criminology & Public Policy*, 9(1): 183–94.

Vollmer, A. (1930). 'The scientific policeman', *The American Journal of Police Science*, 1(1): 8–12.

Vollmer, A. (1933). 'Police progress in the past twenty-five years', *Journal of Criminal Law & Criminology*, 24(1): 161–75.

Weisburd, D. and Braga, A.A. (2006). *Police Innovation: Contrasting Perspectives*, Cambridge: Cambridge University Press.

Weisburd, D. and Neyroud, P. (2011). *Police Science: Toward a New Paradigm*, New Perspectives in Policing, Cambridge, MA: Harvard Kennedy School of Government.

Weisburd, D., Telep, C.W., Hinkle, J.C. and Eck, J.E. (2010). *The Effects of Problem-Oriented Policing on Crime and Disorder*, Crime Prevention Research Review, no. 4, Washington, DC: US Department of Justice, Office of Community Oriented Policing Services.

Welsh, B.C. (2006). 'Evidence-based Policing for Crime Prevention', in D. Weisburd and A.A. Braga (eds) *Police Innovation: Contrasting Perspectives*, pp. 305–321, Cambridge: Cambridge University Press.

4 Some solutions to the evidence-based crime prevention problem

John E. Eck

While attending the Campbell Collaborative annual meeting in Washington, DC, two evidence-based researchers fell in love. Under the influence of forest plots, they decided to take a trip north to Maine to see some real forests. They drove to Mt. Katadin in the center of the state, but somewhere near Meddybemps, Maine, they discovered they were lost. So they stopped at a general store. On the store's commodious porch sat two grizzled old men, colloquially known as 'geezers', smoking pipes.

Approaching the geezers, the researchers asked for directions to the famous mountain. One geezer looked at the other without expression. The second took a deep suck on his pipe and while expelling the smoke said: 'You cannot get there from here'.

Evidence-based crime prevention (including evidence-based policing) attempts to generalize from a few well-executed evaluations to the outcomes of future prevention practice. It wants to make sound statements of the form: 'Given this set of studies of a prevention practice, whose results we have strong reasons to believe are valid, if you implement this practice you are likely to get results similar to those reported in our review'. 'Here' is a published systematic review or meta-analysis of a practice. 'There' is the expected future outcome from applying this practice. I contend you cannot get there from here, and this paper shows why and what we can do about it.

The standard description of evidence-based policing and crime prevention is that practitioners should base their decisions on the best evidence. That best evidence is from randomized controlled trials or rigorously controlled quasi-experiments. And they should not rely on a single study, but on multiple studies analyzed within a systematic review process and containing a meta-analysis of the findings of all evaluations. I have rather ambivalent feelings about this prescription. On one hand it is hard to deny that if one has findings from a well-executed randomized experiment, one has some very good evidence. It is also hard to deny that a well-executed quasi-experiment with sensible controls also produces findings that cannot be easily discarded. And it is extremely difficult to deny that if one has a large number of such studies, the collective evidence is worthy of attention by policymakers.

On the other hand, it is hard to square the logic of this prescription with the logic of Campbell's distinction between internal and external validity (Campbell and Stanley, 1966; Cook and Campbell, 1979; Shadish, Cook and Campbell, 2002).

Questions of internal validity ask: 'Given the way this study was conducted, can I be confident that its findings actually show a causal connection?' In contrast, external validity questions ask: 'How confident am I that these findings will recur if someone evaluates another example of this program somewhere else and with different subjects?' This distinction is so basic that it is described in almost all research methods texts in the social sciences. The preference for randomized controlled trials and strong quasi-experiments over findings from other studies is based on internal validity considerations. But the question being asked is of generalizability, or external validity. And as Cartwright and Hardie (2012) explain, how a study was conducted does not help answer questions of generalizability.

I have marched in the evidence-based movement. I authored one of the chapters in the now-famous Maryland Report (Sherman et al., 1998). I have participated in several systematic reviews and meta-analyses. I have even conducted a randomized controlled experiment. So I am not against these activities; I find them extremely useful. However, I am not persuaded by my friends and colleagues when they demand, seemingly, that policymakers value evidence from such studies over other research and experience, regardless of context. In particular, I am troubled by efforts to get internal validity to solve problems of external validity.

In this paper, I will describe why evidence-based crime prevention and policing advocates are making a logical fallacy. I will also show why we cannot take the results from meta-analysis as indicators of what policymakers should do. Then I will describe how we can use evaluative research in a more modest, but nevertheless important way.

In the first section, I describe the notions of deduction, induction and falsification. These ideas are at the heart of how we judge the quality of research efforts and at the heart of all modern science. Falsification is an attempt to get around a particularly thorny problem with induction.

In the second section, I describe how falsification applies to internal validity but not to external validity. Internal validity questions are retrospective – they evaluate the quality of existing evidence. External validity questions are prospective – they predict what might occur in the future.

In the third section, I show how commonly described evidence-based practices ignore this distinction between internal and external validity and presume to make general statements based solely on internal validity criterion. As the Maine geezers might have said: 'You cannot get to external validity from internal validity'.

In the fourth section, I show how we can generalize by starting with a strong theory. Theories are general statements or conjectures about how some bit of the world works. Evidence consistent with the theory, including evaluations, implies one is permitted to apply the theory generally. Generality is baked into the theory, but not the evidence.

In the fifth section, I show how using external validity concepts may provide policymakers with better information upon which to make decisions. This information is evidence as well. But it is not the evidence commonly described in evaluation reports or in systematic reviews.

In the final section I summarize my arguments and suggest where we can go from here.

Deduction vs. induction vs. falsification

> (T)he fate of a theory, its acceptance or rejection, is decided by observation and experiment – by the results of tests. So long as a theory stands up to the severest tests we can design, it is accepted; if it does not, it is rejected. But it is never inferred, in any sense, from the empirical evidence. There is neither a psychological nor a logical induction. *Only the falsity of the theory can be inferred from empirical evidence, and this inference is a purely deductive one* (emphasis in original).
>
> Karl Popper, 1992: 54

Modern science is usually understood among scientists as relying on falsification; the rejection of theories that are found to be inconsistent with evidence. The principle of falsification was developed by Karl Popper to address the logical difficulties of induction (Popper, 1992). To understand falsification and why it is superior to induction, we need to revise the distinction between deduction and induction.

Deduction is based on a set of logical principles. One starts with one or more assumptions about the world. These are often called premises. You ask: 'If these premises are true, then what can I expect?' Following basic rules of logic, you draw a conclusion. Here is an example:

Assumption/premise: All criminologists write badly.
Assumption/premise: Here is an article written by a criminologist.
Conclusion: It will, if I were to read it, be badly written.

The validity of the conclusion depends on the validity of the premises and on the correct application of the rules. The conclusion is valid if the assumptions are correct because it follows the rules of logic, but it is factually false because the first statement is not correct. A few criminologists do write well.

Here is an example of deductive reasoning that is incorrect because of the incorrect application of logic:

Assumption/premise: Most criminologists write badly.
Assumption/premise: Here is a poorly written article.
Conclusion: The author of the paper is a criminologist.

The first assumption is true. But the logic is incorrect so the conclusion is invalid. There are plenty of noncriminologists (sociologists and political scientists, for example) who write badly, so there is no good reason to believe, based on the assumptions, that the paper was written by a criminologist.

In contrast to deduction, induction works by the accumulation of evidence, without premises. For example:

Here is a poorly written paper written by a criminologist.
Here is another such paper, also written by a criminologist.
Here is another such paper, with the same type of author.

. . . and so on . . .

And here is yet another poorly written paper written by another criminologist. Conclusion: All criminologists are poor writers.

At each step prior to the conclusion, there is an empirical observation. The observer repeatedly sees the same conjunction of bad writing and a criminologist author. The first observation is interesting, but because it might be an anomaly, the observer draws no conclusions. After many observations, the observer decides that this is not an anomalous conjunction, but a fact of nature. One could also propose a possible conclusion early on (perhaps after the first or second observation) and then add confirmatory evidence. Then after accumulating a great deal of such evidence, we determine that the initial proposed conclusion is correct.

Popper (1992) asserted that science does not advance by accumulating observations. He pointed out that physicists had accumulated a very large number and variety of findings that confirmed Newton's theory of physics. If induction was a useful way of characterizing science, then Newton's theory should be valid. Yet Einstein proposed an alternative; a few studies confirmed it, leading to Einstein's theory supplanting Newton's. How could a few observations disconfirm a theory that was backed by many more observations? Clearly, accumulating evidence, even a great deal of evidence, does not guarantee valid theories.

Popper took advantage of an asymmetry in deduction. If one begins with a universal statement – for example, *all* criminologists are poor writers – then finding yet another observation of confirmatory evidence is of limited use. In contrast, finding a single observation that contradicts the theory falsifies the theory. This is enough to force a change in the theory – for example, dropping the 'all'. The reason this works is because the theory is general – it applies across its domain (e.g., writings of criminologist). A nongeneral theory is of limited utility and uninteresting (e.g., some criminologists are bad writers and some are not, some are so-so writers, and some do not write at all).

Falsification operates on theories and hypotheses. When a scientist applies falsification principles, she is testing a theory or hypothesis to see if she can break it. If she cannot, such a finding allows us to say the theory or hypothesis survived the test. It does not allow us to say the theory or hypothesis is absolutely true. It just survived the test whereas competing theories or hypotheses failed. The operating assumption is that all theories and hypotheses are approximations and educated conjectures, so all will fail eventually. They then get replaced by a stronger theory (which, too, will eventually fail).

For any theory that has useful policy implications, we need to say a bit more than 'the tests so far have failed to falsify the theory.' This is enough for academics who do not get out much. But the practitioner cannot wait until the theory is falsified and a better theory proposed. The practitioner has a target problem that needs a solution now. So the practitioner needs to act based on the best available theory, on the assumption that it is good enough, given what we know now. I will come back to the practitioner perspective later in this chapter, as this perspective is important.

Internal vs. external validity

Falsification is applicable to internal validity but not external validity. Internal validity refers to our confidence that the findings from a particular study are true for the cases studied, during the duration of the study, observed with the measurement processes used and inside the study's setting. It involves a retrospective examination, sort of an audit: the study was conducted, using a particular design, it had specific findings and we have greater or lesser confidence that the findings are valid.

Because internal validity depends on the design, we can anticipate the internal validity before an evaluation is launched. So we can say: 'If I conduct the study with this design, I will have more confidence in the findings (whatever they may be) than I would if I conducted it using this other design'. The vagaries of research make this an approximation of the internal validity of the completed study. Vagaries include subjects dropping out of the study; failures of organizations to deliver the intervention when, where and in the appropriate dose; unexpected changes in the study setting that require modifications to the design; and the final results. Despite these unknowns we can plan studies that have a reasonable prospect of having findings with high internal validity. In the end, however, it is the end results whose validity we examine.

We assess internal validity of a study's findings by asking what the possible causes of the outcome are. Typically, in an evaluation, we are interested in determining if a single intervention (e.g., additional lighting to a crime hot spot) had an impact on an outcome (e.g., crime). If the finding is that the intervention did change the outcome, we ask what else could have done so. There are often several: for example, random variation caused the outcome, measurement changes caused the outcome, environmental factors unconnected with the intervention caused the outcome or even the outcome caused the intervention. If the study is able to eliminate all rival explanations, then we are entitled to believe the intervention caused the change. If the study cannot eliminate any alternative explanations, then its findings have no internal validity. In general, the more alternatives the study can rule out, the more internal validity for the study's findings. This applies to alternative explanations we have evidence for, those we can imagine even if we have no evidence they were the cause and those we cannot imagine but are nevertheless possible (though we do not consider magic and celestial powers, daemons and space aliens).

Campbell and Stanley (1966) classified alternative explanations by putting them into nine sets of 'threats to internal validity'. Study design features – for example, control groups, the number of measurement periods, intervention timing and randomization – can be combined in numerous ways to eliminate entire sets of alternative explanations. The approach Campbell and Stanley pioneered focuses on falsifying alternative explanations, not verifying the main explanation. The approach is like an Agatha Christie drawing room murder mystery. There is an outcome (the dead person) and there are alternative explanations (the people in the drawing room). The detective, in her novels, uses evidence to successively eliminate alternative suspects until there is one left. In an evaluation, we would like to falsify all the alternatives, leaving us with a single cause.

External validity is prospective. It assesses our confidence that if we repeated the experiment we would get similar results. The new experiment may have different cases (e.g., people or places), involve variations in treatment, have different measures of outcome or be applied in another setting (Shadish, Cook and Campbell, 2002). External validity describes expectations of generalizability. Although the researcher can take precautions to make the study as natural as possible to reduce threats to external validity, such precautions cannot eliminate threats. The strongest claims to generalizability are multiple studies in varied settings with different cases that illustrate the possibility that the intervention can work more than once and under different circumstances. However, just because it can work more than once does not provide a sound basis for asserting it will.

Yet we do need to generalize. Aside from the personal interest of the researcher, no one would care a fig about an internally valid study that has no application elsewhere. The study is useless. We read research because we expect to learn something that has application beyond the peculiarities of the study. Internal validity is based on these peculiarities. External validity tries to transcend them.

The illogic of evidence-based practices

The core logic behind evidence-based practice is to accumulate and analyze existing research, usually evaluations, and create a synthetic summary finding. A standard method is to use a systematic review to identify all relevant studies. Another method is to 'weight' each study by the evaluation design used. In this way, internal validity is brought into the synthesis. Studies using designs that cannot eliminate most threats to internal validity may be discarded or be given a low weight. The Maryland Methods Score (Sherman et. al., 1998), for example, gives a single point to studies relying on statistical modeling (e.g., regression analysis) and five points to studies using a randomized controlled trial design. In most meta-analyses, it is common to only examine studies using a randomized controlled trial design and a few forms of quasi-experiments that eliminate most threats to internal validity. Other studies that do not use these designs are discarded, effectively giving them a weight of zero.

The goal of a systematic review, and a meta-analysis, is to do more than summarize the research that has taken place. In itself, this would be interesting, but not very useful. The point of the summary is to show practitioners what they can expect to achieve if they use the intervention reviewed. That is, evidence-based practices are aimed at generalizations from the findings of multiple studies with high internal validity.

There are two difficulties with this logic. First, there is no logical or empirical link between a study's internal validity – a primary criterion for selecting and grading studies for analysis – and external validity – the objective of the synthesis. As I have explained, internal validity only applies to the findings of a specific study. It says nothing about whether the study has implications to other people, places, time periods and settings. That is the role of external validity. But unlike internal validity, there is no way to give assurances that efforts to improve external validity have made a study generalizable. In short, you cannot get to external validity from internal validity.

There might be a way of synthesizing studies by directly examining external validity. It would work something like this. First, identify all relevant studies. Second, select only those studies with a sufficiently high internal validity based on their designs. Third, grade these studies by the degree to which each achieved some level of external validity, using criteria developed by Shadish, Cook and Campbell (2002) and described later in this chapter. Finally, recommend interventions that display high external validity and have dependable findings (high internal validity). What we are grading, unfortunately, are the efforts taken by researchers to improve generalizability, not whether barriers to generalizability have been eliminated. We still do not know if the interventions that pass this test will actually behave as predicted.

The second difficulty with the standard logic has to do with the studies selected for review. The studies in a systematic review are not a probability sample of possible studies. Imagine we had a sound theoretical description of all the possible applications of an intervention. Then we could use a probability sampling process (i.e., simple random sampling, cluster sampling, stratified random sampling or other designs) to select a sample of these hypothetical studies. Once the studies to be conducted are sampled, we would carry them out and make their results public. Then we could synthesize the findings from this representative sample of studies and generalize to all possible interventions. This is impossible, of course, as we cannot define the population from which we would sample.

Unfortunately, we cannot describe all circumstances in which the intervention might be used. In a systematic review or meta-analysis, we have an arbitrary collection of studies that is a nonrandom sample of an unknown and unspecifiable population of possible evaluations. This problem arises not because of the much celebrated 'file drawer problem' – census of published studies leaves out those studies that were conducted but not published. It would exist even if all studies that were conducted were published or if systematic reviewers found all those studies hidden away in dusty file drawers.

The problem arises because researchers study what interests them (or their funders) when they have the ability to carry out the research. Because research is a social phenomenon, there are fads that focus on one narrow topic but ignore most others. In short, all the studies conducted (whether published or not) are a nonrepresentative (arbitrary) sample of all possible studies on the topic.

In our first research courses our instructors warned us not to rely upon findings from samples that are arbitrarily selected – for example, interviews of the 12 people standing at my bus stop. Yet in evidence-based knowledge production, we do the equivalent of this: we examine in great detail the studies that exist. I illustrate this problem in Figure 4.1. There is some imaginary universe of possible circumstances where the practitioners might want to apply the intervention. This is, of course, unknown and hard to define. Within this are multiple populations of

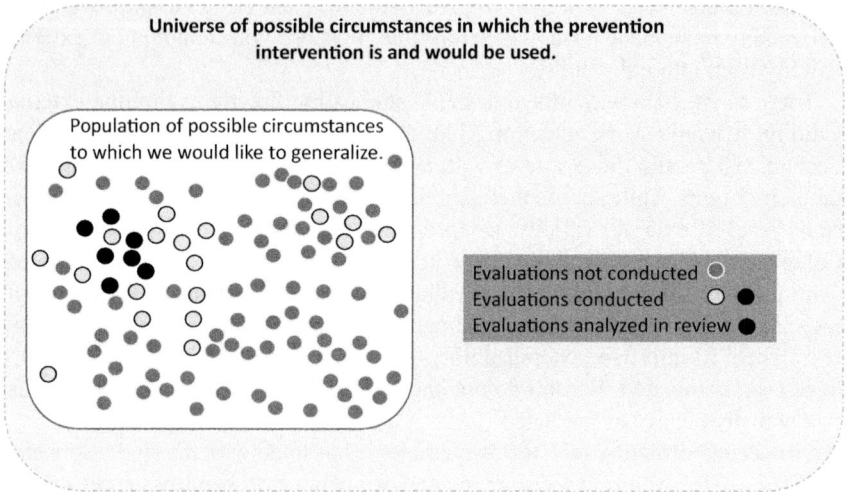

Figure 4.1 Generalizing if reviews were based on sampling theory

circumstances to which the researchers conducting a systematic review or meta-analysis might want to generalize (Figure 4.1 shows only one). Some of the inclusion criteria researchers provide give a partial and often implied definition of this population. Including only studies written in English, for example, hints that the population would encompass English-speaking countries. But this is only a hint and imperfect, as a study conducted in Norway but written in English would be included. Usually, though, this population is not defined. Within this undefined population is a set of possible studies.

But we do not examine possible studies – we study actual studies. It is the set of all actual studies that we use to empirically examine the effectiveness of the intervention. Many of these actual studies cannot be used in systematic or meta-analysis because they do not provide some necessary information (e.g., standard errors) or because the study was not designed with sufficient rigor (e.g., was qualitative, did not have a control condition or was not a randomized trial). Finally, we have a set of studies that seem to fall within the (undefined) population, were conducted in a reasonably rigorous manner and provide the relevant information. We cannot assume that this last group – the set of studies which provide the evidence of effectiveness – is representative of the (undefined) population. Locating all the studies that were conducted does not solve this problem; even if all studies ever conducted were gathered in a review, there is no assurance that this group is anything but an arbitrary set of studies. If this were how someone conducted a survey of voter opinions, we would reject it as likely to be unrepresentative of all voters.

Another lesson our instructors taught us is that large samples are more representative than small samples, assuming a probability sample. Some systematic reviews have numerous studies, but most meta-analyses in crime prevention and policing have relatively few studies.

These problems of nonrepresentativeness and small samples are illustrated in Table 4.1. Drawing on several well-known meta-analyses in policing, I estimated the possible number of studies of the topic and compared this to the number of studies examined in the meta-analysis. The second number is precise, but the first is a gross estimate based on information provided by the authors. When reviewing their studies, I looked for a number of studies the authors seemed to think were relevant to the topic, even if they could not be included in the meta-analysis.

It is obvious that the overall findings from most meta-analyses represent only a small portion of the studies conducted. Only one meta-analysis examined all of the studies found, and this might be because I underestimated the publications identified. Of the other seven studies, none has an analysis rate over 30 percent, and most had a rate of 10 percent or less (the eight meta-analyses had an average rate of 31 percent). Despite the crude estimate of the number of possible studies in the population, this is an underestimate of the problem. The true population would be all the circumstances in which the intervention was applied. Of these, only a few are studied, and only a fraction of these are studied in sufficient rigor to be included in a meta-analysis. And the number of studies analyzed is usually smaller still. Consequently, most meta-analyses in policing and crime prevention have all the generalizability of a qualitative study.

To summarize, we cannot use meta-analytic findings as if the studies examined are representative of a population of possible implementations of a prevention

Table 4.1 Population vs. sample size in meta-analyses

Topic	Publications Identified*	% of Studies Analyzed** (n)	Citation
Focused Deterrence	10	100 (10)	Braga and Weisburd, 2012
Community Policing & Reported Crime	240	27 (65)	Gill et al., 2014
Broken Windows	30	20 (6)	Weisburd, Hinkle, Braga and Wooditch, 2015
Hot-Spots Policing	131	15 (19)	Braga, Papachristos and Hureau, 2014
Antidisorder Tactics	269	10 (28)	Braga, Welsh and Schnell, 2015
Third-Party Policing	160	7 (11)	Mazerolle and Ransley, 2005
Neighborhood Watch	225	5 (12)	Bennett, Holloway and Farrington, 2006
Problem-Oriented Policing	406	3 (10)	Weisburd et al., 2008

* This can only be a rough estimate of the population of studies conducted, as some may not be empirical evaluations and they may contain duplicate accounts of the same intervention.

** I am counting studies (reports and publications), rather than findings. A single study might contain multiple findings. This is because a study usually describes a singular instance of implementation.

program. The set of studies located in these reviews are not probability samples. The proportion of studies examined is usually a small fraction of extant studies. And the numbers of studies examined are small: they are small relative to existing studies, small relative to the hypothetical population and small relative to standard criteria defining a large sample (usually at least 30 cases).

In short, generalizability depends on the use of induction to make a conjecture about future outcomes. Even if we are willing to ignore Popper's misgivings about this, we cannot rely on sampling theory to provide a logical foundation for our recommendations. Internal validity is not inductive; it is a deductive process that is based on falsification, not induction. If multiple studies with high internal validity consistently failed to find support for an intervention, we might reasonably conclude that the intervention does not work.

An alternative way of considering evidence

This contrarian argument seems to lead to the conclusion that we cannot generalize from research. That is not the case. There is another approach that uses falsification rather than induction.

We start with a general theory of a crime problem. The theory, we conjecture, is widely valid within a particular domain (e.g., vehicle theft, or theft of vehicle parts on urban streets, or street robberies on urban streets), but may not be applicable outside the stated domain (e.g., bicycle theft, or theft of vehicles from farms, or commercial robberies). We then ask: 'If this theory is valid, what sorts of interventions would work?' We can then imagine a set of theoretical interventions that would work within the domain. This is presumably how we approach research normally.

In Figure 4.2, the inferences from the theory of the problem to theoretical interventions are shown by downward arrows (a). We decide to try one of these theoretical interventions and create a specific intervention based on the theory (b). This specific intervention, S, is evaluated. The findings from the evaluation of S either support or contradict the conjectures of the theoretical intervention (c). The success or failure of the theoretical intervention has implications for the general theory (d), as well as other specific interventions (e).

We start with a general theory of a crime problem. The theory, we conjecture, is widely valid within a particular domain (e.g., vehicle theft, or theft of vehicle parts on urban streets, or street robberies on urban streets), but may not be applicable outside the stated domain (e.g., bicycle theft, or theft of vehicles from farms, or commercial robberies). We then ask, 'If this theory is valid, what sorts of interventions would work?' We can then imagine a set of theoretical interventions that would work within the domain. In figure X, the inferences from the theory of the problem to theoretical interventions are shown by downward arrows (a). We decide to try one of these theoretical interventions, and create a specific intervention based on the theory (b). This specific intervention, S, is evaluated. The findings from the evaluation of S either support or contradict the conjectures of the theoretical intervention (c). The success or failure of the theoretical intervention

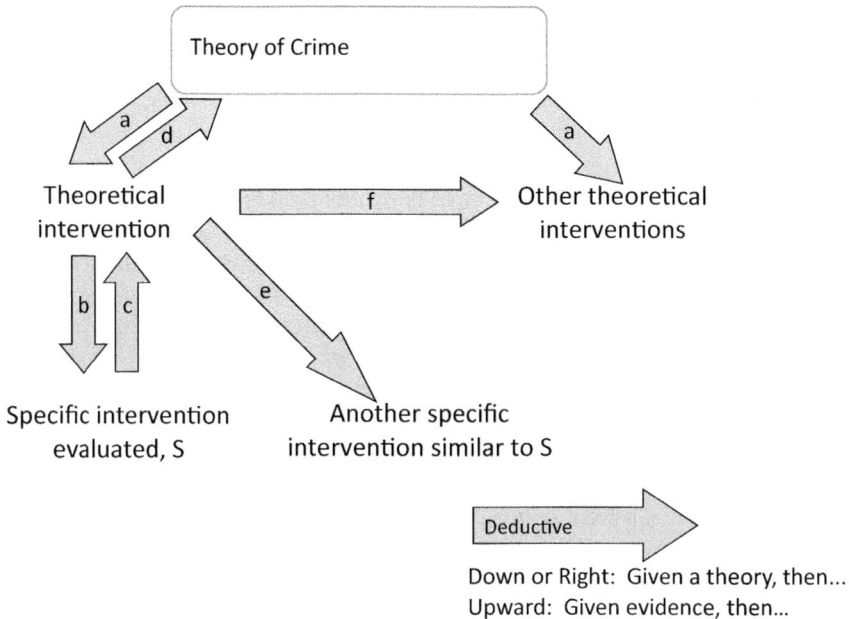

Figure 4.2 Inference based on theory

Source: Eck, John E. 2006. 'When is a bologna sandwich better than sex? A defense of small-N case study evaluations,' *Journal of Experimental Criminology*, 2(3): 345–62.

has implications for the general theory (d), as well as other specific interventions (e). Note that the evaluation findings are not directly generalizable (from S to interventions similar to S). Rather, because the theory is generalizable, the evaluation findings support or contradict that conclusion. Similarly, the outcome of the evaluation of S has no direct bearing on other theoretical interventions. Rather, the evaluation provides implications for the theoretical intervention and the overall theory of the crime problem, and these support or contradict the validity of other theoretical interventions.

Generalizability in this scheme does not come from inductive conclusions of a set of evaluations. Rather, generalizability is baked into the theory. If an evaluation contradicts the specific operationalization of the theory, it implies that the theory is misguided. We are uncertain because the evaluation outcome might be the result of misguided operationalization. That is why we want multiple evaluations: to eliminate the possibility that there was something peculiar about a specific study (e.g., the way crimes were measured or counted). Replication's value is in the falsification of the hypothesis that a particular evaluation's outcome is a peculiarity of the way the study was conducted. Consistent outcomes over multiple studies do not create generalizability, therefore. They eliminate threats to generalizability.

Internal validity counts, but only indirectly. The findings of the evaluation of S influence our confidence in the theoretical intervention (c) to the degree that we are confident that these findings are valid.

This schema suggests that we need to broaden our view of what constitutes evidence. Evidence about the overall theory counts in this schema, though it is discarded in standard evidence-based approaches. This is helpful for selecting interventions when there have been few or no evaluations. We should select interventions from those theories that have been most thoroughly tested relative to theories that have not been tested, have only weak tests or have tests providing ambiguous findings. So even in the absence of evaluations of specific interventions (with high internal validity) we have an evidence-based approach to selecting new interventions. This is critical, as the number of evaluations available for the most tested interventions is usually small, and most crime problems have no tested interventions. However, we do have a strong theoretical foundation within environmental criminology upon which to create plausible interventions. Cemetery crime prevention is a good example. Vandalism of grave yards and theft of metal from monuments in such places is very common. There is not a single evaluation of any intervention to prevent these crimes. However, it is possible to create a set of plausible interventions by drawing upon theories from environmental criminology (Stutzenberger and Eck, 2013).

Note that the evaluation findings are not directly generalizable (from S to interventions similar to S). Rather, because the theory is generalizable, the evaluation findings support or contradict that conclusion. Similarly, the outcome of the evaluation of S has no direct bearing on other theoretical interventions. Rather, the evaluation provides implications for the theoretical intervention and the overall theory of the crime problem. It is these that support or contradict the validity of other theoretical interventions (Eck, 2006).

Generalizability, in this scheme, does not come from inductive conclusions based on a set of evaluations. Rather, generalizability is baked into the theory. If an evaluation contradicts a specific operationalization of the theory, it implies that the theory is misguided. The evaluation, in short, is an attempt to falsify a general theory. Repeated failure to falsify that theory gives us the temporary practical license to act as if that theory, and its implications, is true. It is temporary because we might discover new falsifying evidence later. It is practical in the sense that a policymaker has to act now, on an existing pressing problem, and not wait for more research.

We may be uncertain of a particular study's findings because the evaluation outcome might be the result of a misguided operationalization. That is why we want multiple evaluations: to eliminate the possibility that there was something peculiar about a specific study (e.g., the way crimes were measured or counted). Replication's value is in the falsification of the hypothesis that a particular evaluation's outcome is a peculiarity of the way the study was conducted.

Internal validity counts, but only indirectly in this framework. Internal validity tells us if an evaluation was sufficiently rigorous for us to consider it a strong test of the theory. An evaluation with low internal validity does not provide a strong test, so even if it contradicts the theory, we are loath to give it much credit. An evaluation with high internal validity gives a strong test: if the theory fails such a test, we have confidence the results are the consequence of a weakness in the theory.

This schema suggests that we need to broaden our view of what constitutes evidence. In this schema, evidence about the validity of the overall theory counts. Such evidence is usually discarded in standard evidence-based approaches. So, for example, a descriptive nonexperimental study with findings consistent with the theory, but having no direct bearing on a specific intervention, is useful evidence.

This approach tells us how we should go about selecting interventions. We should select interventions from those theories that have been most thoroughly tested, relative to theories that have not been tested, have only weak tests or whose tests provide ambiguous findings. Even in the absence of evaluations of specific interventions we can have an evidence-based approach.

How does this approach solve the problems I mentioned in the previous section? First, it does not use internal validity to get to external validity. Internal validity describes our confidence that our findings are a solid test of a theory. Multiple evaluations are not used to create generalizability directly. Rather, they are used to show that the evidence for or against a theory is unlikely to be the result of peculiarities within the studies.

Second, it is the theory that provides the generalizability. We start with the assumption that if this theory is valid, then it is generalizable. The only question is whether it is valid. Empirical research is used to test that assumption. All inferences are deductions from either the theory or the evidence or some combination. Multiple studies with similar findings do not give us increasing confidence of the validity of an intervention. Instead, they help eliminate the possibility that a single finding is idiosyncratic to the setting, cases and methods used.

This epistemological solution to the difficulties of generalizing from research has some practical implications, as I have noted. However, its perspective is questionable. It looks at the question of generalizability through the eyes of researchers. This is sufficient if the questions being examined by research are of little practical utility. However, the evidence-based policy movement has been quite clear that they want practitioners to use evidence. In the next section, I look at the problem from the practitioners' perspectives and suggest specific ways researchers can be more helpful.

External validity for practitioners vs. for researchers

Researchers discuss external validity as if it were their concern. For purely academic theories, this is true. However, interesting theories have policy implications, and their evaluations are supposed to inform practices. Researchers should never assume a set of findings are externally valid. Practitioners, on the other hand, often must. To be useful, researchers should provide facts about their specific study that allow practitioners to make a reasonable (though usually perilous) guess as to whether the findings apply to their specific problem. Researchers should look at external validity through the eyes of possible users. After all, it is the practitioner with something at risk (reputation, budget and so forth). The researcher is unaffected by these decisions.

Shadish, Cook and Campbell (2002) describe five dimensions of external validity: units, treatments, outcomes, settings and mechanism based on Cronbach's (1982) typology. *Units* are the cases examined in a study or evaluation. If someone used the same intervention on other people or places, would they get the same findings?

Treatments are the various operationalizations of the theoretical intervention. There are usually multiple ways of implementing a single theoretical intervention. If someone applied a variant of the intervention tested, would they get similar findings?

Outcomes describe how the dependent variable is measured. Here, too, there are often several ways to measure the problem. The most obvious difference is between victimization surveys and official police reports of crime. We can also imagine multiple ways to ask questions about victimization in a survey. And there are multiple ways police record crime. So we can ask, if someone repeats this study but uses a different measure of the same outcome, would they get similar findings?

Settings are the context within which the treatment is applied to units. Time and space help define settings, as do populations, the physical environment, daily routines, traditions and much more. If this intervention is applied elsewhere, would we see the same findings?

Mechanisms are the processes triggered by the treatment that produce the outcomes for the units within a setting. Situational crime prevention specifies five general mechanisms: *risk, reward, effort, provocations* and *excuses*. If an intervention increases risk in one setting, but increases effort or reduces reward in other settings, will the outcome be different?

In an earlier article (Eck, 2010), I showed how failure to give details about these five dimensions left practitioners in the dark as to whether a study is applicable. A practitioner is not interested in whether a study is widely applicable. They want to know if it applies to their particular circumstances (Cartwright and Hardie, 2012). A study that applies to very few other settings might be very appealing to the few practitioners in these settings.

Although we can never be sure that a particular intervention is useful until it has been used, practitioners are not looking for certainty; they want a reasonable bet. The fact that crime prevention intervention worked elsewhere is useful in that this shows the intervention can work (as opposed to an idea that never works). In contrast, information that shows that it often works is not sufficient. That is because the practitioner making the decision is not working in the 'average' agency; he is working in a very specific agency, with very specific problems, in very specific settings. The practitioner needs more information than the mean effect size or proportion of evaluations showing good outcomes.

Consider, for example, the standard forest plots shown in meta-analytic reviews. The plots show some evaluations with strong positive and statistically significant results, other evaluations with small but significant results, studies with inconclusive (not statistically significant) results and evaluations with negative results that are statistically significant. The mean effect size shows the weighted average. A savvy practitioner, reading such a plot, will wonder: 'If my agency used this intervention, what would my results be? It would probably not be the mean effect size, but would my results fall within the 95 percent confidence interval of the mean, or would my results be an outlier?' Unfortunately, there is insufficient information in most systematic reviews to help this practitioner. Dividing evaluations into groups – those that were implemented in context A and those implemented in context B, for example – provides some useful information. But there are usually too few studies to make strong assertions about when and where an intervention is effective.

Practitioners need other information too. Researchers should describe their units, treatments, outcomes, settings and mechanisms in sufficient detail that a reasonably intelligent practitioner could judge the applicability of the findings to their problem. Someone might argue that practitioners do not have the training to make that judgment from a piece of research. And they may be correct. However, the practitioner will make such decisions whether they are trained or not. Further, the researcher is not in a better position to make that judgment. They are mostly ignorant of the specific conditions facing practitioners. And, finally, it is the practitioner who will be held accountable for failure (if anyone is), not the researcher.

In short, we should think of external validity being the primary concern of the users of research. Much as a car manufacturer tries to anticipate the needs of customers, it is the customer who puts down the money and suffers the success or failure of their purchase. This is why governments often act when they find car manufacturers have hidden information from customers about a vehicle's performance or have exaggerated its performance.

Currently, most research is written for other researchers. The short summaries written for practitioners do not give many of the details practitioners need. A typical research summary goes to some length explaining the use of a randomized trial, but does not explain clearly the units studied, or the outcome measures used, or the treatments applied, or the setting enveloping the study, or the mechanism triggered. The intervention might have worked brilliantly by standards of internal validity, but absent information about these other factors, the internally valid findings are useless.

In another chapter in this volume, Bowers and colleagues describe the EMMIE framework: an acronym for *Effect, Mechanism, Moderators, Implementation* and *Economics* (Johnson, Tilley and Bowers, 2015). This framework overlaps substantially with the external validity framework, as illustrated in Table 4.2. All of the external validity elements (rows) deal with aspects of the question: Does the intervention produce the desired effect? Both frameworks address mechanism. Settings are a form of moderator–environmental factors that influence how the intervention performs. Finally, implementation deals with 'who' or 'what' is being treated (units), how they are treated (treatments) and how performance is evaluated (outcomes). EMMIE, however, also draws attention to the cost and

Table 4.2 Elements of external validity and EMMIE

	Effect	Mechanism	Moderators	Implementation	Economics
Units					
Treatments					
Outcomes					
Settings					
Mechanism					

Shaded cells indicate overlapping interests.

benefits of the intervention (economics), something external validity ignores. In short, by describing the five elements of external validity one contributes to EMMIE, but only in part. Alternatively, if one starts with EMMIE, attention to external validity elements helps explicate four of the EMMIE dimensions. Both frameworks demand that researchers take practitioners as important members of their readership and not just talk to other researchers about their narrow academic interests.

What is to be done?

> William Bratton conceded, 'You're not going to find the scientific study that can support broken-windows one way or the other'. He added: 'The evidence I rely on is what my eyes show me', and he pointed to 'the reduction of fear' that he sees in rejuvenated neighborhoods like Times Square'.
>
> (Auletta, 2015)

Clearly, evidence is essential for sound crime prevention policy. The debate is not over the need for evidence; no one disputes the utility of evidence. If you ask for the evidence supporting the most absurd crime prevention proposal, its advocates will give you evidence. But their evidence is not what I or most readers of this chapter would accept as evidence. It is usually anecdotal or based on what some other 'expert' asserts. The debate is over how scientific evidence should be used wisely; what one can say or do when the scientific evidence is absent, ambiguous or contradictory. Critics of an evidence-based policy do not argue that evidence is irrelevant. Rather, they argue that the researchers ignored other evidence or failed to look for other evidence.

The debate is over what evidence should matter and how that evidence should be applied. Mainstream advocates of evidence-based crime prevention policy usually ignore any evidence supporting the theory from which interventions are drawn. This is a mistake. Such evidence might not be definitive, but it can help, particularly when there is little else upon which to base policy. Mainstream advocates rely too much on internal validity to grade evidence. Internal validity is a useful criterion, but it is not enough, and it certainly says nothing about generalizability.

In this paper I have made the following argument: the standard practice is to use inductive reasoning where it is not applicable and to use internal validity to make claims about external validity. Generalizing from a few or many evaluations, regardless of their internal validity, is fraught with problems. Instead, we should start with the theory from which the interventions were derived. A theory is a general statement. Applications derived from that theory carry that attribute. The question, then, is not whether a theoretically derived intervention is generalizable, but whether the intervention and its theory are valid.

I have also argued published studies typically provide insufficient information for practitioners that they can judge the utility of research. Currently, researchers advocating for evidence-based prevention ignore the difficult task facing practitioners. Just because a practice works more times than not, or that it is useful on average, does not mean that it will work and be useful in a particular setting operationalized in a particular way. Practitioners need to have more information so they can make a calculated bet for or against the intervention.

While writing this chapter, the Associated Press (AP) published the results of their investigation into dental floss. 'The federal government has recommended flossing since 1979, first in a surgeon general's report and later in the Dietary Guidelines for Americans issued every five years. The guidelines must be based on scientific evidence, under the law,' stated the article (Donn, 2016). It goes on to say:

> The AP looked at the most rigorous research conducted over the past decade, focusing on 25 studies that generally compared the use of a toothbrush with the combination of toothbrushes and floss. The findings? The evidence for flossing is 'weak, very unreliable,' of 'very low' quality, and carries 'a moderate to large potential for bias.
>
> 'The majority of available studies fail to demonstrate that flossing is generally effective in plaque removal,' said one review conducted last year. Another 2015 review cites 'inconsistent/weak evidence' for flossing and a 'lack of efficacy'.'
>
> (Donn, 2016)

Should you, dear scientific evidence–based reader, stop using dental floss? And if you are not willing to stop, what does this tell you about the difficulties of applying evidence? If there was a strong theory of gums that implied flossing was not useful, would these results be more meaningful? And if the article reporting these results told us something about the people who were tested and their diets, could you make a more reasoned guess as to what we should do after a meal? But the article told us nothing about the theory or the experimental subjects. So we are at a loss as to how to use this report.

Many of the practices practitioners consider or apply are like teeth flossing. They seem reasonable, but the evidence is weak, very unreliable, of very low quality and carries a moderate-to-large potential for bias. Even more practices have no scientific evidence at all if we only consider experimental and quasi-experimental evidence as being scientific. There is no reason to believe we will be flooded with such evidence any time soon, yet practitioners need to practice. So unless you are willing to tell practitioners to stop all those practices, just as you are willing to stop flossing your teeth, you will need to rethink your stance on evidence. Paying closer attention to theory may be the most practical solution.

Acknowledgements

Special thanks to Johannes Knutsson and Lisa Tompson for encouraging me to write this paper, and to Nick Tilly for his thoughtful response. Thanks to Shannon Linning, who caught many of the errors in the text; those she did not catch are mine alone.

References

Auletta, K. (2015, 7 September). 'Fixing Broken Windows: Bill Bratton Wants to Be America's Top Cop. His Critics Say That His Legacy Is Tainted', *The New Yorker*,. Retrieved from www.newyorker.com/magazine/2015/09/07/fixing-broken-windows (accessed 9 August 2016).

Bennett, T., Holloway, K. and Farrington, D.P. (2006). 'Does neighborhood watch reduce crime? A systematic review and meta-analysis', *Journal of Experimental Criminology*, 2(4): 437–58.

Braga, A.A., Papachristos, A.V. and Hureau, D.M. (2014). 'The effects of hot spots policing on crime: An updated systematic review and meta-analysis', *Justice Quarterly*, 31(4): 633–63.

Braga, A.A. and Weisburd, D.L. (2012). *The Effects of 'Pulling Levers' Focused Deterrence Strategies on Crime*. Retrieved from http://campbellcollaboration.org/lib/project/96/ (accessed 6 March 2014).

Braga, A.A., Welsh, B.C. and Schnell, C. (2015). 'Can policing disorder reduce crime? A systematic review and meta-analysis', *Journal of Research in Crime and Delinquency*, 52(4): 567–88.

Campbell, D.T. and Stanley, J.C. (1966). *Experimental and Quasi-experimental Designs for Research*, Chicago: Rand McNally.

Cartwright, N. and Hardie, J. (2012). *Evidence-Based Policy*, Oxford: Oxford University Press.

Cook, T.D. and Campbell, D.T. (1979). *Quasi-experimentation: Design and Analysis Issues for Field Settings*, Skokie, IL: Houghton-Mifflin.

Cronbach, L.J. (1982). *Designing Evaluations of Educational and Social Programs*. San Francisco, CA: Jossey-Bass.

Donn, J. (2016, 2 August). 'Medical Benefits of Dental Floss Unproven', *Associated Press*. Retrieved from http://bigstory.ap.org/article/f7e66079d9ba4b4985d7af350619a9e3/medical-benefits-dental-floss-unproven (accessed 3 August 2016).

Eck, J.E. (2006). 'When is a Bologna sandwich better than sex? A defense of small-N case study evaluations', *Journal of Experimental Criminology*, 2(3): 345–62.

Eck, J.E. (2010). 'Policy is in the details: Using external validity to help policy makers', *Criminology & Public Policy*, 9(4): 859–66.

Gill, C., Weisburd, D., Telep, C.W., Vitter, Z. and Bennett, T. (2014). 'Community-oriented policing to reduce crime, disorder and fear and increase satisfaction and legitimacy among citizens: A systematic review', *Journal of Experimental Criminology*, 10(4): 399–428.

Johnson, S.D., Tilley, N. and Bowers, K.J. (2015). 'Introducing EMMIE: An evidence rating scale to encourage mixed-method crime prevention synthesis Reviews', *Journal of
Experimental Criminology*, doi: 10.1007/s11292-015-9238-7

Mazerolle, L.G. and Ransley, J. (2005). *Third Party Policing*, New York: University of
Cambridge Press.

Popper, K.R. (1992). *Conjectures and Refutations: The Growth of Scientific Knowledge*,
London: Routledge.

Shadish, W.R., Cook, T.D. and Campbell, D.T. (2002). *Quasi-Experimental Designs for
Generalized Causal Inference*, Skokie, IL: Houghton-Mifflin.

Sherman, L.W., Gottfredson, D.C., McKenzie, D.L., Eck, J.E., Reuter, P. and Bushway, S.
(1998). *Preventing Crime: What Works, What Doesn't, What's Promising*, Washington,
DC: U.S. Department of Justice, Office of Justice Programs.

Stutzenberger, A.L. and Eck, J.E. (2013). *Preventing Vandalism & Theft in Cemeteries*.
Unpublished report. School of Criminal Justice, University of Cincinnati.

Weisburd, D., Hinkle, J.C., Braga, A.A. and Wooditch, A. (2015). 'Understanding the
mechanisms underlying broken windows policing: The need for evaluation evidence',
Journal of Research in Crime and Delinquency, 52(4): 589–608.

Weisburd, D., Telep, C.W., Hinkle, J.C. and Eck, J.E. (2008). *The Effects of Problem-
Oriented Policing on Crime and Disorder*. Retrieved from www.campbellcollaboration.
org/lib/project/46/ (accessed 3 August 2016).

5 Multiple research methods for evidence generation

Mike Maxfield, Yuchen Hou, Jeffrey A. Butts,
Jennifer M. Pipitone, Latifa T. Fletcher
and Bryce Peterson

Rachel Boba (2010) introduced the helpful phrase 'practice-based evidence' to the police research literature. Widely used in psychiatry and other health fields that employ counseling, practice-based evidence is evident in policing research as the systematic study of routine practices, change, and their impacts. Problem-oriented policing, Compstat, and similar accountability systems are examples of ways to generate practice-based evidence in policing. This approach departs from the concept of developing evidence-based practice through experiments that center on the internal validity of causal inferences. Similarly, practice-based evidence generation is less concerned with producing generalizable findings than solving local problems in context.

The generation of practice-based evidence draws on a wide range of research designs and measurement strategies. These include, but are not restricted to, experimental and quasi-experimental designs. This chapter describes the scope and nature of design and measurement strategies that can produce practice-based evidence. Discussion centers on four broad dimensions of social research: *problem identification, measurement, causal process*, and *generalization*. Research begins with problem identification and definition. All research raises questions of measurement, something that is critical for research on policing. Some types of police-generated data are most commonly used for measures of crime or public safety. Other important strategies are surveys and observation.

Explanatory and evaluation research are concerned with understanding some sort of causal process or mechanism, how things work. Evidence-based policing usually addresses this through narrowly defined experimental and quasi-experimental methods. Practice-based evidence recognizes two other approaches. First is focusing on specifically defined problems in specific contexts, much like the scientific realism described by Pawson and Tilley (1997). Second, causal processes can be inferred when outcomes match very specific, theory-based, a priori expectations.

When we are interested in whether or not our findings represent some larger population or can apply in some other situations, our attention centers on generalization. Systematic reviews of evidence, usually evidence that meets some methodological criteria, imply that practices widely supported by evidence can be generalized to other settings. But applied research on policing sometimes focuses more narrowly on solving specific problems in specific places. Some parts of responses to problems may be applied elsewhere, but the interest is more on solving a specific problem than producing generalizable knowledge. Another dimension of generalization is sampling. Traditional social science research most values probability samples that are not always possible or necessary in generating practice-based evidence.

This chapter describes tools for researchers to address the tasks of problem definition, measurement, causal processes, and generalization. We begin with an extended example of developing practice-based evidence in community-based youth justice organizations in New York City. Then we expand on the four basic dimensions of research tools and discuss how these might be applied to develop practice-based evidence on an important and evolving intervention in policing.

Our discussion of these concepts may seem a bit pedantic at times, especially to more experienced researchers. This stems from our intent to describe basic research principles and operations in a way less burdened with the language and traditions of researchers. For example, the litany of validity is not much more than a way of understanding measurement, causal processes, and generalization. But chanting *validity* and *designs* to control validity threats sometimes signals expert hegemony, implying that reliable evidence can only be obtained in highly technical and often expensive ways.

Evidence generation

Thinking about these four dimensions of research – problem definition, causal process, measurement, and generalization – guided the Evidence Generation initiative at the Research and Evaluation Center at John Jay College of Criminal Justice. It evolved into a good example of practice-based evidence described by Boba (2010). The Evidence Generation mission was also inspired by Liberman's (2009) argument for a critical view of evidence-based thinking. Liberman begins by reminding readers of Campbell's (1969) view that social policies should be viewed as experimental, and expected outcomes as hypotheses. Despite the off-putting reference to the American Society of Criminology in the article's title, Liberman was clearly onto something. In our words, evidence generation:

> is **not** simply an effort to expand the use of evidence-based programs. We help agencies and programs develop their own evidence. We work on growing new evidence in support of innovative models, whether the models are designed to affect client behavior, to improve systems, or to influence law, policy, and practice.
>
> (https://johnjayrec.nyc/evgenmission/, retrieved March 31, 2016.
> Emphasis in original)

The principal goal of the initiative was to provide technical assistance to non-profit organizations that served justice-involved youth in New York City. In the United States, such nonprofits are increasingly required by their funders to provide evidence-based services or to evaluate the effects of their programming. We helped them develop the capacity to do this and referred to the organizations we worked with as *affiliates* in an effort to signal more of a collaborative than consultative relationship.

To a great extent funding sources specified certain requirements for data collection, and even the data management software that was to be used. Our efforts had to work around such requirements, but we also found we could clarify mandates from funders and help affiliates reduce the burden of complying with requirements.

At the same time, evidence generation recognizes that different organizations in New York City serve populations and communities that are not always represented in the canon of evidence-based or proprietary programs. For example, we worked with one small organization we will call Sleepy Hollow. Sleepy Hollow served youth from parts of Harlem. Among other things, they sought help in developing after-school programs from a vendor based in Utah. Utah programming had been widely adopted in western cities in California, Colorado, and other states. The company's print and web-based promotional information featured happy-looking (white) teenagers riding horses, target shooting, and hiking in desert or mountain environments. Thinking about causal processes in context, we advised Sleepy Hollow staff that the mechanisms at work in communities in the American west could not be readily transferred to Harlem.

Another affiliate in Brooklyn, Wired for Success, adopted a more targeted approach that drew on resources unique to New York City. Wired was also small and focused on developing basic job and social skills for justice-involved youth. After two months of workshops, participants were placed in paying internships. Many of these were in small theater companies and other organizations in the entertainment sector. Others were placed with publishers and legal services organizations. These sectors offer interesting, rewarding opportunities for minority youth who lack advanced training. A senior staff person at Wired is also a successful singer, model, and performer.

We helped Sleepy Hollow, Wired for Success, and 10 other organizations satisfy reporting mandates and learn more about what happened to their participants after programming. We developed a standard but flexible process of engagement that began by helping organizations clarify goals, resources, and constraints and then systematically lay them out. Details are available on a website,[1] but Figure 5.1 summarizes what became our seven-step process of working with Affiliates.

Step 1 was inspired by the *Standardized Program Evaluation Protocol* (Lipsey et al., 2010). Our *Protocol for Evidence Generation* (PEvGen) was a tool to assess basic features of an organization's information and data management systems, together with how thoroughly they were documented. Step 1 was established during the project's second year and was never fully developed. It was intended mostly as a lead-in to step 2.

New York is awash with small community-based organizations staffed by a few people, together with larger nonprofits that have hundreds of staff in many

Seven-Step Process for Engaging with Affiliates

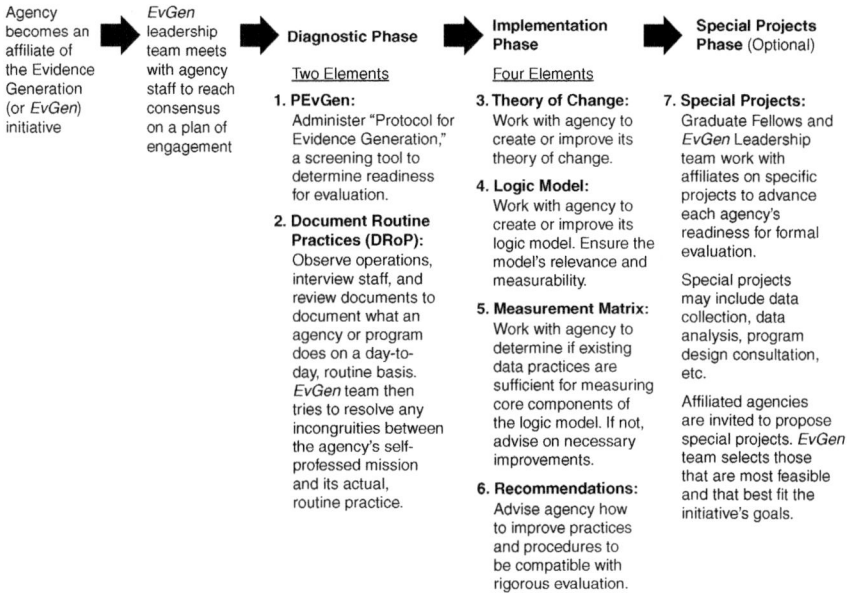

| Agency becomes an affiliate of the Evidence Generation (or *EvGen*) initiative | ➤ | *EvGen* leadership team meets with agency staff to reach consensus on a plan of engagement | ➤ | **Diagnostic Phase** | ➤ | **Implementation Phase** | ➤ | **Special Projects Phase** (Optional) |

Diagnostic Phase

Two Elements

1. **PEvGen:**
   Administer "Protocol for Evidence Generation," a screening tool to determine readiness for evaluation.

2. **Document Routine Practices (DRoP):**
   Observe operations, interview staff, and review documents to document what an agency or program does on a day-to-day, routine basis. *EvGen* team then tries to resolve any incongruities between the agency's self-professed mission and its actual, routine practice.

Implementation Phase

Four Elements

3. **Theory of Change:**
   Work with agency to create or improve its theory of change.

4. **Logic Model:**
   Work with agency to create or improve its logic model. Ensure the model's relevance and measurability.

5. **Measurement Matrix:**
   Work with agency to determine if existing data practices are sufficient for measuring core components of the logic model. If not, advise on necessary improvements.

6. **Recommendations:**
   Advise agency how to improve practices and procedures to be compatible with rigorous evaluation.

Special Projects Phase (Optional)

7. **Special Projects:**
   Graduate Fellows and *EvGen* Leadership team work with affiliates on specific projects to advance each agency's readiness for formal evaluation.

   Special projects may include data collection, data analysis, program design consultation, etc.

   Affiliated agencies are invited to propose special projects. *EvGen* team selects those that are most feasible and that best fit the initiative's goals.

Figure 5.1 Seven-step process for engaging with affiliates

Source: Evidence Generation initiative. Research & Evaluation Center, John Jay College of Criminal Justice, New York, NY.

sites throughout the city. Our engagement with each affiliate began with efforts we called *Documenting Routine Practices* (DRoP). As graduate student fellows learned about what organizations did, why, and how they did those things, they generated documentation that in most cases did not previously exist. Some larger organizations had detailed manuals and regulations, but these mostly expressed how tasks were intended to be done, not what actually happened. DRoPs were put together from graduate student interviews with staff, observation of programming, and examination of various documents. As stated in step 2 of Figure 5.1, 'EvGen team tries to resolve incongruities between an agency's self-professed mission and its routine practices'.

After things were worked out, such documentation became a valuable stand-alone product. We encouraged organizations to review and revise DRoP documents as needed and to include appropriate excerpts in their applications to funders or reports to oversight agencies.

Steps 3 and 4 are familiar items from standard evaluation literature. A theory of change states three things: a problem, a planned general approach to addressing the problem, and the expected effect. This was a key part of problem identification and beginning to articulate a causal process. Graduate student fellows worked closely with Affiliates to prepare theories of change that were meaningful, yet realistic and succinct. Theories of change were generally restricted to 200 words or less. Here is an excerpt from Wired:

> Youth involved in the juvenile or criminal justice system face unique challenges that make it difficult for them to complete their education and develop employability skills. To address these challenges, [Wired's] curriculum focuses on the development of four core life skills combined with employability training and prepares youth for placement in a paid internship. By supporting and guiding youth through the entire internship process, [Wired] aims to provide youth with the support and guidance necessary to (1) achieve personal transformation, (2) ignite motivation for learning, and (3) increase employability skills.

Logic models used the DRoP and theory of change documents to link resources, inputs, outputs, and outcomes. We drew on several resources in the evaluation literature (for example, Kellogg Foundation, 2004) to develop detailed models of what each organization did and expected results. Some affiliates had done this, but as with DRoP, student fellows developed their own based on what the organization was doing and how those things were being done. Some existing logic models were neither realistic nor useful. Many were what we termed 'saturated', where everything is related to everything else.

The measurement matrix in step 5 laid out logic model inputs, outputs, and outcomes in rows, with columns indicating whether the information was being collected, its source, and ratings of how reliable the source was and how critical each measure was. The latter distinguished measures that may have been simply required from those that were truly important to get right. Another column indicated possible sources of information if it was not currently being collected.

Recommendations in step 6 suggested steps the affiliate could take to improve data collection, reports that should be produced, or other items to build their capacity for evidence generation, including comparison strategies (discussed later). After this process of standard engagement our work with many affiliates ended. Others briefly described special projects that built on earlier engagement and that would involve more customized collaboration. Examples are noted in step 7 of Figure 5.1.

As another important part of the EvGen initiative we convened quarterly workshops that brought all organizations together. Workshops covered topics we had learned were of interest to several organizations and often featured staff from each organization as presenters. The workshops produced a number of 'Aha!' moments where staff from organizations learned from each other. For example, many organizations used a records management system designed for nonprofit organizations that was required by funders. Staff from one organization were particularly skilled at making data entry and reporting templates and led a workshop that was highly valued by other participants. Two other workshops that stemmed from collective interests spawned collaboration with a New York State agency to produce criminal history follow-up information and a guidebook to help organizations locate former participants.

The evidence generation process centered on developing local evidence that was not intended to be *generalizable*, but turned out to be useful as organizations learned from each other. Theories of change and logic models clarified *problem identification* and stated expected *causal processes*. Working with affiliates we developed *measures* to serve their individual needs and operations. These measures reflected our understanding of record-keeping processes, as much as possible incorporating this knowledge into data collection procedures. For some special projects, such as criminal history follow-ups, we developed crude comparison strategies that provided some evidence of a *causal process*.

It is important to note that the main goal was to build an affiliate's capacity to generate evidence about what they did and with what effect. We did not work as consultants. That distinction was not always easy to maintain, especially with smaller organizations who expected the EvGen process to collect data and write reports about program impact. More information, including samples of our work with affiliates, can be found at: https://johnjayrec.nyc/evgen/.

We now turn to a more focused consideration of problem identification, causal process, measurement, and generalization. Our discussion illustrates how these concepts can frame the generation of evidence about police body-worn video cameras.

Problem definition

Framing research questions is one of the most important parts of designing research. Problem definition begins at the outset, but is frequently revised as problems become better understood while data and other experiences are accumulated. Researchers think of this in terms of framing research questions and a first step toward developing empirical measures. The large and growing literature on problem-oriented policing devotes a great deal of attention to defining and better understanding policing problems (e.g. Scott, 2015).

Very specific problem statements are usually preferred in problem-oriented policing. Clarke and Eck (2005) include 11 different types of offenses and activities under the general label 'car crime'. Fifteen separate problem guides, developed by the Center for Problem-Oriented Policing, describe different conceptualization of problems involving vehicles. Problems involving theft of and from cars in parking facilities are different from those presented by theft of and from cars on residential streets and driveways.

Similarly, the mechanism-in-context perspective described by Pawson and Tilley (1997) especially values laying out very specific mechanisms. Growing interest in evaluating police body-worn cameras (BWCs) offers a timely example similar to the closed-circuit TV (CCTV) mechanisms described by Pawson and Tilley.

Lum and associates (2015) examined 42 completed or ongoing empirical studies, including both quantitative and qualitative projects. Four completed studies and 15 of 30 on-going projects employed randomized controlled trials. The review by Lum et al. helpfully identifies seven general areas for research on BWC and 30 possible research questions within those areas. The seven areas are (Lum et al., 2015: 12–13):

- Impact of BWC on officer behavior
- Impact on citizen behavior
- Impact on criminal and internal police investigations
- National prevalence and use of BWC

- Officer attitudes and BWC
- Citizen and community attitudes
- Impact on police organizations

Among the 30 research questions are several that have not yet been addressed by completed or ongoing projects, including officer compliance with constitutional standards, changes in crime or fear of crimes, and changes in agency policies with respect to use of force and police–citizen contacts (Lum et al., 2015: 20). This represents an unusually careful and detailed presentation of different approaches to defining possible impacts of BWCs. The report by Lum et al. generated a solicitation for evaluations of these specific research questions by the Laura and John Arnold Foundation (LJAF):

> Specifically, LJAF seeks proposals for research on major gaps in our knowledge about BWCs as identified by the recent LJAF report by Lum et al. (2015). . . . The LJAF will prioritize funding to specific areas of research that were identified by the report as under-researched (see Tables 5.2 and 5.4 of the Lum et al. report for more information).
>
> (Laura and John Arnold Foundation, 2016: 1)

Reviewing many of the completed studies described by Lum et al. suggests examples of mechanisms to guide the definition of different consequences of BWCs in encounters between police and people. What follows are examples of mechanisms and contexts extracted from descriptions of selected evaluations and feasibility studies of BWCs.

1   The 'self-awareness' mechanism.

   BWC may play a social surveillance role in changing people's conduct to more socially desirable responses. This mechanism can affect police and citizens somewhat differently (Ariel, Farrar and Sutherland, 2015).

2   The 'oversight' mechanism.

   BWCs can be a form of supervision in that recorded encounters will be reviewed by supervisors. As a consequence, police are more likely to obey administrative directives.

3   The 'compliance' mechanism.

If activating a BWC begins with a verbal notification, that notification may encourage citizens to comply with police directives and have a calming effect in potentially volatile encounters (Peters and Eure, 2015).

4   The 'rational choice' mechanism.

The fact that interactions captured by BWC can become evidence in criminal proceedings may impel police and citizens to make more rational decisions. Police seek to avoid complaints, lawsuits, and disciplinary actions. Citizens could similarly regulate their own behavior because the use of BWC makes them more vulnerable to criminal prosecution.

5   The 'symbolic interaction' mechanism.

BWCs could have a symbolic effect even if not activated. In this case the BWC may be preconceived by the police and citizens as a symbol of police legitimacy, accountability, and transparency. This symbolic mechanism may elicit a signal that both of the police and citizens may conduct civilized behaviors. In that case, a proactive contact initiated by police may be met with a cooperative response from citizens, and vice versa.

6   The 'expectation' mechanism.

In the view of citizens, the deployment of a new technology is expected to enhance the quality of services provided by the police. If citizens do believe BWCs will be effective, their satisfaction with the police services may improve. Police may expect more respectful behavior from citizens and expect fewer bogus complaints. On the other hand, negative expectations from the police would affect their acceptance of BWCs and eventually undermine the beneficial outcomes that might otherwise be generated (Ready and Young, 2015).

Some of these mechanisms are more evident in evolving policies regarding BWCs, whereas others have been less often considered. For example, the oversight mechanism potentially extends the capacity to supervise officers. Recorded interactions may also be useful in training.

The way different BWC mechanisms operate may also vary by the context in which they are being considered or deployed.

1   The 'community-based' context.

BWCs are mostly outfitted for police patrol officers who encounter people mainly in public settings and private households. Compared to the fixed physical contexts in which CCTV mechanisms are embedded, BWC mechanisms may vary across communities and between public and private settings.

2   The 'trigger' context.

> Much of police work is reactive, where officers respond to calls for service. In such cases victims or witnesses will be more grateful for police intervention than in proactive situations where police decide to intervene.

3   The 'culture' context.

> Officers' perceptions on this new technology are diffused through their shared experiences and views about BWCs, producing convergence in expectations and attitudes (Young and Ready, 2015).

4   'Subculture' context.

> Police subculture may oppose BWCs and encourage steps to disable cameras, images, or sound. Subculture effects may be stronger in departments or regions with more influential unions. Or differential support may exist, where problem officers are opposed to BWCs, whereas other officers are supportive or neutral.

5   The 'policy' context.

> The adoption of new technology raises new policy issues. Written rules and protocols are required for the proper use of BWC and the review of BWC recordings. Police behaviors and attitudes may be different for mandatory and discretionary activation policy. Unions may demand to play a role in setting policies.

6   The 'political' context.

> Expectations and use of BWC can vary based on the degree of consensus among city leadership, the community, and police. The degree of media scrutiny and oversight by state or federal authorities may also affect BWC use and impact.

It should be easy to see how different combinations of mechanisms and contexts could be reflected in, or ignored, in research designed to evaluate BWCs. Included are questions about which officers will wear BWCs, whether use is voluntary or mandatory, policies or guidelines on what and when to record, and how to handle equipment malfunctions. Finally, identical equipment and policies can be expected to produce different results in communities where political consensus is widespread and those where BWCs are implemented in response to federal oversight.

These observations suggest that irrespective of the evolving base of evidence about BWC effects and operation, individual jurisdictions should be prepared to generate their own evidence as cameras are implemented. The way the BWC problem is defined and the contexts in which BWCs will be deployed are likely to vary enough that the generation of local evidence will be required.

Causal process

Although laying out mechanisms and their contexts is a key part of problem definition, mechanisms are equally helpful for understanding causal processes. The Evidence Generation initiative illustrated how theories of change and logic models are useful when specifying expected causal processes.

It is unfortunate that much discussion surrounding evidence-based policing or other policy centers on questions about research design, while advocating a narrow class of designs. Readers will be familiar with and weary of advocacy by and challenges to experiments and meta-analysis of research findings. Experiments and meta-analyses can be useful, but cannot be universally applied to testing interventions and weighing evidence accumulated over a number of research studies. In fact, one tends to drive the other. Systematic reviews and meta-analysis are best suited to assess research studies that are similar in design. So in order to pool findings across a number of studies, those studies must meet certain specified design standards.

An even more long-standing, tiresome, and surprisingly resilient area of contention is the distinction of qualitative and quantitative research. Each camp has a handbook (Piquero and Weisburd, 2010; Copes and Miller, 2015) and advocates (Hough, 2014; Jacques, 2014). It is more useful to think of the Q words as descriptors of different kinds of measures rather than different approaches to doing research. Quantitative measures can be tabulated or ordered, whereas qualitative measures are categories. Even categories can be counted and compared, something that we do in coding open-ended responses to questionnaires or content analysis, and sometimes making sense of focus group transcripts. Viewing measurement in this way focuses attention more on developing the best available measures, rather than declaring that qualitative or quantitative research will be done. Maruna (2010) and Sullivan and McGloin (2014) offer good observations on 'mixed method' designs and exploiting advantages of different kinds of measures, respectively.

Comparison strategies

Maxfield (2001) suggests thinking about comparison strategies as tools for addressing two fundamental evaluation questions: (1) Did you get what you expected? and (2) Compared to what? Random assignment is one such strategy for answering the 'compared to what' question, but others are more generally applicable and usually sufficient for generating evidence for local needs. Three nonexperimental comparison strategies are familiar: *nonrandom comparison groups*, *cohorts*, and *pre-test post-test comparisons*. Five others are less well known: preintervention scores, implementation effort, specified objective, cliff-edge effect, and data signatures.

- *Preintervention scores.* This is sort of a good-news version of regression to the mean. We can have more confidence in causal processes when interventions produce change in extreme cases. A meta-analysis of juvenile justice interventions found greater improvements in high-risk juveniles. This was explained in terms similar to regression to the mean. 'High-risk juveniles by definition are likely to have high re-offense rates and thus have the most room for improvement if they receive an effective intervention' (Lipsey et al., 2010: 23). It is easy to see a counterpart in police interventions – areas with high crime and disorder problems have the most room for improvement. With respect to BWCs, it is reasonable to expect greater improvements in community relations from areas where community views of police are especially negative.

- *Implementation effort.* Emerging dose–response research in corrections illustrates this approach (Loughran et al., 2009; Sperber, Latessa and Makarios, 2013). Similarly, larger 'doses' of programming have greater effects in juvenile justice interventions (Lipsey et al., 2010: 27). Examining the effects of restricting access to control residential burglary, Bowers and associates (2004) found the rate of burglary decline accelerated as more gates were installed in alleyways. Again, applications in policing are readily apparent. Increasing the number of police or the duration in particular places is an example of implementation effort. With respect to BWCs, patrol areas where virtually all police wear BWCs could be compared to areas where they are deployed among a smaller percentage of officers.
- *Cliff-edge effect.* Very large changes in outcome measures or changes in very specifically defined outcome measures exhibit what Nagin and Weisburd (2013) call high evidentiary value. They cite one classic example of sharp drops in motor vehicle fatalities and serious injuries following the deployment of breathalyzers in Great Britain (Ross, 1973). Another example is the virtual elimination of cell phone fraud in the United States following technology change that made it impossible to clone handset signals (Clarke et al., 2001).
- *Specified objective.* Based on a management by objectives principle, setting a performance goal, then comparing actual results to that goal can be evidence of a causal process. This is not a strong comparison strategy, but can nevertheless be useful if performance goals are reasonable and based on appropriate measures. Many dangers are evident, some of which are discussed in the measurement section.
- *Data signatures.* Eck and Madensen (2009) describe how very specifically defined interventions that target precise populations and are expected to produce certain patterns of outcomes can enhance confidence in causal processes. This combines some elements of dose–response and cliff-edge effects as a comparison strategy, and is similar to what Shadish et al. (2012) refer to as pattern matching. Farrell et al. (2015) draw on signatures to account for patterns in the international crime drop.

Small-claim process

Eck makes a very useful distinction between small-claim and large-claim interventions: 'For the many small-scale, small-claim crime prevention interventions, internal validity is of limited importance and external validity is unimportant'

(Eck, 2002: 95). When police or other officials target an individual or small place and detect the intended reduction in crime or disorder, there often can be no other plausible explanation for observed change. Eck describes examples from problem-oriented policing, where tailoring interventions to small-scale problems produces change. Rival explanations may be considered to some extent, but reducing problems is most important. Similarly, it would be nice if a successful intervention at one place produced similar results in another, but it is not necessarily expected that a small-scale intervention in one place can produce any sort of larger-claim evidence about effectiveness. This touches on the question of generalization.

Small-scale, small-claim interventions produce evidence that can be good enough to understand a local causal process. Nonexperimental evaluations of BWCs could focus on detailing all possible mechanisms and assessing effects intensively in relatively small areas. Officers and supervisors might review videos jointly, discuss what was shown and not shown, and draw tentative conclusions about how well videos captured an individual incident. Another interesting set of questions is whether BWCs appear to have stronger effects on certain types of police–citizen interactions. Katz et al. (2015) found that following the implementation of BWCs in Phoenix, Arizona, family violence incidents were more likely to produce charges and guilty verdicts, suggesting that video and audio records of often volatile incidents can be especially useful.

Measurement

Agency records

The quality of measures in policing has always been important for basic and applied research on policing, but is often framed in terms of data availability. Police records of calls for service, incidents, arrests, and use of force reports are usually more available than alternative measures. Police records are collected as a matter of routine, though they may not be routinely available to researchers. Such data are much more likely to be available for collaborative research, action research, or other research partnerships.

Most discussion of possible errors in police data collection processes considers nonreporting error, and less commonly, nonrecording error. Victim surveys produce estimates of nonreporting, but nonrecording is trickier to assess. Another way to describe nonrecording is crimes known to police but not retained by police record-keeping systems. The relatively limited research on nonrecording often focuses on a type of corruption stemming from police efforts to suppress crime data. One of the most prominent examples of claims about crime data suppression is a critique of the New York City Police Department by Eterno and Silverman (2012). More generally, Donald Campbell wrote: 'The more any quantitative social indicator is used for social decision-making, the more subject it will be to corruption pressures' (Campbell, 1976: 49). Campbell began by describing voting as an important social indicator that is widely subject to corruption, then mentioned police complaints and clearance rates.

Use of BWCs produces another type of nonrecording problem that underscores the potential complexities of measurement. Peters and Eure (2015) describe preliminary procedures for investigating incidents that were not recorded or where recording was interrupted. Nonrecording can apply to video, audio, or both. Questions can also emerge from camera angles and sound, especially incidents when two or more officers are involved but some are not wearing BWCs. Nonrecording can be intentional, unintentional, or situational – where important parts of an encounter cannot be recorded. Katz et al. report what they interpret as a high proportion of noncompliance in activating BWC recording, with less than 50 percent of incidents recorded for officers wearing cameras (Katz et al. 2015: 42). More generally, Ariel et al. (2015) discuss nonrecording as a concern with treatment fidelity. A police chief from Florida described an example:

> We had an officer who had several questionable incidents in the past, so we outfitted him with a camera. Right in the middle of an encounter with a subject, the camera goes blank, and then it comes back on when the incident is over. He said that the camera malfunctioned, so we gave him another one. A week later he goes to arrest a woman, and again, the camera goes blank just before the encounter. He claimed again that the camera had malfunctioned. So we conducted a forensic review of the camera, which determined that the officer had intentionally hit the power button right before the camera shut off.
> (Miller, Toliver and Police Executive Research Forum, 2014: 8)

It is useful to consider that agency-produced indicators such as crime rates, arrests, court dispositions, probation violations, criminal history records, and the like measure four types of variation:

- The underlying concept of interest. Reported burglaries or car thefts reflect these events. Probation agency records of recidivism partly measure reoffending by persons on probation. Arrests for drug offenses in a neighborhood are partly affected by drug use and sales in that area.
- Error stemming from behavior of victims or others in detecting or deciding whether or not to report an incident. Shoplifting is an example of a crime that is often not detected. Victim surveys are widely used for estimating nonreporting.
- Error stemming from behavior of staff in justice agencies. Burglaries and car thefts reflect police decisions to record and retain reports of these offenses. Research has indicated that victim and neighborhood characteristics are associated with recording decisions (Warner, 1997; Boivin and Cordeau, 2011). Recidivism measures reflect activities by probation officers so that more active officers are more likely to detect reoffending. Individual police or police commanders may decide to place more or less emphasis on drug arrests in a particular area.
- Unknown error. Especially with agencies that handle a large number of incidents or cases, technical, clerical, and other errors are certain to crop up. Many police agencies are paying more careful attention to the locations of

offenses, but small errors in recording location on incident forms can produce misleading data. On the other hand, unknown error tends to increase inversely with the extent to which data are routinely used. The more regularly supervisors and leaders monitor data, the better able they are to recognize unknown error.

Using agency records to develop measures therefore requires examining the records critically and closely. Many local agencies incorporate some sort of audit procedures where state or local oversight organizations will periodically examine local records for accuracy. If this is the case, it is more likely that the error portion of agency data will be reduced. Periodic victim surveys can monitor reporting rates and estimate whether they are more common for certain types of offenses affecting certain kinds of victims. Victim surveys can also produce a forward records check by searching police records for incidents victims claim to have reported.

Asking questions

Question-based measures are used for two general reasons. First, there may be no other practical way to measure the concept. Perceptions, attitudes, opinions, other feelings, and knowledge are the main categories of things that can be most readily measured by asking questions. BMW research questions formulated by Lum et al. include attitudes about privacy and police officer job satisfaction. Ready and Young (2015) examined police perceptions of technology in the evaluation of BWCs in Mesa, Arizona.

The second reason is that question-based measures may be cheaper or more readily available than direct measures. The prevalence of drug use among high school students could be measured through urinalysis, but is largely impractical. Instead, surveys are regularly administered to obtain self-reports of drug use. Victimization surveys measure experiences that might be observed or that might appear in administrative data. Depending on victimizations that are observed (and not necessarily reported) would overlook even more incidents that may not be present in police records.

Surveys gather responses from relatively large numbers of individuals to questions presented in a standard way. Open-ended interviews and focus groups are better for getting more detailed information about operations in a command or conditions in a small area. Focus groups are good at getting two types of measures. First, focus groups are often used to collect information about which little is known, sometimes to help develop questionnaire items for a survey. The second type of measure is almost the opposite. Focus groups can shed further light on patterns of responses to surveys. For example, assume a community survey finds that 80 percent of area residents feel that teenagers and young people presented no problems in the area, whereas 12 percent were very concerned about disorderly teenagers. A sample of that 12 percent could be selected and convened as a focus group to delve more deeply into the specific nature and sources of respondent concerns.

Observation

Environmental criminologists and their allies probably use measures based on direct observation more than other criminal justice researchers. Applications range from simple counting systems to systematic social observation, with CCTV and motion-sensor cameras somewhere in between. Public health researchers were among the first to consider how systematically recorded images such as Google Street View could provide evidence for neighborhood conditions (Badland et al., 2010). Kurti and associates (2013) collected discarded cigarette packets in their research on illegal cigarette markets (Kurti, von Lampe and Thompkins, 2013). Plouffe and Sampson (2004) observed characteristics of parking lots with high rates of auto theft. Urinalysis is a form of observation, and community urinalysis of wastewater has come to be used to assess drug use for areas served by sewage treatment facilities (Burgard and Field, 2014). Highly local and time varying samples collected at a Swiss music festival revealed a weekend effect, with cannabis and cocaine spiking in samples and the first detected methamphetamine use (Benaglia, 2015). Though it is unlikely police or others conducting small-scale research would be eager to collect and analyze such data, opportunities for triangulation are available (van Wel et al., 2016).

Observation-based data are frequently cited in the problem-oriented policing literature, and, of course, gathering information by observation is a basic tool in policing. Observation for research is different in some important ways. First, it is more systematic, as in the term systematic social observation. Environmental surveys, like interview surveys, use protocols to record information, are conducted in a more or less uniform way, and are often collected from some sort of sample.

The Lowell, Massachusetts hot-spot experiment by Braga and Bond (2008) offers a good example of efforts to validate agency records. Police data on calls for service for disorder problems were triangulated with systematic social observation, addressing the question of how problems reported in police records compared to problems observed by researchers. In this way observation data can be used to triangulate measures to verify written records or suggest problems with written records. The question of nonrecording in use of BWCs is an example. In their study of car-mounted video cameras used by the New Jersey State Police, Maxfield and Andresen (2004) accompanied state police offers on road patrol to observe camera use. They discovered intermittent sound problems that signaled accidental nonrecording, as well as officers who intentionally turned off microphones during encounters.

Generalization

External validity is another term that is often misunderstood and misused. It is also sometimes deployed to justify meta-analysis. Thinking about generalization can be more useful. Can interventions or responses to problems be used in other settings or places? Will the self-awareness mechanism for BWC use operate differently for senior and less experienced law enforcement officers? Can evidence that something works in one city indicate it will work in other cities? The answer to the second question is often 'no', and is best reflected in tenets of problem-oriented policing to understand how similar problems become different in different settings. The limited need for generalizability is also illustrated in the importance of studying mechanisms in context, not assuming that all causal processes will operate similarly in different contexts (Pawson and Tilley, 1997). Recalling Eck's discussion of small-claim, small-scale evaluation, generalization across settings is not always possible or necessary.

In a different way, generalization is important in selecting samples of people, places, or other things to measure. Probability samples are strongest for making statistical estimates, but not necessary or appropriate for other purposes. Researchers trying to sample elusive populations for which no sampling frames exist have devised work-arounds that can be especially useful in generating evidence about police effectiveness.

Respondent-driven sampling takes advantage of hidden networks to locate elusive subjects. Dombrowski and associates (2012) describe how they used such techniques to find methamphetamine users in New York City. Recognizing that New York City's stop-question-frisk tactics targeted people in public places in specific neighborhoods, Fratello and associates (2013) used street sampling techniques in areas with high rates of stops in a type of victimization survey. This is a form of site-intercept sampling that roots questions about generalization in places where people of interest are likely to be found and is well suited as a tool for gathering information about place-based problems and interventions (Bush and Hair, 1985). Similarly, Blount-Hill and Butts (2015) describe how respondent-driven sampling in New York City's Cure Violence program yielded a large number of young minority males in high-violence neighborhoods.

Another approach to generalization in evaluating BWCs is to make observations in settings that score high or low on measures of interest. Rather than trying to generalize across all areas in a large city, the cameras can be first deployed in selected areas that recognize possible mechanisms at work. This is the approach described by Grossmith (2015) and colleagues in their evaluation of BWCs in London. Areas included in the sample had relatively high rates of crime and high rates of stop-and-search. Because one measure of interest was a reduction in complaints against police, areas that had low rates of complaints were excluded.

Evaluations of BWCs exhibit different views on generalization. One is illustrated by the LJAF call for rigorous evaluations to produce a better catalog of evidence. Another is to recognize that BWCs may be more useful in specific types of incidents, or that guidelines on their use must recognize differences in incidents or settings. Though it is easy to overstate the value of shared experiences, police departments learn from each other, and may adapt BWC use and policies to meet local needs (Miller et al., 2014). This is an example of practice-based evidence.

Conclusion

Community-based nonprofit organizations differ from law enforcement organizations in countless ways. Resources and flexibility are especially important examples. It is difficult to imagine directly transferring something like John Jay's

Evidence Generation initiative to a large or moderate-sized police department. However, the basic research tools are widely used, if not acknowledged in the terms used here. Problem-oriented policing, Compstat-like accountability systems, place-based interventions, special event management, and even traffic engineering and enforcement consider the principles of problem definition, process, measurement, and generalization.

We have illustrated how these principles drove our approach to evidence generation for community-based organizations. They can similarly be used in figuring out how to implement body-worn cameras and how to assess their impact. Although the Laura and John Arnold Foundation (2016) explicitly cites randomized trials as the preferred approach to evaluation, their solicitation acknowledges that other approaches may be appropriate. Only a relative handful of law enforcement agencies will host these evaluations, but many more can be expected to consider or implement some form of BWC technology. In doing so, they will almost certainly consult the growing body of evidence. Given the extreme decentralization of U.S. law enforcement, most departments will have to adapt the technology and its management in some way. Like our Evidence Generation Affiliates, departments will differ in important ways, which means that practice-based evidence will be necessary to implement and assess BWCs.

Butts (2015) compares evaluating social policies to pointing a flashlight in a dark room, where one can only see what is illuminated by the flashlight's beam. He writes:

> Research evidence does not emerge from a pristine and impartial search for truth. The evidence we have today is the fruit of previous research investments made by policymakers and funding bodies with goals, beliefs, values, and preferences. Funding provides the flashlight and points it as well. To say that a program or practice is "evidence-based" means that the odds of success are reasonably good. The findings of existing evaluations are like small beams of light in a dark room. They are not sufficient for making all the choices required to formulate and implement social policies. Naive lawmakers who demand irrefutable evidence for every funding decision are simply afraid of the dark.

Practiced-based evidence and more flexible approaches to evidence generation are potential ways to expand the field of view illuminated by the flashlight.

Acknowledgement

We thank Kate Bowers for thorough and helpful comments on an earlier draft of the chapter.

Note

1 John Jay Research and Evaluation Center. 'Evidence Generation'. Retrieved from https://johnjayrec.nyc/evgen/

References

Ariel, B., Farrar, W. A. and Sutherland, A. (2015). 'The effect of police body-worn cameras on use of force and citizens' complaints against the police: A randomized controlled trial', *Journal of Quantitative Criminology*, 31: 509–35.

Badland, H. M., Opit, S., Witten, K., Kearns, R. A. and Mavoa, S. (2010). 'Can virtual streetscape audits reliably replace physical streetscape audits?', *Journal of Urban Health: Bulletin of the New York Academy of Medicine*, 87(6): 1007–16.

Benaglia, L. (2015, 24 August). *Assessing Intra- and Inter-Day Variations in Illicit Drugs Consumption during a Music Festival*, University of Lausanne Doctoral School. Diablerets, Switzerland.

Blount-Hill, K.-L. and Butts, J.A. (2015). *Respondent-Driven Sampling: Evaluating the Effects of the Cure Violence Model with Neighborhood Survey*, New York: Research and Evaluation Center, John Jay College of Criminal Justice, City University of New York.

Boba, R. (2010). 'A practice-based evidence approach in Florida', *Police Practice and Research*, 11: 122–8.

Boivin, R. and Cordeau, G. (2011). 'Measuring the impact of police discretion on official crime statistics: A research note', *Police Quarterly*, 14: 186–203.

Bowers, K.J., Johnson, S.D. and Hirschfield, A.F.G. (2004). 'Closing off opportunities for crime: An evaluation of alley-gating', *European Journal on Criminal Policy and Research*, 10: 285–308.

Braga, A.A. and Bond, B.J. (2008). 'Policing crime and disorder hot spots: A randomized controlled trial', *Criminology*, 46(3): 577–607.

Burgard, D.A., Caleb, B.-G. and Field, J. (2014). 'Working upstream: How far can you go with sewage-based epidemiology?', *Environmental Science and Technology*, 48: 1362–8.

Bush, A.J. and Hair, J.F. Jr. (1985). 'An assessment of the mall intercept as a data collection method', *Journal of Marketing Research*, 22: 158–67.

Butts, J. (2015, 18 October). *Cursing the Darkness* [Linked In Post]. Retrieved from www.linkedin.com/pulse/cursing-darkness-jeffrey-butts?trk=prof-post (accessed 4 April 2016).

Campbell, D.T. (1969). 'Reforms as experiments', *American Psychologist*, 24: 409–29.

Campbell, D.T. (1976). Assessing the Impact of Planned Social Change (Occasional paper series, 8), Western Michigan University, Kalamazoo Evaluation Center, Retrieved from www.eric.ed.gov/PDFS/ED303512.pdf.

Clarke, R.V. and Eck, J.E. (2005). *Crime Analysis for Problem Solvers in 60 Small Steps*, Washington: U.S. Department of Justice, Office of Community Oriented Policing Retrieved from www.popcenter.org

Clarke, R.V., Kemper, R. and Wyckoff, L. (2001). 'Controlling cell phone fraud in the US: Lessons for the UK 'foresight' initiative', *Security Journal*, 14(1): 7–22.

Copes, H. and Miller, J.M. (eds). (2015). *The Routledge Handbook of Qualitative Criminology*, London and NY: Routledge.

Dombrowski, K., Khan, B., Wendel, T., McLean, K., Mishula, E. and Curtis, R. (2012). 'Estimating the size of the methamphetamine-using population in New York City using network sampling techniques', *Advances in Applied Sociology*, 2(4): 245–52.

Eck, J.E. (2002). 'Learning from Experience in Problem-Oriented Policing and Situational Prevention: The Positive Functions of Weak Evaluations and the Negative Functions of Strong Ones', in N. Tilley (ed) *Evaluation for Crime Prevention*, Crime prevention studies, vol. 14, pp. 93–117, Monsey, NY: Criminal Justice Press.

Eck, J.E. and Madensen, T.D. (2009). 'Using Signatures of Opportunity Structures to Examine Mechanisms in Crime Prevention Evaluations', in J. Knutsson and N. Tilley (eds) *Evaluating Crime Prevention Initiatives*, Crime prevention studies, vol. 24, pp. 48–59, Monsey, NY: Criminal Justice Press.

Eterno, J.A. and Silverman, E.B. (2012). *The Crime Numbers Game: Management by Manipulation*, Boca Raton, FL: CRC Press.

Farrell, G., Laycock, G. and Tilley, N. (2015). 'Debuts and legacies: The crime drop and the role of adolescent-limited and persistent offending', *Crime Science*, 4(16), doi: 10.1186/s40163-015-0028-3

Fratello, J., Rengifo, A.F., Trone, J. and Velazquez, B. (2013). *Coming of Age with Stop and Frisk: Experiences, Self-Perceptions, and Public Safety Implications. Technical Report* [Tech. Rep.], New York: Vera Institute of Justice.

Grossmith, L., Owens, C., Finn, W., Mann, D., Davies, T. and Baika, L. (2015). *Police, Camera, Evidence: London's Cluster Randomised Controlled Trial of Body Worn Video*, London: College of Policing and the Mayor's Office for Policing and Crime.

Hough, M. (2014). 'Confessions of a recovering 'administrative criminologist': Jock Young, quantitative research and policy research', *Crime Media Culture*, 10: 215–26.

Ioannidis, J.P.A. (2005). 'Why Most Published Research Findings Are False', *PLoS Med*, 2: e124. doi: 10.1371/journal.pmed.0020124

Jacques, S. (2014). 'The quantitative-qualitative divide in criminology: A theory of ideas' importance, attractiveness, and publication', *Theoretical Criminology*, 18: 317–34.

Katz, C.M., Choate, D.E., Ready, J.R. and Nuno, L. (2015). *Evaluating the Impact of Officer Worn Body Cameras in the Phoenix Police Department*, Phoenix, AZ: Center for Violence Prevention and Community Safety, Arizona State University. Retrieved from http://johnjayrec.nyc/2016/01/20/justicetech/.

Kellogg Foundation. (2004). *Logic Model Development Guide: Using Logic Models to Bring Together Planning, Evaluation, and Action*, #1209, Battle Creek, MI: W.W. Kellogg foundation.

Kurti, M.K., von Lampe, K. and Thompkins, D.E. (2013). 'The illegal cigarette market in a socioeconomically deprived inner-city area: The case of the South Bronx', *Tobacco Control*, 22: 138–40.

Laura and John Arnold Foundation. (2016). *Building a Rigorous Research Base for Body Worn Cameras*. Retrieved from www.arnoldfoundation.org/wp-content/uploads/Building-a-Rigorous-Research-Base-for-Body-Worn-Cameras.pdf

Liberman, A.M. (2009). 'Advocating evidence-generating policies: A role for the ASC', *The Criminologist*, 34: 2–5.

Lipsey, M.W., Howell, J.C., Kelly, M.R., Chapman, G. and Carver, D. (2010). *Improving the Effectiveness of Juvenile Justice Programs: A New Perspective on Evidence-Based Practice*, Washington, DC: Center for Juvenile Justice Reform, Georgetown Public Policy Institute, Georgetown University.

Loughran, T.A., Mulvey, E.P., Schubert, C.A., Fagan, J., Piquero, A.R. and Losoya, S.H. (2009). 'Estimating a dose-response relationship between length of stay and future recidivism in serious juvenile offenders', *Criminology*, 47(3): 699–740.

Lum, C., Koper, C., Merola, L.M., Scherer, A. and Reioux, A. (2015). *Existing and Ongoing Body Worn Camera Research: Knowledge Gaps and Opportunities*, [Report for the Laua and John Arnold Foundation], Fairfax, VA: Center for Evidence-Based Crime Policy, George Mason University.

Maruna, S. (2010). 'Mixed Method Research in Criminology: Why Not Go Both Ways?', in A.R. Piquero and D. Weisburd (eds) *Handbook of Quantitative Criminology*, pp. 123–40, New York: Springer-Verlag.

Maxfield, M.G. (2001). *Guide to Frugal Evaluation for Criminal Justice*. Final report to the National Institute of Justice. Washington, DC: U.S. Department of Justice, Office of Justice Programs, National Institute of Justice, www.ncjrs.gov/pdffiles1/nij/grants/187350.pdf

Maxfield, M.G. and Andresen, W.C. (2004). *Evaluation of New Jersey State Police In-Car Mobile Video Recording System*, Final report to the Office of the Attorney General, Newark, NJ: School of Criminal Justice, Rutgers University.

Miller, L., Toliver, J. and Police Executive Research Forum. (2014). *Implementing a Body-Worn Camera Program: Recommendations and Lessons Learned*, Washington, DC: Office of Community Oriented Policing Services.

Nagin, D.S. and Weisburd, D. (2013). 'Evidence and public policy: The example of evaluation research in policing', *Criminology and Public Policy*, 12: 651–79.

Pawson, R. and Tilley, N. (1997). *Realistic Evaluation*, Thousand Oaks, CA: Sage.

Peters, M.G. and Eure, P.K. (2015). *Body-Worn Cameras in NYC: An Assessment of NYPD's Pilot Program and Recommendations to Promote Accountability*, New York: New York City Department of Investigation, Office of the Inspector General for the NYPD.

Piquero, A. and Weisburd, D. (eds). (2010). *Handbook of Quantitative Criminology*, New York: Springer-Verlag.

Plouffe, N. and Sampson, R. (2004). 'Auto theft and theft from autos in parking lots in Chula Vista, CA: Crime analysis for local and regional action,' in *Understanding and Preventing Car Theft*, M. G. Maxfield and E. V. Clarke (Eds) Crime Prevention Studies, vol. 17, pp. 147–171, Monsey, NY: Criminal Justice Press.

Ready, J.T. and Young, J.T. (2015). 'The impact of on-officer video cameras on police-citizen contacts: Findings from a controlled experiment in Mesa, AZ', *Journal of Experimental Criminology*, 11: 445–58.

Ross, H.L. (1973). 'Law, science, and accidents: The British road safety act of 1967', *Journal of Legal Studies*, 2: 1–78.

Scott, M.S. (2015). *Identifying and Defining Policing Problems*, Problem-Oriented Guides for Police. Problem-solving tools No. 13. Washington, DC: Office of Community-Oriented Policing Services.

Shadish, W.R., Cook, T.D. and Campbell, D.T. (2002). *Experimental and Quasi-Experimental Designs for Generalized Causal Inference*. Boston, MA: Houghton Mifflin.

Sperber, K.G., Latessa, E.J. and Makarios, M.D. (2013). 'Establishing a risk-dosage research agenda: Implications for policy and practice', *Justice Research and Policy*, 15: 123–41.

Sullivan, C.J. and McGloin, J.M. (2014). 'Looking back to move forward: Some thoughts on measuring crime and delinquency over the past 50 years', *Journal of Research in Crime and Delinquency*, 51(4): 445–66.

van Wel, J., Gracia-Lor, E., van Nuijs, A., Kinyua, J., Salvatore, S. and Castiglioni, S., et al. (2016). 'Investigation of Agreement between Wastewater-based Epidemiology and Survey Data on Alcohol and Nicotine Use in a Community', *Drug and Alcohol Dependence*, 162: 170–175. doi: http://dx.doi.org/10.1016/j.drugalcdep 2016.03.002

Warner, B.D. (1997). 'Community characteristics and the recording of crime: Police recording of citizens' complaints of burglary and assault', *Justice Quarterly*, 14: 631–50.

Young, J.T. and Ready, J.T. (2015). 'Diffusion of ideas and technology: The role of networks in influencing the endorsement and use of on-officer video cameras', *Journal of Contemporary Criminal Justice*, 31: 243–61.

6 How to morph experience into evidence

Ken Pease and Jason Roach

I think people in this country have had enough of experts.

Michael Gove, June 10, 2016.[1]

In this chapter we present in outline form an alternative to the currently favoured way of reaching conclusions about policing impact. For most police services, large-scale events, particularly those which have proven problematic, are followed by post hoc evaluation (with all the problems which attend hindsight). By contrast, routine evaluation of their everyday work and initiatives is unusual.

Consider a public meeting about crime prevention hardware. One speaker is the world's leading academic expert on the topic. The other is a local mid-ranking police officer. To whom will more questions be addressed by the audience? Having observed situations of this kind, our contention is that the academic would be well advised to take a book to read during that part of the proceedings. We make three assertions, the third flowing from the first two:

1   Police officers may be persuaded by the experience of other officers, but seldom by academic research, however extensive and sophisticated. Collegiality among police officers is an enduring feature of police culture (see Loftus, 2010). Most officers are not aware of, are not taught about and choose not to seek out relevant academic research. When launching local initiatives, their first action tends to be the arrangement of visits to similar initiatives in other forces, rather than taking to the journals.
2   Implicitly, universities, government and the public value police experience so highly as to offset expertise of other kinds in recruitment decisions and policy development. To test this claim, please check the academic records of former police officers appointed to high academic roles. It is clear that police experience overrides what may be thought of as unacceptably low levels of research competence and theory awareness.
3   Any attempt to make the craft of policing more data based should start with an acknowledgement of the first two propositions and work through their implications. The present chapter represents an initial audacious (probably premature and unpopular) start on this task. It outlines an approach which yokes policing experience to a statistically defensible method of uncertainty reduction.

There is now a Society for Evidence-Based Policing. That title seems to us insulting. Unless one charges the police with behaving randomly, the issue is not whether, but how, evidence is adduced, tested, weighed and applied in problem situations. Our assertion about the primacy of experience in placing a value on police pronouncements has profound implications. It means that the emphasis for researchers of policing issues requires an appreciative stance towards police craft as the appropriate point of departure. The imposition of the alien conventions of the academic worldview will enjoy transient success only insofar as it is helpful for career progression. It was ever thus. One of us recalls, forty years ago, more than one neophyte cop reporting his tutor constable asserting: 'First thing is to forget everything you heard at training school'.

The failure of the body of applicable academic studies to gain substantial traction in police work may be tentatively attributed to the following circumstances:

- That evaluations are not seen to derive from the *experience* of police officers.
- That the choice alternatives between which the police officer is daily faced are typically not recognisable in the results of set piece research.
- That research evaluations come as predigested entities and do not require the mental work necessary for iterative improvements.
- That research results come long after practitioner reputations have been staked and organisation funds expended assuming scheme success.
- That ownership of consolidation or maintenance of successful schemes carries less kudos than innovation (see 'Killing the Cubs' later).

Malcolm Sparrow (2016) makes a similar argument against the evidence-based policing (EBP) movement as currently understood, with social scientists posing the questions and identifying the truths to which police practice should cleave. He identifies the problems as follows[2]:

- The EBP process is too slow to inform operational policing decisions.
- EBP mounts evaluations of extant strategies, thus not extending, and possibly narrowing, the policing repertoire by excluding novel approaches.
- By concentrating on large aggregated data sets, EBP neglects important micro-level choices crucial to success.
- By emphasising large data and complex designs, the rate of experimentation under EBP is reduced.
- EBP perpetuates traditional mind-sets by privileging approaches which attract senior-level support and funding.

Put brutally, our starting point is that the craft of policing is seen by its practitioners as primarily the gaining of skill through the personal or vicarious acquisition of experience *as a police officer*. Research evidence is neither personal nor vicarious experience. It comes from those who have never undergone the rite of passage of dealing with aggressive, vomit-caked revellers over weekend nights in city centres, or accompanying parents identifying the dead bodies of their children. The attempt to make policing more evidence based has so far been flawed in failing to engage with that truth. The task, in the writers' view, is to apply a process of decision optimisation. This should flow from the experience-centred perspective of the police. It should use experience-based evidence as the most promising point of departure for refinement of police decision-making. It should adhere to a process recognisable to science that will yield improvements which are cumulative across time and managements.

Things *are* (pretty much) what they used to be

The reader may detect a tension in the foregoing. Police experience is highly valued by the public (and respected by the writers). Yet we are suggesting change. What needs changing?

The former UK Prime Minister David Cameron was moved to call the police 'the last unreformed public service' (see Ignatans and Pease, 2014). Looking back over the fifty years or so which represent our combined lives working in police stations and around police officers, we discern only modest change while the context of policing has changed markedly. The experience of someone reporting a crime today remains recognisable from what it was in 1970, whereas a call to Tesco today will reveal their awareness of your address, customer history and probably the location of your birthmarks. Mapping applications in policing are new, but why do police maps so often cover 24-hour periods despite the widely different areal distributions of crime across the three shifts? Such details are telling in showing the disconnect between police data and the operational decisions which they could inform. Why is it still the case that any researcher accessing police data invariably has to spend so long editing it because of poor data quality control? This has a profound consequence for in-house analysts, who are often reduced to producing the most basic of reports because of poor data quality, when doing a professional job would require extensive data editing, which the pace of police work does not permit. Any police claim that practice is data driven is belied by the inadequacy of current police data quality assurance. There is a coating of the policing vocabulary with words from the criminological literature like 'cocooning', 'reassurance', and 'routine activities'. Now, after every serious crime, TV news will include a clip of a senior police officer proclaiming 'officers have been deployed to provide reassurance'. This is a reflex response designed to show that something is being done. It neglects research showing that the effect of seeing police officers is highly contingent on setting and circumstance (Unsworth et al., 2012). Spatial location of events has become far more precise, alongside extensive digitisation of police data. Algorithm-based predictive patrolling has gained an insecure foothold in a few police areas. Crime on the streets has declined across the Western world, but that was little or none of the police's doing, however frequent the proud announcement of local declines. Much of the crime problem has migrated to cyberspace, and to a large extent is still not reflected in police training and resourcing, which remains determinedly territorial in its organisation.

Perhaps more persuasive in demonstrating that evidence has not been cumulative in its impact beyond more than a few cherry-picked examples is a small exercise one of us set up some years ago which has not been published. A colleague (Enid Roberts) was asked to identify from the Popcenter website those UK projects which had enjoyed success in the Goldstein award competition. She contacted the forces concerned to ask who was now responsible for the successful work, either as a continuation of the project or its mainstreaming into force business. She was (charmingly) persistent and got forwarded to various people in the forces concerned, but *without exception* the successful projects had faded as completely and sadly as Ozymandias' great edifice in the eponymous Shelley poem. *So even within-force experiences of success do not survive.* It could, of course, be that the reason why forces did not know what had happened to their successes was because they were now seamlessly incorporated into practice, but we very much doubt that. Some of the successes were relatively recent, and Enid was persistent.

In this admittedly discursive section, we have sought to argue that esteem for police experience has not yielded the cumulative changes in policing expertise and sensitivity to changing context that allows complacency. To sum up our argument, the move towards cumulatively evidenced policing should start, and its most feasible route lies through the respect for, but refinement of, lessons learned via policing experience itself.

Killing the cubs

So why do successful policing initiatives more often than not pass away? Senior police officers are powerful. Ambitious senior police officers will set their stall out for promotion by doing new things rather than consolidating older things. Obviously new things must be tried, but successful programmes must not be neglected, or worse. We see the resulting fragmentation of progress as a major problem in policing. Consider the lion. A lion finds a lioness attractive. She already has cubs. He sees off her partner, the father of the cubs. He then kills the cubs. He's not going to waste time and energy nurturing progeny which do not carry his genes. This genetic selfishness runs across many human parenting phenomena. One theory for the near-unique phenomenon of concealed ovulation in humans is that it helpfully introduces ambiguity into paternity issues (Mummy's baby, Daddy's maybe – Roach and Pease, 2013). In a raft of brilliant Canadian work by Margo Wilson and Martin Daly, we find many suggestive parallels (see Roach and Pease, 2013 for an overview). Stepfathers are disproportionately dangerous to their stepchildren (indeed more than 100 times more so than biological fathers). Female onlookers disproportionately stress the similarity of newborns to putative fathers, not the mother, and so on. Thus is paternal protection assured by diminishing the suspicion of having been cuckolded. What is the parallel between the lion, the stepfather and the police chief? Please bear with us.

Like the lion, the ambitious police officer, having achieved command, will be tempted, consciously or because of enthusiasm for his or her as yet unrealised ideas, to let the initiatives of his or her predecessor wither, however successful. Our original Kirkholt burglary reduction work enjoyed success (Pease, 1991). In its second phase, under different management, one of us noticed that the cocooning (i.e., the engagement of immediate neighbours and security uprating) of burgled homes was no longer happening. When this was queried, the officer in charge of this phase remarked derisively, 'We've moved a long way beyond that'. Ron Clarke, doyen of situational crime prevention research, tells a similar story from a different force. A comparable fate befell the extension of the repeat victimisation work to domestic violence. PC Sam Lloyd, Graham Farrell and one of us established a process which was ahead of what typically happens even now (Lloyd et al., 1994). It guaranteed that a first officer attending a domestic incident knew what legal protections were in place. The scheme also introduced pendant alarms and single-number mobile phones for recent victims. The victims were our loudest supporters. When the project ended, the system quickly fell into disuse. A more recent example comes from Greater Manchester Police, where Inspector Vinny Jones and analyst Matt Fielding produced an excellent programme of predictive patrolling, which fell into disuse upon the departure of the divisional commander who has supported their work. Vinny retired, and Matt resigned in frustration. So many promising cubs have perished unnecessarily.

A suggestive sidelight on this metaphorical cub killing is that the reader will observe that more publicity is given to police initiatives when they start than when they later demonstrate success. Cynically, the ideal career trajectory for the ambitious officer is to kill your predecessor's promising cubs, make a song and dance about the birth of your own cubs, then get promoted (to head of the pride) before someone comes along to kill your cubs. The parallel with cub killing becomes less clear at that point, but the head of the pride who has achieved the position having left a trail of dead cubs now has the influence and control over resources to thwart potential rivals and their cubs.

In brief, our view of the present state of affairs is that policing experience rather than social science research is so embedded as what is to be valued in operational decisions that experience has to be the starting point for progress. Yet it is metaphorical cub killing and political infrastructure of policing which makes the accumulation of knowledge about what works best so imperfectly realised. In what way, if any, can academics help, with humility appropriate to their marginal position in police esteem?

The remainder of this chapter suggests how to establish a mind-set which encourages innovation *and* consolidation of innovation across time and local management. The route proposed here sounds indirect and arcane but has practitioner experience as its starting point. The reader may argue that cub killing is a feature of many organisations. We agree. We think our proposed remedy has wider application, but one has to start somewhere.

Conditional probability

If one of us eats mushrooms the chances of throwing up later are high. If mushrooms are not eaten, the chances of throwing up are low. If one drinks in O'Malleys Shamrock bar in Derry tonight and listens to the music, then the chances of getting into a fight are low. If one goes into the same bar wearing a bowler hat and an orange sash, then a fight is almost certain. All skilled behaviour (arguably all behaviour) can be represented as internalised assessments of conditional probability, that is, assessments of what is likely to happen if one takes one or other course of action. If you really need a reference for that observation, you are a hopeless academic incapable of introspection, but to humour you try the classic Miller, Galanter and Pribram (1960).

Wisdom comes with the establishment of a set of conditional probabilities which are modified in the light of experience. The tennis player notes that one opponent has a problem with drop shots to the backhand corner and increases the use of such shots. In the conventional phrasing, her approach is *conditional on* the opponent being played. The chef comes to know that the oven he uses requires less cooking time than the recipe book suggests.

There are many alternative ways of making the same fundamental, almost self-evident point. Kelly's (1950) theory of personality has as its fundamental postulate, paraphrased here as 'a person's processes are channelized by the way in which (s)he anticipates events'. In other words, what you do depends on your set of internalised conditional probabilities of the consequences. At its simplest, the acquisition of skill consists of a process of predicting likely outcomes, observing the actual outcomes and revising conditional probabilities. Sometimes this happens after one event (the burnt child avoids the fire), sometimes it takes a lifetime (as in the honing of artistic talent). Perfect (in the real-world elusive) performance is achieved when expected and actual outcomes coincide. This is an overly simple depiction of the real world but will do for now. This process is already recognisable in the musings and actions of skilled police officers. The adage that you can have a thirty-year police career or a one-year police career repeated thirty times is a way of thinking about this point. The 'one-year career thirty times' officer will learn a set of tactics early in the career and apply them thereafter. The 'thirty-year career' officer revises actions in the light of outcomes, that is, constantly reworks the conditional probabilities applied. What are the attributes of an evaluation approach which would be suitable for policing – one in which practitioner experience morphs into transferable and scientifically defensible evidence? We explain what should comprise such an approach in the sections that follow.

Prediction based

In his brilliant book *The Signal and the Noise*, Nate Silver introduces Bayesian analysis which we describe later by reference to gambling. The successful gambler is one with the best understanding of the variables on which the outcome is conditional. Perhaps the outcome of a football match is most successfully anticipated taking into account the recency of the manager's appointment, the number of players coming to the end of their contracts and the identity and recent performances of the referee.[3] The gambler who weighs these appropriately wins more often because he has optimised the conditional probabilities which comprise their skill set. That said, the second writer's grandad had a 'system' for predicting winning racehorses based on the optimisation of conditional probabilities only known to him. Needless to say, although he very rarely won, he never questioned the validity and reliability of his system.

Iterative

It should allow refinement of implementation as circumstances change without the criticisms that arise when a scheme to be evaluated is changed during the course of the evaluation.

Scalable

It should be applicable across the range of implementer roles. Initiatives consist of a range of people making a series of interlocking decisions. Set piece evaluation tends to collapse these into a single entity.

Accessible

Comprehension of the process should require no expertise beyond that to be expected from the average practitioner.

If these criteria are worth recalling, the acronym PISA might help, keeping in mind a leaning edifice that is thought worth preserving.

Bayes-less speculation

Although we believe Bayesian statistics to represent the way forward for policing evaluations, we do not need to mention Bayes at all to describe the bones of the evaluation process we favour, which simply reflects the way in which people learn skills. Learning chess, for example, involves learning which moves improve the chances of success. Each move is a prediction of consequences. In our proposed policing application, Bayesian statistics simply formalises and makes public what the more skilled officer does already. It consists simply in requiring people (of all ranks) making decisions on tactics or strategy *to predict* what will happen in the immediate future and the variables (conditions) under which it will occur. These predictions have to be specific (greater or less crime of a particular kind, more or fewer arrests or whatever is of interest). These will be compared with outcomes and the exercise repeated until predictive accuracy stabilises at a higher level than it began. A refined version of this approach satisfies the criteria of prediction based, iterative, scalable and accessible. It mirrors the position of the successful gambler with the important difference that the police may themselves be able to influence the outcome of the next match once the conditioning variables are identified![4]

Bayes' camp

Although there is no need to locate the approach suggested here with the Bayesian tradition in statistics, there are substantial reasons for doing so. First we need a brief and simplified canter over the statistical ground.

There are two major statistical traditions: frequentist and Bayesian. The frequentist approach is probably the one which academics experienced as students (with perhaps a brief nod towards Bayes). The frequentist approach reaches conclusions about differences between groups on the basis of presumptions about the population distribution from which they are drawn. This requires the drawing of an adequately sized sample and its analysis. The conclusions are reached at the end of the process. The Bayesian approach starts with a guess about the future based on experience, research and/or intuition. This guess or experience-based estimate is known as the prior. It then takes outcomes into account in revising the initial judgement. This is the posterior probability. The posterior can then be used as the next prior and the next outcome examined to yield another posterior judgement. Recall Nate Silver's characterisation of the successful gambler as an example of the process. But Bayesian statistics is a broad church and has developed complex and sophisticated variants. Perhaps it is simply better here to describe its history and give one example of what the simplest kind of Bayesian approach might yield. We are aware that the iterative core of the approach is not conveyed by the example. The reader is invited to think of it as a single stage in an iterative process.

At this stage we digress on the assumption that the reader is unfamiliar with the history of statistical analysis and of Bayes' rule in particular. This is an attempt to show that Bayesian analysis is a major, respectable and arguably increasingly dominant analytic approach. Thomas Bayes was an eighteenth-century Presbyterian minister. His work was published posthumously by his friend Richard Price and developed by Pierre-Simon Laplace. The Bayesian approach has been out of favour for most of the intervening period. The use of Bayesian statistics in the code-breaking work of Alan Turing and colleagues at Bletchley Park in World War II evoked interest, albeit much later because of remaining security limitations on what entered the public domain (Megrayne, 2011). Neglect of Bayes in the twentieth century was not least a result of opposition from R.A. Fisher of University College London, frequentist giant and hammer of the Bayesians. Fisher was a genius (immortalised by the F ratio initialised for him). It is perhaps no coincidence that Fisher's early brilliance was displayed in the analyses of plant yields at Rothamsted research station. Plants do not learn skills or accommodations in complex situations. Fisherian techniques are arguably more adapted to plants than people. A recent statistical text now asserts: 'It is curious and re-assuring that the overwhelmingly dominant Fisherian approach is now giving way in the 21st century to a Bayesian approach that had its genesis in the 18th century' (Kruschke, 2015: 100).

Bayesian approaches take many forms, but at their centre is the notion that one proceeds on facts and inferences one already has rather than making comparisons with hypothetical population distributions. It changes conclusions as outcomes dictate. There has been an explosion of applications of the Bayesian approach across a diverse range of topics. In the *Oxford Handbook of Applied Bayesian Analysis* (O'Hagan and West, 2010), the word the editors use repeatedly to describe the chapters is 'showcase', emphasising the point that there is a huge untapped range of applications which are possible. The range of techniques spawned by the original insight is impressively documented in the handbook. The editors' opening sentence confirms: 'The diversity of applications of modern Bayesian analysis at the start of the 21st century is simply enormous'. Bespoke software for Bayesian analysis now exists.[5] Just Google 'Bayesian methods in cancer research' 2016 and you will get an avalanche of results. We choose just one such reference because of its author, David Spiegelhalter, who is a leading proponent of Bayesian methods and deviser of the free WinBUGS software for use in Bayesian analysis (Spiegelhalter, 2006). There has been a flood of 'how to' books for Bayesian analysis coinciding with increased interest and recognition of relevance (e.g. Gelman et al., 2015; Downey, 2014; Kruschke, 2014 and Yau, 2015). This chapter cannot even begin to teach Bayesian skills. It does aspire to demonstrate why you should want to.

There are many ways of characterising the difference between frequentist and Bayesian approaches. One is to say that frequentist approaches ask how likely are the data given the theory, whereas the Bayesian approach asks how likely is the theory given the data. The frequentist approach favours experiments and requires adequate sample sizes to reach conclusions. The last decade has seen a major movement from frequentist to Bayesian thinking. There are both negative and positive reasons for this. Perhaps a key paper making for worries about frequentist conventions is Ioannidis (2005). Its title is *Why Most Published Research Findings Are False*. The paper is short and complex and sets out the circumstances under which published results are most likely to be wrong. The contributory factor, which it will suffice to name here because it will already be familiar, is the $p < .05$ convention for statistical significance. Do twenty analyses and one will be significant by chance. The suspicion for the p value as a measure of anything worth measuring has now gone so far that some peer-reviewed journals ban the p value.[6] Examination of p values in published psychological research shows an implausibly large number of analyses which 'just made it' to the .05 level (otherwise known as torturing the data until they confess).

In the Bayesian approach any data can lead to a change of view, allowing change of judgements on the basis of single events, impossible when sample data have to be compared against a presumed population.

Another advantage of a Bayesian approach, crucial in the present context, is its encouragement for constant reassessment of confidence in the truth of a proposition. A randomised control trial (RCT) is difficult to mount and stands in the literature for lengthy periods while the reality of the policing practices which it purports to represent change. Put crudely, having to wait for long periods doing the same thing before one can be told it was all useless while sensing what improvements could be made is an offence against reason. In a work in progress, it will be argued that Bayes is the unacknowledged and unused formal underpinning of realist evaluation. One of the frustrations of recent years has been mails or phone calls from police officers doing a Masters course at one of our older universities saying they want to mount an RCT. In a classic 'putting the cart before the horse' scenario, one of us recently asked a student asking to do this 'What about?' They replied, 'I haven't decided yet'. Thus do presumptions about the efficacy of policing tactics begin.

How many promising initiatives have thus been prematurely discarded on the basis of a p value when its implementers know what could have been done to make it work on the basis of their experience in implementation? A young inspector to whom one of us talked a few weeks ago described how his bosses rejected his idea on the basis of an RCT that had been carried out on the topic. He spoke persuasively to one of us about what he thinks had happened in the RCT and how he was confident that he could make his idea work. We believe him.

For the statistically interested reader, we recommend a masterly video presentation of Bayes' rule and its spin-off benefits.[7] The video takes its examples from diagnosis in medicine, but can be thought of in terms of any judgement which can be right or wrong. Will there be more or less pub violence next week? Will there be more or less when there are high-visibility patrols? Will there be more or less when extra bar staff are recruited? The process involves anticipating (prior), seeing what happens, changing anticipation (posterior) and perhaps refining what is done until you understand the variables on which the phenomenon is conditioned.

In Chapter 8 of Silver's (2013) book *The Signal and the Noise*, he emphasises that the Bayesian approach is fundamentally a mind-set rather than a statistical approach. He uses gambling as apt because the stake is the outward and visible sign of belief. The more you believe, the higher the stake you place. Likewise the more effort and time a police officer invests in a task, the greater her 'stake'. His interview with a highly successful gambler describes the latter's way of working. He takes all the evidence and weighs it, places a bet according to belief and adjusts his belief according to whether the outcome is as he bets. By an iterative process of evidence weighing, he wins more than he loses.[8] One can think of police work as a gamble in exactly the same way. Time and resources deployed are the stake. The odds are relevant. It may be worthwhile taking a modest punt on an outcome with long odds of success, for example, with attempts to reduce serious crimes, such as homicide, that are low in prevalence but high in social harm.

To reprise, the advantages of the Bayesian approach include the following:

1 It starts with judgements and belief made by practitioners. This is ideally informed by the research literature, just as the gambler's bet is better informed by statistics.
2 It uses any information rather than relying on set piece experiments.
3 It provides quick feedback to enable adjustments of judgement.
4 It is iterative in revising degree of belief in propositions.
5 It requires implementers to think about mechanisms.

The objection to Bayesian thinking on the basis of the subjectivity of prior probabilities seems perhaps strange with hindsight. Often there is enough evidence to get a reasonable data-based prior probability. Where there is not, given some basic rationality in revising belief levels in the light of experience, belief levels will converge, whatever the initial starting point. Figure 6.1 shows this with initial beliefs of 25 percent, 50 percent and 75 percent and a rational terminal belief level of 95 percent (few things in life are 100 percent certain). It shows evidence increments along the abscissa. The curve would be less smooth with each piece of non-confirmatory evidence, but the convergence would be as shown.

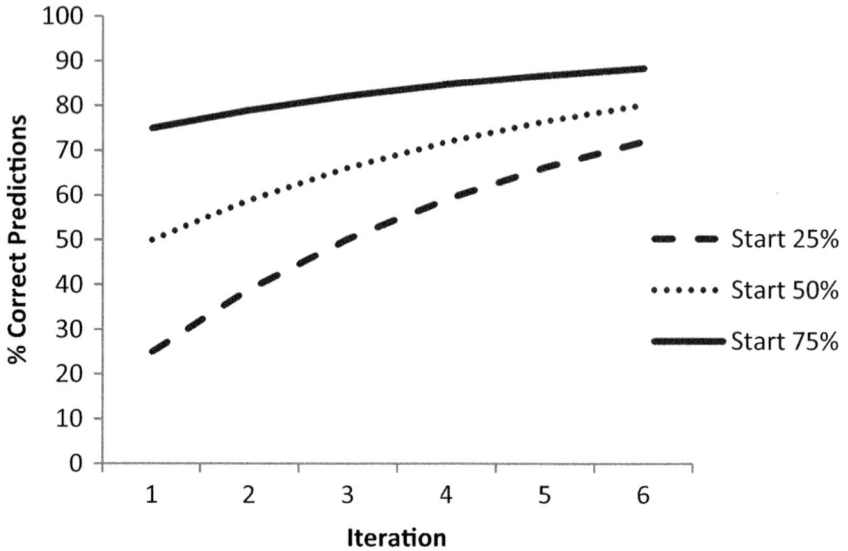

Figure 6.1 Convergence of belief in steps of 20 percent movement towards an end point with each evidence increment

Paddling in Bayes

If the proliferation of 'how to' books is welcome and we are trying to understand the arena of Bayesian modelling, that is a work in progress, and in any event the application we envisage to reducing uncertainty in policing is very simple. As Nate Silver emphasises, the central point of Bayes is the idea that you gather as much evidence as you can, then you act on it and see what happens, work out some extra evidence that might be relevant, check that out and so on until you get as good a prediction as it is possible to get or decide your premises are wrong and try a different tack. We see this process as one which some police officers already pursue. The first writer had the privilege of working with Sgt. Ian Wilson of Cheshire Police on his Operation Shield work on traceable liquids. His approach was pure Bayes. He saw a pattern of burglaries in his home area, articulated reasons for it and deployed traceable liquids and associated signage as if his reasoning were correct. Burglary numbers fell, and the patterns changed so that a modified hypothesis, including speculative travel to crime patterns, which led to modified deployment of the signage. Never satisfied, he refined his actions on the basis of changes in burglary patterns, for example, in their times.

Finally, it would help to look at a policing problem in the format that Nate Silver presents. Let us take the probability of serious injury or death by domestic violence following a domestic violence call for service.

Table 6.1 is based insofar as is possible on the risk assessment instrument with the best reviewed predictive validity (Messing and Thaller, 2013). After a call to

Table 6.1 Anticipation of serious injury/death in domestic violence: Bayes estimates

Prior Probability		
Probability of Later Serious Injury/Death	x	10%
Risk Assessment		
Probability of Accurately Predicting Later Injury/Death	y	65%
Probability of Wrongly Predicting Later Injury/Death	z	50%
Posterior Probability		
Probability of Later Injury/Death Given Prediction of Later Injury/Death	$\dfrac{xy}{xy+z(1-x)}$	13%

deal with domestic violence the risk assessment is administered. Row 1 shows that after 10 percent of all such calls there is a further call resulting in serious injury or death. The next row shows that the predictor accurately identified 65 percent of those who suffer subsequent serious injury or death. This is known as the *sensitivity* measure. The next row looks at the proportion of people who are wrongly predicted to suffer subsequent serious injury or death. It is 50 percent. If confused at this point, remember that the denominator for the 65 percent figure was the number of people suffering subsequent serious harm, and for the 50 percent figure the denominator is the number of predictions of serious harm. The two figures are different. The bottom row shows the proportion of people who, on the basis of the figures noted, will actually go on to suffer later harm having been predicted to do so. This comes out at a (probably surprisingly low) figure. Eighty-seven percent of those predicted to suffer will not go on to do so. This is the test of specificity. The proportion is low because (thankfully) only a minority of victims go on to suffer harm. The 'false alarm rate' is a huge problem in resource-strapped organisations like the police.

To put that illustration in context, what would one do operationally? Surely it would be to revise the predictor so as to increase specificity with no loss of sensitivity. Specificity matters less if the action taken is not intrusive and/or expensive.

Chapter summary and a big 'so what?'

In our ideal world, what should happen next?

1   We hope to have awakened interest sufficiently to invite a force to collaborate in testing some initiatives in a Bayesian way. These initiatives should be sampled across ranks. That is to say, a Police Community Support Officer with a belief about a very local problem should be as eligible as an area commander with a belief about an area-wide problem. The purpose of the trial would be

to establish and roughly quantify the belief, clarify the mechanism which would be relevant were the belief to be vindicated, and hence which kinds of evidence would lead the belief to be revised (in either direction). There would be no comparison groups or any of the other apparatus of frequentist evaluation – simply assessment of the emergent data signature. This may sound wholly unscientific, but it is precisely the process that can build upon a long and largely neglected classic in cognitive psychology (Bruner, Goodnow and Austin, 1956).

2   Work in process (Laycock and Pease, 2017) seeks to tease out how adoption of a Bayesian approach would fit into the approach to evaluation with which it appears to have most in common, although the traditions have never, to our knowledge, been placed alongside each other. The evaluation style in question is known as realist evaluation. Where the Bayesian approach speaks of gambles or predictions, the realist approach speaks of guesses, but the sense is the same. A recent book on realist evaluation (Pawson, 2013) lacks any reference to Bayes, but one could cut and paste paragraphs from that book into introductory texts on Bayes and no one would notice. Realist evaluation is seen as a suitable vehicle for introducing Bayesian thinking into the evaluation of police work, and more widely.

Of course, if colleagues hate everything we have written, then one of us will likely assume the foetal position and tend to his allotment instead, while the other looks at the current vacancies at a large supermarket chain. Mind you, we would still have a high posterior probability of being right while planting carrots or pushing trolleys.

Notes

1 Deacon, M. (2016). 'Michael Gove's Guide to Britain's Greatest Enemy. . . The Experts', Retrieved from www.telegraph.co.uk/news/2016/06/10/michael-goves-guide-to-britains-greatest-enemy-the-experts/ (accessed September 2, 2016).
2 The criticisms are a selection from Sparrow's list and have been reworked for brevity by the present authors, hopefully retaining the thrust of the Sparrow argument.
3 Always the most important factor for Arsenal Manager Arsene Wenger.
4 Astute readers may see here an echo of the Compstat process. Compstat is retrospective; the approach here is predictive.
5 www.mrc-bsu.cam.ac.uk/software/bugs/the-bugs-project-winbugs/ (accessed September 5, 2016).
6 https://thepsychologist.bps.org.uk/liberating-or-locking-away-our-best-tools (accessed May 20, 2016).
7 www.youtube.com/watch?v=TfeaZ_26iQk&feature=youtu.be&list=PLpl-gQkQivXiB mGyzLrUjzsblmQsLtkzJ (accessed September 5, 2016).
8 Unless he is the second writer's grandad.

References

Bruner, J., Goodnow, J. and Austin, G. (1956). *A Study of Thinking*, New York: Science Editions.
Downey, A.B. (2014). *Think Bayes*, Sebastapol, CA: O'Reilly.

Gelman, A., Carlin, J.B., Stern, H.S., Dunson, D.B., Vehtaru, A. and Rubin, D.B. (2015). *Bayesian Data Analysis*, London: CRC Press.

Ignatans, D. and Pease, K. (2014, 26 June). 'Smoke, mirrors and the decline in public confidence', *Police Professional*, 24–25.

Kelly, G. (1950). *A Theory of Personality*, New York: Norton.

Kruschke, J.K. (2014). *Doing Bayesian Data Analysis*, London: Elsevier.

Kruschke, J.K. (2015). *Doing Bayesian Data Analysis*, 2nd edition, London: Academic Press.

Loftus, B. (2010). 'Police occupational culture', *Policing and Society*, 20: 1–20.

Loyd, S., Farrell, G. and Pease, K. (1994). *Preventing Repeated Domestic Violence: A Demonstration Project on Merseyside*, London: Home Office.

Megrayne, S.B. (2011) *The Theory That Would Not Die*, London: Yale University Press.

Messing, T. and Thaller, J. (2013). 'The average predictive validity of intimate partner violence risk assessment instruments', *Journal of Interpersonal Violence*, 28: 1537–58.

Miller, G., Galanter, E. and Pribram, K. (1960). *Plans and the Structure of Behaviour*, New York: Holt, Rinehart and Winston.

O'Hagan, A. and West, M. (2010). *The Oxford Handbook of Applied Bayesian Analysis*, Oxford: Oxford University Press.

Pawson, R. (2013). *The Science of Evaluation*, London: Sage.

Pearl, J., Glynmour, M. and Jewell, N.P. (2016). *Causal Inference in Statistics*, New York: Wiley.

Pease, K. (1991). 'The Kirkholt project: Preventing burglary on a British public housing estate', *Security Journal*, 2: 73–77.

Roach, J. and Pease, K. (2013). *Evolution and Crime*, London: Routledge.

Silver, N. (2013). *The Signal and the Noise*, London: Penguin.

Sparrow, M. (2016). *Handcuffed*, Washington, DC: Brookings Institution Press.

Spiegelhalter, D. (2006). 'Incorporating Bayesian ideas into health care evaluation', *Statistical Science*, 19: 156–74.

Unsworth, P., Alexander, R. and Pease, K. (2012). 'Signal crimes and signal policing', *Police Journal*, 85: 161–8.

Yau, C. (2015). *R Tutorial with Bayesian Statistics Using OpenBUGS*, Palo Alto, CA: Yau.

7 Reviewing evidence for evidence-based policing

Kate Bowers, Lisa Tompson, Aiden Sidebottom, Karen Bullock and Shane D. Johnson

Evidence-based policing has widespread appeal. It calls for a shift from ways of working that are led by experience to that which is informed by the best available research evidence. Yet research evidence can, of course, take many forms and be of varying quality. In this chapter we consider the main sources of research evidence available to support decision-making in the crime prevention field. We begin by discussing four main sources of research evidence: practitioner reports, primary evaluation studies, systematic reviews, and reviews of reviews. We then focus on a sample of systematic reviews of single crime prevention interventions and, using the EMMIE framework (Johnson, Tilley and Bowers, 2015), we explore the extent to which these reviews adequately report information on the **E**ffect of intervention, the **M**echanisms through which interventions are believed to work, **M**oderators that may influence the impact of intervention, **I**mplementation issues that may impede or facilitate the intervention, and the **E**conomic costs of interventions. Based on this exercise and similar efforts to review the evidence base for crime prevention, we next outline five features that we argue increase the value of evidence reviews in support of crime prevention. Finally, we discuss some practical steps to increase the likelihood of future evidence reviews incorporating these features.

Looking for evidence

In this section we review four sources of research evidence from the perspective of the practitioner, whose decision-making the evidence base is ultimately intended to inform.

Practitioner reports

We start with what is likely to be most familiar to our practitioner: reports written by and for practitioners. Taking a variety of forms, we focus on those that involve the routine assessment and evaluation of crime prevention initiatives that practitioners may conduct either themselves or in collaboration with researchers. Such evaluations are conducted for a variety of reasons; for example, to meet the requirements of funders, to satisfy the host organisation/s that an investment was worthwhile, or as part of a problem-solving project. Examples include the Tilley

Award entries in the UK (see Bullock et al., 2006) and the Goldstein Award entries in the United States (see Scott, 2000; Rojek, 2003). The Tilley and Goldstein Award schemes seek to acknowledge excellence in problem-oriented policing and require entrants to pay attention to evaluation. Consequently, they are especially useful in this context.

Practitioner reports are potentially good sources of information about the effectiveness of local-level crime prevention interventions. They may contain information that is both useful and digestible to practitioners but that might be overlooked by other evaluators. For example, Bullock et al. (2006) found material about implementation was available in just over 40 per cent of the 150 Tilley Award reports that they examined. This material provided useful lessons for practitioners hoping to avoid problems at the development and implementation stages of new projects.

There are two common problems with practitioner reports. The first relates to methodological quality. Research suggests that, at best, the methodological quality of practitioner reports is variable and oftentimes poor (Bazemore and Cole, 1994; Read and Tilley, 2000; Scott, 2000; Bullock *et al.*, 2006). In discussing quality it is important to distinguish between two different forms of evaluation (see Eck, 2016). Process evaluations track the development and implementation of an intervention, and hence focus on what was done and how. Outcome evaluations estimate the impact of an intervention on crime (or other outcomes), assuming the intervention has been implemented.

Process evaluations may lack necessary detail if practitioners have not understood the need to maintain detailed project records. They may see doing so to be too time consuming, intrusive, and peripheral to their day-to-day job (Bullock et al., 2002; Forrest et al., 2005). Whatever the reason, process evaluations often do not contain sufficient information to enable project replication. There are also recurrent problems with outcome evaluations. For example, it has been shown that practitioner reports often lack sufficient data, give little consideration to alternative explanations for observed effects or to possible side effects, and pay scant attention to how initiatives may have produced their effects (Read and Tilley, 2000; Bullock et al., 2006).

A second problem is that although practitioner reports might be made available on an organisation's website, at conferences, or through informal networks, they are unlikely to be visible or accessible to other practitioners. A notable exception are the previously mentioned Tilley and Goldstein Award entries that are publically available by the U.S.-based Center for Problem-Oriented Policing (see www.popcenter.org), a web-based resource containing copious materials regarding what techniques are effective in reducing crime and in what circumstances, along with materials regarding the implementation of problem-oriented policing.

Academically motivated primary evaluation studies

Practitioners may draw on the results of academically motivated primary evaluations to guide their decision-making; these being assessments of the impact of a crime prevention intervention at a given point in time, conducted by academic, government, or other professional researchers. Such evaluations might investigate the processes through which an intervention was delivered, demonstrable crime prevention effects, unintended consequences, and cost effectiveness. To illustrate, two of us (Bowers and Johnson) conducted an impact evaluation of the effectiveness of fitting gates to networks of alleys running along the back of terraced properties to reduce opportunities for offending. We found that, relative to a reference area, burglary reduced by approximately 37 per cent in the areas where alley gates were implemented, that there was a diffusion of crime control benefits to properties in the immediate surrounding areas, and that the scheme yielded savings of £1.86 for every £1 spent (Bowers et al., 2004).

There are three central concerns about primary evaluation studies: quality, accessibility, and interpretability. First, addressing quality, evaluations vary in terms of their internal validity – the extent to which they are able to demonstrate cause-and-effect relationships (Campbell and Stanley, 1963). Many evaluations examine observed crime trends before and after an intervention is implemented but fail to consider whether any observed change was generated by the intervention or another (potentially unknown) factor. Threats to internal validity can be mitigated by establishing appropriate control groups. Superior to before and after evaluation designs, such quasi-experimental designs are, however, subject to selection bias. Areas or individuals assigned to treatment and control groups might differ in ways that might affect the outcomes observed.

Selection bias can be addressed by randomly allocating people or places to treatment and control conditions using a randomised control trial design (RCT), often seen as the 'gold standard' evaluation design (Sherman et al., 1997). That said, where conducted properly, quasi-experimental studies can rule out most (if not all) threats to internal validity (Eck and Madenson, 2009; Nagin and Weisburd, 2013). Moreover, where interventions are tailored to the peculiarities of specific locations, as is called for in problem-oriented policing (see Goldstein, 1990), randomly allocating interventions to areas that did not experience the crime problems of interest would be of little value, even if the internal validity of the evaluation were high. Our aim here is not to debate which type of evaluation methodology is the best – this will vary according to the situation. Instead, our point is that methodological adequacy is important but varies across primary evaluation studies.

A second issue concerns the accessibility of primary evaluations. The results of academic studies are typically published in academic journals. Although access to academic journals is progressively changing due to open access publishing, many journals remain inaccessible to those not affiliated with a university (such as police practitioners) due to the expensive subscription fees. That the results of primary evaluations will be published at all, however, is not guaranteed. It is widely accepted that positive results are more attractive to the academic community, to funders, and to journal editors (Franco et al., 2014) and are therefore more likely to be published and appear in multiple outlets (Rothstein et al., 2005). In contrast, studies yielding negative or null findings are less likely to be published and may never be submitted for publication – the so-called 'file drawer problem' (Rosenthal, 1979). Fortunately, the issue of null findings is becoming more widely acknowledged in academia, and there are efforts to rectify this. For example, the *Journal of Experimental Criminology* now encourages the submission of high-quality null-finding evaluations in a short report format.[1]

A third concern relates to the interpretability of primary evaluations. All evidence, to some extent, requires interpretation: a judgement of its relevance to the presenting problem and context. It may be difficult for practitioners, who cannot realistically be expected to have the expertise necessary to interpret (often complex) statistical data or esoteric academic jargon to make sense of the findings of evaluations. Even where findings can be accessed and understood, interpreting the results of multiple studies, which may be contradictory, can be difficult. Evaluation reports may or may not provide the sorts of contextual data that would inform practitioners about whether an intervention, demonstrably effective or otherwise, would likely be suitable for their local context and available resources. Considering the process of implementation, primary evaluations may or may not provide practitioners with the information necessary to successfully deliver an intervention (Bullock et al., 2006).

Before moving on, it is worth rehearsing the different groups who might undertake primary evaluations. Some are generated by academics, others by practitioners, some by academic–practitioner partnerships, and others still by consultancies or paid contractors. Each of these groups will have their own interests and incentives, and these should be considered by the reader. These interests will, for example, influence the degree to which the findings are produced by impartial advisors, the technical quality of the research, the likely medium of publication, and the financial resourcing of the exercise. For a more detailed account of some of these potential pitfalls see Tilley (1999). A key point is that insufficiently funded evaluations undertaken by researchers lacking in appropriate methods training can lead to both partial and misleading results.

Systematic reviews

Keeping abreast of developments in the evaluation literature is difficult for busy practitioners. Systematic reviews are an important means of distilling the research evidence to support decision-makers. They require that each step of the review process be conducted in a transparent way so as to enable future replications. The process of conducting a review is characterised by explicit objectives and a rigorous searching and screening process whereby primary studies are accepted or rejected on the basis of explicit eligibility criteria, with exclusions justified and documented (Farrington et al., 2001). The quality of the candidate studies are usually critically appraised before the data from them are marshalled to produce new knowledge that is 'greater than the sum of the individual studies' (Gough and Thomas, 2012: 39).

Where the data from primary studies are sufficiently similar and it is statistically appropriate, quantitative methods such as meta-analysis can be used to produce estimates of the overall effectiveness of an intervention. A meta-analysis weights the effect sizes of individual studies by their respective sample sizes and variance (i.e., the reliability of the estimated effects), thus producing a pooled effect size (and estimate of the precision of that statistic) that reflects the reliability of the findings. In combining samples across multiple studies, meta-analysis increases statistical power, thus enabling an overall effect of an intervention to be detected (should one exist). This is a key advantage of this method and one reason why systematic reviews with meta-analyses are the dominant source of evidence in other allies of evidence-based practice, most notably medicine. Pooling data from multiple primary evaluation studies provides a quantitative summary of the evidence as it relates to a given topic at a set point in time and, crucially, absolves practitioners of the tricky task of making sense of sometimes contradictory evidence from different studies.

An informative meta-analysis will also explore those factors which might feasibly *moderate* the effect of an intervention. That is, the meta-analyst will specifically look to code information on factors deemed to influence the outcomes produced by the intervention under review. For example, does closed-circuit TV (CCTV) work better in car parks or residential areas, or does cognitive-behavioural therapy work better for male or female offenders? This information can then be used to partition the studies into meaningful subgroups, and pooled effect sizes can be computed for each, revealing whether these factors are relevant to the observed effect. More sophisticated analytical techniques (e.g., meta-regression, multilevel modeling, or Bayesian analysis) can be used to make causal inferences about the degree to which these factors moderate the effect.

Systematic reviews are important for communicating high-level research findings to practitioners and policymakers. Yet, there are good reasons why in crime reduction, unlike in medicine, systematic reviews are not a mainstay of professional practice. First, high-quality primary evaluations are rare and for some topics virtually absent (e.g., organised crime, terrorism, modern slavery). Although 'empty'[2] systematic reviews may be useful for researchers, they are of little utility to practitioners. Second, there is a tendency for systematic reviews to focus on studies published in scientific journals. Failure to consult the 'grey literature' of government and practitioner reports, which comprises a sizable proportion of the crime reduction literature (Wilson, 2009; Tompson and Belur, 2015), may give rise to biased findings and neglect potentially important information. Finally, the methods used to quantitatively synthesise data from primary studies can be complex, and effectively communicating these methods to a lay audience is challenging. The inclusion of 'plain English' executive summaries is now increasingly common in a bid to help overcome this issue.

Reviews of reviews

The next section of this chapter will discuss strategies for reviewing the quality of evidence, focusing in particular on systematic reviews. For completeness, however, it is important to acknowledge that 'reviews of systematic reviews' or 'meta-reviews' are an additional source of research evidence (Gough and Thomas, 2012) that might plausibly inform crime prevention decision-making. Reviews of reviews can take several forms. They may act as an umbrella review on a particular topic (for example, the prevention of drug use in young people; see Canning et al., 2004), a particular approach to crime reduction (see, for example, Bowers and Johnson, 2016 who undertake a review of reviews employing situational crime prevention measures), or as a way of summarising existing reviews across an entire field (such as the *Preventing Crime: What Works, What Doesn't, What's Promising* by Sherman et al., 1997).

Reviews of reviews have their own strengths and weaknesses. They have the significant advantage of being a 'one-stop shop' for busy practitioners and academics. They can also usefully present evidence in a consistent format across a number of topics, making the comparison of ideas and outcomes much quicker and easier. Ultimately, their value relies on the quality of the research reports that they draw on and in this case they are further removed from the original context – they depend on the systematic reviewer's interpretation of the original primary evaluations, which, of course, might be biased or incomplete. This is why it is essential to consider the quality of the underlying evidence, to which subject we now turn.

To summarise the types of evidence discussed in this section and to document the key features of each in terms of strengths and weaknesses, we have compiled Table 7.1 for reference.

Table 7.1 The strengths and weaknesses of different research evidence for practitioners

Source of research evidence	Main purpose	Main strengths	Main weaknesses
Practitioner reports	To convey local knowledge of crime prevention initiatives	• Written in accessible language for practitioners • Can contain contextual information relevant for implementation	• Often use weaker outcome evaluation designs that lack internal validity (e.g. pre-/postintervention designs) • Process evaluations can be incomplete as detailed information not collected/recorded • Little consideration may be given to alternative explanations for observed effects or to possible side effects • Scant attention paid to how initiatives may have produced their effects (mechanisms)

(Continued)

Table 7.1 (Continued)

Source of research evidence	Main purpose	Main strengths	Main weaknesses
Academically motivated primary evaluation studies	To report the impact of initiatives to academic audiences	• *May* be methodologically robust (i.e., have good internal validity) • Will have been critiqued by other academics	• Publishing outlets can be inaccessible • Negative, or null, results may never be published • Language may be inaccessible
Systematic evidence reviews	To synthesise evidence on a given initiative	• Arguably the most reliable form of evidence • Consider the composite findings of an evidence base • Pool the effect to generate an overall conclusion	• Are dependent on the quality of primary evaluations • May not include 'grey literature' (i.e., nonacademic sources) • Language may be inaccessible
Review of reviews	To synthesise evidence across broad topics	• Act as a 'one-stop shop' for practitioners • Consistently display evidence from multiple sources • Can identify quality and evidence gaps	• Are dependent on the quality of systematic reviews, which are in turn dependent on the quality of primary evaluations • Given their breadth such exercises may need frequent updating to remain relevant

Grading evidence

We now turn our attention to efforts to grade research evidence and take stock of evidence rating tools for crime reduction. Apparent in many definitions of evidence-based practice is the notion that some evidence is better than others and that decisions should be informed by the 'best' available evidence. For Sackett et al. (1996: 3), 'Evidence-based medicine . . . is the conscientious, explicit and judicious use of current best evidence in making decisions about the care of individual patients'. For Lawrence Sherman (1998: 3), 'Evidence-based policing is the use of the best available research on the outcomes of police work to implement guidelines and evaluate agencies, units, and officers'.

Distinguishing 'better' from 'worse' evidence is a key requirement for evidence-based practice. To meet this aim, tools have been established to rate the quality of research evidence and the confidence that can be placed in recommendations derived from it. The Canadian Task Force on the Periodic Health Examination is widely credited with producing the original 'hierarchy of evidence' in 1979. Like many subsequent evidence rating scales, it was oriented towards questions of intervention effectiveness (did it work?) and the risk of bias associated with different sources of evidence. RCTs thus received the highest grade, as they are widely considered to be the most trustworthy source of primary evaluation evidence.

Numerous evidence rating systems have since been developed to meet the requirements of specialist fields. A 2002 systematic review (West et al., 2002) identified over 100 evidence rating systems for health care research, pertaining (in descending order) to RCTs (n = 49), systematic reviews (n = 20), observation studies (n = 19), and diagnostic test studies (n = 18).

Until recently, the only evidence rating scale commonly applied to criminological interventions was the Maryland Scientific Methods Scale (SMS). The SMS emerged out of a review of the evidence base for crime prevention (Sherman et al., 1997). It is a simple five-point scale designed to assess internal validity and communicate the results to consumers of that evidence. A summary of the SMS is given in Table 7.2.

According to the SMS, studies that report only a correlation between crime levels and an intervention are deemed 'weak' in terms of causal validity. For example, studies that show that the risk of crime is lower in areas that have Neighbourhood Watch (relative to those that do not) would reach level one. Where there is a 'temporal ordering of cause and effect', evidence is deemed 'moderate'. In our Neighbourhood Watch example, a study would meet this criterion if levels of crime were tracked for the period pre- and postintervention. The use of control groups provides greater evidence of causality, but the type of control group matters. The random allocation of units (e.g., areas or people) to treatment and control groups is designed to eliminate selection bias and, if done correctly, leads to equivalence across groups, meaning that rival (null) hypotheses can generally be

Table 7.2 Maryland Scientific Methods Scale for rating crime prevention evaluations

Least rigorous	1. Correlation between a crime prevention program and a measure of crime or crime risk factors.
	2. Temporal sequence between the program and crime or risk outcome clearly observed, or a comparison group present without demonstrated comparability to the treatment group.
	3. A comparison between two or more units of analysis, one with and one without the program.
	4. Comparison between multiple units with and without the program, controlling for other factors, or a nonequivalent comparison group has only minor differences evident.
Most rigorous	5. Random assignment and analysis of comparable units to program and comparison groups

ruled out. According to the SMS, RCTs are the most rigorous type of evaluation design. Alternative methods of selecting control groups, such as matching areas of intervention to areas with comparable social or demographic characteristics, would receive a moderate rating.

The SMS was proposed as an intuitive, easily communicable method of appraising methodological quality in primary studies. The architects of the SMS do, however, acknowledge a number of limitations. Farrington, Gottfredson, Sherman, and Welsh (2002) discuss how the SMS is silent on 1) the mechanisms through which an intervention might bring about the observed effects, 2) external validity (the extent to which the observed findings are generalisable), and 3) that certain research designs – which may have strong internal validity (e.g., multiple time-series designs) – are not included.

The U.S. National Institute of Justice has launched a more recent initiative to systematically grade the research evidence to support policing and crime prevention at CrimeSolutions.gov. This aims to identify and rate the available evidence on what works to prevent crime and offending. CrimeSolutions.gov focuses on interventions (such as CCTV) rather than problems (such as burglary). For interventions that do not yet have systematic reviews, the methodological adequacy of existing primary evaluations is assessed for rigor and the extent to which interventions were implemented as intended. Findings are then collated to provide an indication of whether the intervention has been shown to work and the strength of the evidence on which this assessment is based. Where systematic reviews do exist, the quality of the review evidence is assessed. In both cases, studies are assessed by expert reviewers using standardised scales that draw on (but are not limited to) the SMS. By presenting findings using a simple evidence rating scale in combination with easy-to-read narratives that describe the intervention, evaluation outcomes, and issues associated with implementation (and, where available, the costs), the aim is to provide practitioners and policymakers with an understanding of what the evidence base suggests.

A similar initiative is underway in the UK as part of the What Works Centre for Crime Reduction hosted by the College of Policing. Work conducted to date has sought to systematically identify, rate, and rank existing systematic reviews of crime prevention interventions, as well as to carry out new systematic reviews to fill knowledge gaps where existing reviews are out of date, limited in scope, or otherwise do not sufficiently inform crime prevention practice. In the next section we describe the evidence rating scale – EMMIE – generated by the What Works Centre for Crime Reduction and report the results of applying this scale to a sample of systematic reviews.

Applying EMMIE to grade systematic review evidence

CrimeSolutions.gov and the UK What Works Centre have broadly similar objectives: that of identifying, grading, and synthesising research evidence in a manner that best supports the needs of decision-makers. An important difference between the approach of the UK What Works Centre and other similar exercises is that systematic reviews are systematically rated not just on methodological adequacy – which is, of course, vital – but along other dimensions that are also important to practitioners and policymakers. As mentioned in the introduction, the EMMIE framework was designed to gather evidence (or acknowledge the absence of it) on five key dimensions (encapsulated by the acronym 'EMMIE'): (a) the Effect of the intervention, (b) the causal Mechanism(s) through which interventions are intended to work, (c) the factors that Moderate intervention effectiveness, (d) the articulation of practical Implementation issues, and (e) the Economic costs of intervention (Johnson et al., 2015).

These five elements of EMMIE were selected to ensure that reviews do not just focus on quantitative outcomes ('Effect') following the intervention of a crime prevention scheme. This limited focus fails to acknowledge that the impact of social interventions may vary substantially in different contexts (these act as 'moderators' for likely outcomes) and when different mechanisms are 'fired' (for example, the use of CCTV as a visible deterrent in a car park compared to the submission of CCTV evidence to convict for a common assault in a town centre). Implementation is distinct from, but related to, these issues and continues to be highly challenging in this field (see, e.g., Knutsson and Clarke, 2006). This is because gathering and mobilising agencies and individuals; gaining appropriate funding; accessing the correct tools and equipment; garnering public support, consent, and involvement; dealing with administrative red tape; and negotiating unanticipated issues are all complex and time-consuming undertakings. Finally, information on cost effectiveness and cost/benefit are of huge interest to practitioners and policymakers, but collecting detailed information on both the inputs to (for example, staff time, equipment costs, consumables) and outputs of a crime prevention scheme (number of hours delivered, number of physical measures installed) is rarely done in the sort of systematic way that would be of use to others planning similar exercises.

A coding instrument was devised to systematically rate systematic reviews along the dimensions of EMMIE (see Tompson et al., 2015). This instrument included around 100 fields on which evidence was either extracted (the EMMIE-E codes) or quality-graded (the EMMIE-Q codes). As part of the What Works Centre for Crime Reduction, this instrument has been used to appraise the quality of 87 systematic reviews on crime prevention (for details on how the reviews were identified see Bowers et al., 2014). Here we present the results for a subset of police-relevant reviews (n = 6) to illustrate the quality of evidence pertaining to interventions and strategies that the police might reasonably be able to implement, whilst acknowledging that a far wider spectrum of crime prevention interventions exist that can be implemented by, or with, other agencies. The topics of the systematic reviews were (in descending order): sobriety checkpoints (3), hot-spots policing (1), second responder programmes (1), and street-level drug law enforcement (1).

The quality scores for Effect varied across the six systematic reviews, although four reviews were seen to score three or four, indicating that they had sufficiently considered elements of validity that might bias the reliability of the effect reported (Table 7.3). Mechanism was less well covered. Four of the six reviews made a broad statement of how the intervention was believed to work, one did not mention mechanisms at all, and one provided a detailed review. Moderators were covered

Table 7.3 The quality scores for six policing and partnership systematic reviews on each EMMIE dimension

EMMIE dimension	Quality score	N reviews
Effect	1. Considered no elements of validity	0
	2. Considered 1 element of validity	1
	3. Considered 2 elements of validity	1
	4. Considered 3 elements of validity	2
	5. Considered 4 or 5 elements of validity	2
Mechanism	0. No mention	1
	1. Broad statement	4
	2. Detailed review	1
	3. Formal model and predictions	0
	4. Tested using data	0
Moderator	0. No mention	0
	1. Ad hoc description	1
	2. Post hoc test of moderators	1
	3. Theory-based description	2
	4. Theory-led data analysis	2
Implementation	0. No account	0
	1. Ad hoc comments	4
	2. Systematic efforts to document	1
	3. Detailed evidence-based account	1
	4. Complete evidence-based account	0
Economics	0. No mention of costs	6
	1. Only direct costs/benefits estimated	0
	2. Direct and indirect costs/benefits estimated	0
	3. Marginal/opportunity costs	0
	4. Costs by bearer	0

a little more thoroughly. Four of the systematic reviews used existing theory (or empirical evidence) to describe or test factors that could moderate the effect of the initiative. Efforts to document implementation factors that might impede or facilitate a crime prevention initiative were rare, with only one systematic review doing so in an evidence-based manner (actually providing quantitative or qualitative information on what happened), and most systematic reviews provided only ad hoc comments on this dimension (and hence inconsistently documented evidence across evaluations). Lastly, information on economics was entirely absent from these reviews. This is by no means atypical for crime prevention studies; an exercise on a larger number of systematic reviews in the field demonstrated that there is a significant paucity of financial information reported (Johnson et al., 2016).

Requirements of 'good' systematic evidence reviews

In this section we discuss what can be gleaned from the coding exercise presented earlier and translate these lessons into recommendations for what a 'good' systematic evidence review should include, taken here to mean useful to decision-makers.

1. Evidence reviews need to cover EMMIE

The previous section highlights the need for systematic reviews in crime prevention to collect and report evidence (or the lack of it) on each of the dimensions of EMMIE. We therefore recommend that each of these elements is considered by those producing systematic reviews in the field. Although this will make the coding of reviews more intensive, we believe the gain to crime prevention practice would be significant. Hence, in principle, instead of purely knowing whether a given intervention has been shown to be effective in preventing crime, practitioners will have knowledge about how and where an intervention is most likely to work, what the implementation challenges are likely to be, and information on expected costs. We contend that this additional information will enable decision-makers to make better judgements about the potential for success given their particular local conditions. Note we present this both as an aspiration and as a method for organising existing information. A big hurdle to achieving this goal is the observation that primary studies seldom report information beyond effect in great detail (see Sidebottom et al., 2015) and that standard systematic reviews often select studies largely based on research design, which may preclude studies with useful noneffect information from being included.

Fortunately, the lack of information on possible mechanisms and moderators in systematic reviews is beginning to be more widely acknowledged and addressed. For example, the Campbell Collaboration now seeks reviews to be more explicit in terms of mechanisms and logic models (see Policies and Guidelines[3]). A recent example is a systematic review of candidate mechanisms to explain the effect of broken-windows policing undertaken by Weisburd et al. (2015). Combined with renewed pressure from academics such as Cartwright and colleagues (Cartwright and Hardie, 2012) for evaluation studies to collect information beyond just intervention effectiveness, we are cautiously optimistic that reviews with a wider breadth of evidence will begin to become available.

2. Evidence reviews should make the 'holes' explicit and assess the quality of what is available

EMMIE offers the opportunity to systematically rate a wider range of evidence types. For example, when reporting information about the calculation of an effect size, detailed guidance on how to report the results of systematic literature searches, explaining the statistical meta-analysis procedure taken, assessing the reliability of results given the extent of the evidence used, and reporting any biases in the procedure (such as coder bias or publication bias) is already available (see Egger, Davey Smith, Schneider, and Minder, 1997; Duval and Tweedie, 2000; Gwet, 2014). However, once assimilated across primary studies, assessing the quality of implementation information, descriptions of the various contexts, and likely mechanisms is not commonly done. The EMMIE coding tool encourages quality appraisal across a fuller range of relevant dimensions, rather than assigning primacy to just the 'effect' of an intervention.

One question is whether the assessment of information along these lines should be an activity undertaken by systematic reviewers themselves, given their knowledge of the primary evidence available, or by those at a policy level who are assessing the quality of competing systematic reviews. We would argue that assessment at both these levels is useful – the former would make the latter more expedient and would also ensure that those undertaking reviews are cued to look for various pieces of information in primary studies and to do this with a critical eye. Neither should the quality of the systematic review and the quality of the primary evidence be conflated. Thorough reviews can come back with 'nil returns', and this is useful to acknowledge in quality assessments.

As discussed in Table 7.3 and elsewhere (Bowers et al., 2014) research conducted for the UK College of Policing (COP) has demonstrated that there are considerable holes in the evidence base on crime prevention. Holes result from no evidence being available in primary studies and from systematic reviews that do not report information where it is available. It would be useful if systematic reviews made this distinction clear. Use of EMMIE would encourage such reporting.

3. Reviews should summarise available primary studies for practitioners

There is wide variation in the degree to which reviews give contextual details or narratives about each of the evaluations that they summarise. Some include a basic 'one-liner' for each intervention, others include tables summarising the (reviewer-deemed salient) features of primary studies, and others provide longer narrative-based summaries. The latter give textual detail but take up space and might not record primary evaluation evidence systematically and accessibly. We recommend a systematic way of reporting narrative or contextual information on primary interventions, presented in a format where easy comparisons are possible. A possibility is to apply EMMIE at the *primary* study level to do this. Each primary study could be summarised on the five key elements and a summary table to enable comparison across primary studies. Structured narratives could be added. These have been made available at the systematic review level for the What Works Centre Crime Reduction Toolkit and could be sensibly applied to primary evaluations as well (see http://whatworks.college.police.uk/toolkit/Pages/Toolkit.aspx).

4. Reviews should be written with practitioners in mind

We have mentioned that some academic products can be difficult for practitioners to interpret. Good examples of accessible academic writing for practitioners include the Pop Center problem-solving and response guides. These synthesise evidence from multiple sources (practitioner and academic reports) in a way that speaks directly to practitioner needs. These are not conducted systematically, as defined herein, but are thorough and comprehensive. Working outside these conventions means they do not require the academic jargon of formal systematic reviews – which makes them immediately more accessible, allows more room for the inclusion of tacit knowledge (Tilley, 2006) or 'golden nuggets' of information from many sources (independent of the *overall* quality of the original evidence), and affords more flexibility in their presentation. Some guides focus on interventions (or responses), others on particular crime or disorder problems. The Center for Problem-Oriented Policing problem-solving guides include summaries of each response (as part of an appendix outlining the different possible approaches) setting out whether it appears to work, how it works, the conditions under which it works best, and any considerations that are necessary in terms of potential barriers to effective implementation.

This speaks to our earlier argument that more than the 'effect' needs to be considered and highlights the final point we will make here: that *summaries* really matter. Many practitioners will only read a summary, so it really needs to contain the key information and be clear. It is for this reason that there are often guidelines for systematic review summaries – such as those offered by Campbell Collaboration – although arguably these have a tendency to focus on methods and quantitative effect sizes rather than contextual information for practitioners. Fortunately academics are becoming more mindful of difficulties with communicating key messages concerning evidence to practitioners. The principles associated with 'translational criminology' are becoming more generally understood and recognised. Translational criminology is a field in its own right which seeks to translate scientific discoveries into policy and practice through studying knowledge dissemination (Laub, 2011).

5. Reviews should be amenable to being integrated into knowledge 'hubs'

When focusing on the search for the best intervention with which to address a specific crime problem, practitioners might need to review the potential of multiple interventions from several systematic reviews. When constructing a systematic review, thought could usefully be given to how easily the evidence from one systematic review can be integrated with reviews of potential alternatives.

A key activity of the What Works Centre has been to summarise information at the intervention level in a consistent way (based on EMMIE) across different systematic reviews. As mentioned earlier, although other exercises in integrating this type of information exist, we focus on our experiences with the production of the online Crime Reduction Toolkit (whatworks.college.police.uk/ toolkit/). Some reviews were more easily streamlined in the integration process than others; for example, comprehensive reviews and those that used the 'common language' of crime prevention practice (see Ekblom, 2010). Conversely, in some reviews, even basic information about where and when the intervention took place were hard to find or missing. Similarly, across countries and places descriptions of the actors involved can vary (for example, 'PCSOs' in the UK are a type of police officer with specific duties and powers). Reviews written in languages other than English are often missed in such integration exercises. Finally, for reviews that do focus on problems rather than interventions, and therefore review multiple approaches, it is often difficult to distinguish the specific information at the intervention level that would be necessary for integration into a knowledge hub organised by intervention.

Some suggestions on practical steps to improve the value of evidence reviews for crime prevention

We have listed five features which we believe would increase the practical value of evidence reviews for crime prevention. Our suggestions to encourage future reviews to incorporate these features are as follows.

1. Develop reporting guidelines for crime prevention reviews

Presently, there is no agreed-upon standard for the reporting of systematic reviews in criminology. According to the Enhancing the QUAlity and Transparency Of health Research (EQUATOR) network there are now over 250 reporting guidelines in the medical sciences. A direct response to the seemingly pervasive inadequacies of much research reporting which threaten to stifle replication and waste resources, these guidelines aim to improve the completeness and consistency of reporting.

It is not that criminologists are ignorant to the existence of reporting guidelines or that they are immune to the sorts of shortcomings they are designed to overcome. Far from it. In their appraisal of 62 published RCTs using the CONSORT statement, Perry, Weisburd and Hewitt (2010) identified several recurrent omissions and reporting deficits, with over half of the reviewed studies receiving a 'low' rating for the quality of reporting.

Guidance on what should be included when reporting a systematic review is already available in the form of the PRISMA statement. PRISMA originated in medicine, however, and therefore does not fully capture all the issues that are important in the reporting (and conduct) of systematic reviews in criminology (see Sidebottom and Tilley, 2012). EMMIE provides a convenient framework around which to generate reporting guidelines for crime prevention reviews, in addition to modifying those reporting guidelines already available.

2. Encourage supplementary online materials

The type of evidence review which we are advocating likely contains more words than a standard evidence review. This might not sit well with academic journals, the main outlets for systematic reviews. To address this issue we might take the lead from other disciplines which increasingly allow for supplementary material to be attached to a published article.

3. Lobby researchers, practitioners, and policymakers to speak EMMIE

Ultimately we need to make sure practitioners engage with the drive to improve the evidence base. Much work is still required to cultivate a culture in which research evidence that speaks to the dimensions of EMMIE is a) routinely collected and reported by evidence producers (i.e., researchers) and b) routinely and explicitly sought by evidence consumers (i.e., practitioners and policymakers). There are a number of fronts on which activity is required here. Practitioners need to (a) know where to look for evidence, (b) have an appetite to use it, (c) understand it sufficiently to use it successfully in evidence-based practice, (d) be aware of the current limitations of what is available, and (e) be motivated to collaborate in exercises to improve evidence. This is a tall order, but is one that we believe we should be collectively moving towards.

Conclusion

This chapter has considered the role of research evidence in support of crime prevention decision-making. We have highlighted different forms of research evidence and discussed their respective strengths and weaknesses. We explained the role that research design plays in determining the reliability of evaluation evidence. In considering the task of grading the quality of research evidence, both in crime prevention and in other fields, we argued that the majority of such exercises concentrate only on rating the quality of the process of generating the effect size (outcome). Although essential, we argue that this does not go far enough in speaking to other key requirements for good practice. Information on how interventions work, for whom, under what conditions, with what input, and at what cost needs to not only be systematically reported but also rated for quality. We need to mobilise the crime prevention community to see the value of doing this and to engage in exercises to fill the existing gaps in the evidence base.

Notes

1 Personal communication from current editor Lorraine Mazerolle.
2 An 'empty' systematic review is one in which no publications meet the criteria outlined by the authors for inclusion. Typically, the result of this includes the inability to perform a meta-analysis which statistically summarises the average effectiveness of an intervention.
3 The Campbell Collaboration both commissions and provides a library of systematic reviews of the research evidence in social policy, including criminal justice. www.campbellcol laboration.org/artman2/uploads/1/C2_Reviews_policy__guidelines_draft_5–1–13.pdf.

References

Bazemore, G. and Cole, A. (1994). 'Police in the laboratory of the neighbourhood: Evaluating problem-oriented strategies in a medium sized city', *American Journal of the Police*, 13(3): 119–48.

Black, N. and Donald, A. (2001). 'Evidence based policy: Proceed with care commentary: Research must be taken seriously', *British Medical Journal*, 323: 275–9.

Bowers, K.J. and Johnson, S.D. (2016). 'Situational Crime Prevention', in D.P. Farrington and D. Weisburd (eds) *What works in Crime Prevention and Rehabilitation: Lessons from Systematic Reviews*, New York: Springer.

Bowers, K.J., Johnson, S. and Hirschfield, A. (2004). 'Closing off opportunities for crime: An evaluation of alley-gating', *European Journal on Criminal Policy and Research*, 10(4): 285–308.

Bowers, K.J., Tompson, L. and Johnson, S.D. (2014). 'Implementing information science in policing: mapping the evidence base', *Policing: A Journal of Policy and Practice*, 8(4): 339–52, doi: 10.1093/police/pau052

Bullock, K., Erol, R. and Tilley, N. (2006). *Problem-Oriented Policing and Partnership*, Cullompton: Willan Publishing.

Bullock, K., Farrell, G. and Tilley, N. (2002). *Funding and Implementing Crime Reduction Projects*, Home Office Online Report 13, London: Home Office.

Campbell, D.T. and Stanley, J.C. (1963). 'Experimental and Quasi-Experimental Designs for Research on Teaching,' in N.L. Gage (ed) *Handbook of Research on Teaching*, pp. 171–246. Chicago, IL: Rand McNally.

Canning, U., Millward, L., Raj, T. and Warm, D. (2004). *Drug Use Prevention among Young People: A Review of Reviews*, London: Health Development Agency.

Cartwright, N. and Hardie, J. (2012). *Evidence-Based Policy: A Practical Guide to Doing It Better*, New York: Oxford University Press.

Duval, S. and Tweedie, R. (2000). 'Trim and fill: A simple funnel-plot – based method of testing and adjusting for publication bias in meta-analysis', *Biometrics*, 56(2): 455–63.

Eck, J.E. (2016). 'Evaluation for Lesson Learning', in N. Tilley and A. Sidebottom (eds) *Handbook of Crime Prevention and Community Safety*, 2nd edition, London: Routledge.

Eck, J.E. and Madensen, T. (2009). 'Using Signatures of Opportunity Structures to Examine Mechanisms in Crime Prevention Evaluations', in J. Knutsson and N. Tilley (eds) *Evaluating Crime Reduction Initiatives*, Crime Prevention Studies, vol. 24, pp. 59–48, Monsey, NY: Criminal Justice Press.

Egger, M., Davey Smith, G., Schneider, M. and Minder, C. (1997). 'Bias in meta-analysis detected by a simple, graphical test', *British Medical Journal*, 315(7109): 629–34.

Ekblom, P. (2010). *Crime Prevention, Security and Community Safety using the 5Is Framework*, London, UK: Palgrave Macmillan.

Farrington, D.P., Gottfredson, D., Sherman, L.W. and Welsh, B. (2002). '*The Maryland Scientific Methods Scale*', in D. Farrington, D. MacKenzie, L. Sherman and B. Welsh (eds) *Evidence based Crime Prevention*, pp 13–21, London: Routledge.

Farrington, D.P., Petrosino, A. and Welsh, B.C. (2001). 'Systematic Reviews and Cost-Benefit Analyses of Correctional Interventions', *The Prison Journal*, 81(3): 339–59.

Forrest, S., Myhill, A. and Tilley, N. (2005). *Practical Lessons for Involving the Community in Crime and Disorder Problem-Solving*, Home Office Development and Practice Report 43, London: Home Office.

Franco, A., Malhotra, N. and Simonovits, G. (2014). 'Publication bias in the social sciences: Unlocking the file drawer', *Science*, 345(6203): 1502–5.

Goldstein, H. (1990). *Problem-oriented policing*, New York: McGraw-Hill.

Gough, D. and Thomas, J. (2012). 'Commonality and Diversity in Reviews', in D. Gough, S. Oliver, and J. Thomas (eds) *An Introduction to Systematic Reviews*, pp. 35–65, London: Sage.

Gwet, K.L. (2014). *Handbook of Inter-Rater Reliability*, 4th edition, Gaithersburg: Advanced Analytics, LLC.

Hope, T. (2004). 'Pretend it works: Evidence and governance in the evaluation of the Reducing Burglary Initiative', *Criminal Justice*, 4(3): 287–308.

Johnson, S.D., Bowers, K.J., Tompson, L., Laycock, G., Tilley, N. and Sidebottom, A. (2016, April). *What Works to Reduce Crime, How Does It work, and What else Do We Need to Know?* Denver: Academy of Criminal Justice Sciences.

Johnson, S.D., Tilley, N. and Bowers, K.J. (2015). 'Introducing EMMIE: An evidence rating scale to encourage mixed-method crime prevention synthesis Reviews', *Journal of Experimental Criminology*, doi: 10.1007/s11292-015-9238-7

Knutsson, J. and Clarke, R.V. (eds) (2006). *Putting Theory to Work*, Crime Prevention Studies, vol. 20, pp. 163–97, Monsey, NY: Criminal Justice Press.

Laub, J.H. (2011, October). 'Strengthening NIJ: Mission, science and process', *NIJ Journal*/Issue No. 268: 16–21.

Liberati, A., Altman, D.G., Tetzlaff, J., Mulrow, C., Gøtzsche, P.C., Ioannidis, J.P., Clarke, M., Devereaux, P.J., Kleijnen, J. and Moher, D. (2009). 'The PRISMA statement for reporting systematic reviews and meta-analyses of studies that evaluate health care interventions: Explanation and elaboration', *Journal of Clinical Epidemiology*, 62: 1–34.

Nagin, D. and Weisburd, D. (2013). 'Evidence and public policy: The example of evaluation research in policing', *Criminology and Public Policy*, 12: 651–79.

Perry, A.E., Weisburd, D. and Hewitt, C. (2010). 'Are criminologists describing randomized controlled trials in ways that allow us to assess them? Findings from a sample of crime and justice trials', *Journal of Experimental Criminology*, 6(3): 245–62.

Raynor, P. (2008). 'Community penalties and home office research: On the way back to "nothing works"?', *Criminology and Criminal Justice*, 8(1): 73–87.

Read, T. and Tilley, N. (2000). *Not Rocket Science? Problem Solving and Crime Reduction*, Crime Reduction Research Series Paper 6, London: Home Office.

Rojek, J. (2003). 'A decade of excellence in problem-oriented policing: Characteristics of the Goldstein award winners', *Police Quarterly*, 6(4): 492–515.

Rosenthal, R. (1979). 'The file drawer problem and tolerance for null results', *Psychological Bulletin*, 86(3): 638–41.

Rothstein, H.R., Sutton, A.J. and Borenstein, M. (eds). (2005). *Publication Bias in Meta-Analysis: Prevention, Assessment and Adjustments*, Chichester, UK: John Wiley & Sons, Ltd.

Sackett, D.L., Rosenberg, W.M.C., Gray, J.A.M., Haynes, R.B. and Richardson, W.S. (1996). 'Evidence based medicine: What it is and what it isn't', *British Medical Journal*, 312: 71.

Scott, M. (2000). *Problem-Oriented Policing: Reflections on the First 20 Years*, Washington, DC: US Department of Justice, Office of Community Oriented Policing Services.

Sherman, L.W. (1998). 'Evidence-Based Policing', in *Ideas in American Policing*, Washington, DC: Police Foundation.

Sherman, L.W., Gottfredson, D., MacKenzie, D., Eck, J.E., Reuter, P. and Bushway, S. (1997). *Preventing Crime: What Works, What Doesn't, What's Promising*, Washington, DC: US Department of Justice Office of Justice Programs.

Sidebottom, A. and Tilley, N. (2012). 'Further improving reporting in crime and justice: An addendum to Perry, Weisburd and Hewitt (2010)', *Journal of Experimental Criminology*, 8(1): 49–69.

Sidebottom, A., Tompson, L., Thornton, A., Bullock, K., Tilley, N., Bowers, K.J. and Johnson, S.D. (2015). *Gating Alleys to Reduce Crime: A Meta-Analysis and Realist Synthesis*, Report submitted to the College of Policing. Retrieved from http://whatworks. college.police.uk/About/Documents/Alley_gating.pdf

Tilley, N. (1999). 'Project evaluation: problems and pitfalls', in A. Marlow and G. Pearson (eds) *Young People, Drugs and Community Safety*, Russell House: Lyme Regis.

Tilley, N. (2006). 'Guidance and Good Practice in Crime Prevention', in J. Knutsson and R. Clarke (eds) *Putting Theory to Work*, Crime Prevention Studies, Monsey, NY: Criminal Justice Press.

Timmermans, S. and Berg, M. (2003). *The Gold Standard: The Challenge of Evidence-based Medicine and Standardization in Health Care*, Philadelphia: Temple University Press.

Tompson, L. and Belur, J.B. (2015). 'Information retrieval in systematic reviews: A case study of the crime prevention literature', *Journal of Experimental Criminology*, doi: 10.1007/s11292-015-9243-x

Tompson, L., Bowers, K.J., Johnson, S.D. and Belur, J.B. (2015). *EMMIE Evidence Appraisal Coding Tool*, London, UK: UCL Department of Security and Crime Science. Retrieved from http://discovery.ucl.ac.uk/1462093/

Weisburd, D. (2000). 'Randomized experiments in criminal justice policy: Prospects and problems', *Crime & Delinquency*, 46(2): 181–93.

Weisburd, D., Hinkle, J., Braga, A. and Wooditch, A. (2015). 'Understanding the Mechanisms Underlying Broken Windows Policing: The Need for Evaluation Evidence', *Journal of Research in Crime and Delinquency*, 52(4), 589–608.

West. S, King, V, Carey, T.S., Lohr, K., McKoey, N., Sutton, S. and Lux, L. (2002 April). *Systems to Rate the Strength of Scientific Evidence. Evidence Report/Technology Assessment No. 47*, Prepared by the Research Triangle Institute – University of North Carolina Evidence-based Practice Center under Contract No. 290–97–0011. AHRQ Publication No. 02-E016, Rockville, MD: Agency for Healthcare Research and Quality.

Wilson, D.B. (2009). 'Missing a critical piece of the pie: Simple document search strategies inadequate for systematic reviews', *Journal of Experimental Criminology*, 5(4): 429–40.

8 Evidence-based policing as a disruptive innovation

The Global Policing Database as a disruption tool

Lorraine Mazerolle, Elizabeth Eggins,
Angela Higginson and Betsy Stanko

Evidence-based policing (EBP) is, arguably, one of the biggest contemporary watersheds in the history of policing (see Dunham and Alpert, 2015; Lum and Koper, 2015). In the language of Christensen's (1997) theory of disruptive innovation, EBP is a policing knowledge process that is part of the broader digital reform movement across the world (Helbing, 2015), dislodging the incumbent craft-based mode of doing police business. The dislodging of this model – which relies on learning largely based on knowledge acquired through on-the-job, hands-on experience of police work – started over three decades ago with the onset of the professional era in policing (see Kelling and Moore, 1989). Yet the onset of EBP during the mid-1990s created new opportunities for the professionalisation of police, where scientific evidence started to be created by police and was placed directly in the hands of police and police policymakers. The establishment of police research collectives in the late 1970s (e.g., U.S. Police Executive Research Forum and Home Office Police Research Group), the proliferation of problem-oriented policing starting in the early 1990s (see Scott, this volume), followed by the release of the U.S. report titled *What Works, What Doesn't and What's Promising* (Sherman et al., 1997), pinpoints the start of the EBP movement. Sherman et al.'s report arguably offered the first comprehensive review of the best available scientific evidence to guide criminal justice policy and practice, including policing. Fast forward nearly 20 years, and EBP continues on an upward trajectory and is an important catalyst in the dislodging of the incumbent craft model of policing.

What might it take for EBP to truly become a disruptive innovation? In this chapter we argue that EBP initiatives are collectively situated to dislodge the police's historical sole reliance on craft to guide policing practice. For example, police mission and value statements are now informed by the language of evidence-based approaches (see Queensland Police Service, 2014); police-led Societies of Evidence-Based Policing (in the UK, Australia, New Zealand, Canada and the United States), along with the concomitant society conferences, are growing in size every year; and police master's programs, workshops and masterclasses offered by institutions such as Cambridge University, University of Queensland, University College London and George Mason University are advancing the capacity of police to engage in producing their own science and dislodging the craft-based approach to policing. One other family of EBP initiatives involves the creation of online tools that enable consumption and diffusion of police evidence. Given that the use of scientific research is foundational to the evidence-based policing movement (see Weisburd and Neyroud, 2011; Neyroud and Weisburd, 2014), a high-priority goal of the EBP movement is to place the research evidence in the hands of practitioners and policymakers (Telep and Lum, 2014). In this chapter, we argue that police practitioners' access to online, open-access, plain English summaries of the vast policing scientific literature, brought together in easy-to-search websites, is a key EBP enabling initiative, radically changing the capacity of police to access the science of their own profession. Just as the proliferation of automatic teller machines transformed the banking industry (see Christensen et al., 2015), easy, web-based access to police science is, we argue, creating opportunities for police to be active consumers and producers of police science, shifting the balance away from police reliance on craft to guide practice.

In policing, open-access websites such as the Campbell Collaboration (see www.campbellcollaboration.org), the Lum-Koper Matrix (see http://cebcp.org/evidence-based-policing/the-matrix/), Crime Solutions (see www.crimesolutions.gov), the Crime Reduction Toolkit (see http://whatworks.college.police.uk/toolkit/Pages/Toolkit.aspx) and the Center for Problem-Oriented Policing (see www.popcenter.org) collectively offer police comprehensive information about what is known about the effectiveness of police practices. One other website, the Global Policing Database (GPD) (see www.gpd.uq.edu.au), is a relative newcomer. The GPD is yet to reach its completed state, but is an evolving resource that is updated with evidence while the systematic compilation process is underway. As such, both during its compilation and upon its completion, the GPD will be a valuable addition to the family of policing evidence websites. All of these websites are sourced in different ways, with different criteria driving the inclusion (and exclusion) of studies that form the corpus of available evidence. We argue that these websites form one cornerstone for police adopting EBP, leading ultimately to the disruption of the incumbent, craft mode of police business, particularly as these websites become more sophisticated, offer quality, plain English summaries and become widely disseminated. This chapter focuses on the genesis of the GPD, a tool that aims to provide the broadest range of robust evaluation evidence for police and policing. The chapter begins with an overview of the GPD, describes the search methodology that was used to populate it and provides an analysis of the studies that were both included and excluded from the GPD beta version. We conclude with a discussion of how the GPD and other similar online tools are potential game-changers, enabling the EBP movement to become the dominant, mainstream approach to policing.

Overview of the Global Policing Database

The Global Policing Database (GPD) is an initiative of the University of Queensland, Queensland University of Technology and the London's Mayor's Office of Policing and Crime (MOPAC), with funding support from the Australian Research Council and the UK College of Policing (see Higginson et al., 2015). The GPD aims to capture the largest corpus of published and unpublished experimental and quasi-experimental evaluations of policing interventions conducted globally since 1950, and is distinguished from other repositories of police evaluation research in three key ways.

First, the GPD is not limited to interventions that police themselves undertake to control or prevent crime problems. Rather, our definition of 'police intervention' includes interventions where police could be the primary implementers, a partner in the intervention or the recipients of the intervention. Second, the GPD is not limited to studies using crime and disorder outcomes. Rather, the GPD places no limits on the type of outcome measures used to evaluate police interventions. As such, the GPD includes studies that evaluate police interventions using outcomes such as crime, disorder, psychological and physiological measures of well-being and perceptions of police. Third, the GPD places no limits on the language of the documents, making the resource truly global in nature. These three features make the GPD a comprehensive resource of evaluative police research that can be used by a large range of policymakers, practitioners and researchers to advance evidence-based policy and practice in policing.

With over 350,000 abstracts identified for the period 1950 to 2014 (see Figure 8.1), construction of the GPD is a painstaking task that has, so far, culminated in the release of the beta version in mid-2015 (see www.gpd.uq.edu.au), which includes

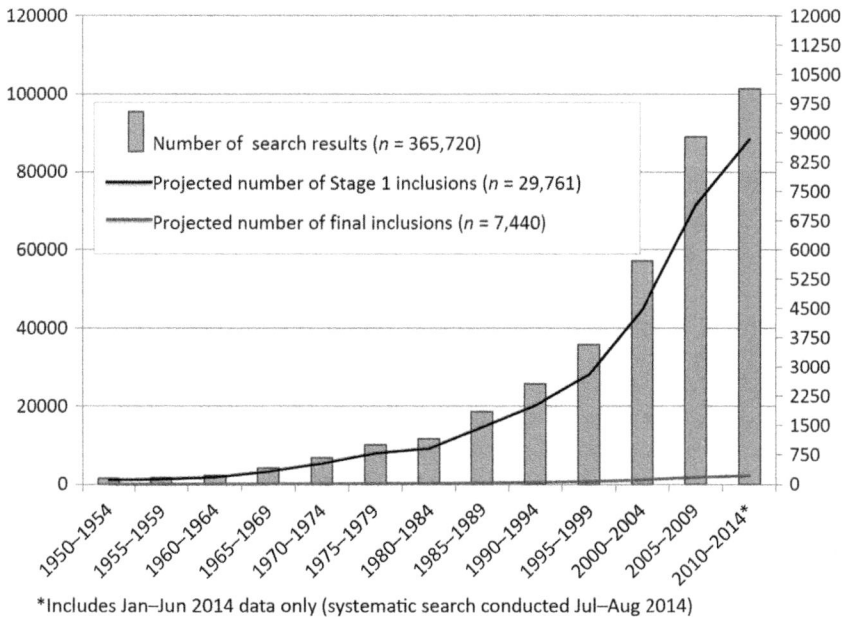

*Includes Jan–Jun 2014 data only (systematic search conducted Jul–Aug 2014)

Figure 8.1 Number of GPD search results by year (1950–2014)

*Includes Jan–Jun 2014 data only (systematic search conducted Jul–Aug 2014)

80 eligible studies from January to June 2014 only. With the beta release of the GPD, police can assess the foundations for what will ultimately be a comprehensive web-based and searchable database. The research team continues to systematically search, retrieve and screen published and unpublished studies that report quantitative impact evaluations of any type of policing intervention, moving backwards from mid-2014 to January 1, 1950. Figure 8.1 demonstrates the exponential growth in research relating to police, from just over 20,000 items captured by the systematic search in the period 1990–1994, to over 100,000 items captured in the period 2010–2014. The task of populating the GPD back to 2010 is expected to be completed by the end of 2016, with initial eligibility screening completed back to 2005.

> The scope of the GPD differs from the *What Works for Crime Reduction Toolkit* (see Bowers et al., this volume). The tool kit focuses on a synthesis of systematic reviews drawn from both the Campbell and Cochrane Collaboration libraries that include police interventions as well as a host of other crime reduction interventions undertaken by nonpolice agents or agencies. Similar to the GPD, the tool kit is an evolving resource that is updated as evidence is identified and now includes summary EMMIE statements (Effect, Mechanism, Moderator, Implementation, Economic) (see Johnson et al., 2015) of 41 crime-reducing interventions generated from harvesting results from 65 systematic reviews. The GPD is also different from the Lum-Koper Evidence-Based Policing Matrix and the Crime Solutions websites. Unlike Crime Solutions and the Lum-Koper Matrix, the GPD includes studies with outcomes beyond crime and disorder and is populated using systematic search and screening techniques.
>
> (see Higginson et al., 2015)

Search locations and terms

To reduce publication and discipline bias, our search strategy is international in scope, involving searches for literature across a number of disciplines, including criminology, law, political science, public health, sociology, social science and social work. The GPD systematic search strategy was designed to capture a comprehensive range of published (i.e., journal articles, book chapters, books) and unpublished literature (e.g., working papers, governmental reports, technical reports, conference proceedings, dissertations), implemented in five stages. The first stage involved systematically searching a substantial number of bibliographic databases that collectively contain a mixture of published and unpublished literature (see Higginson et al., 2015).

The subsequent stages are currently in progress and entail extensively searching grey literature sources, harvesting the references of eligible studies and previous narrative reviews, and contacting policing experts for feedback and input. The fifth and final search stage will involve comprehensively searching non-English language search locations to ensure the GPD is international in scope. This search will include the 12 most common non-English languages across the globe, such as Chinese, French, German, Spanish, Hindi and Arabic (Higginson et al., 2015).

Several steps were taken to ensure the systematic search had optimum sensitivity and specificity. First, our search was piloted in an iterative process until we were confident that it captured eligible research, whilst not capturing too large a proportion of irrelevant research. In addition, our search strategy included a combination of free-text and controlled vocabulary search terms across a number of search fields (i.e., title, abstract, keywords, indexing terms).

Inclusion criteria

To be included in the GPD, each document must satisfy all three inclusion criteria: timeframe, intervention type and research design. There are no restrictions applied to the types of outcomes, participants, settings or languages considered. In terms of timeframe, we include all policing research conducted after January 1, 1950. For types of interventions, each document must contain a quantitative impact evaluation of a policing intervention. We define a policing intervention as any kind of strategy, technique, approach, activity, campaign, training, directive, or funding/organisational change that involves police in some way. Other non-police agencies or organisations can be involved. Police involvement is broadly defined as police initiation, development or leadership; police as recipients of the intervention or the intervention is related, focused or targeted to police practices; or interventions that are developed by others but delivered by police.

In terms of study design, the GPD includes only quantitative research that uses experimental or quasi-experimental evaluation designs with a valid comparison group or condition that does not receive the intervention. Designs where the comparison group receives 'business-as-usual' policing, no intervention or an alternative intervention (treatment–treatment designs) are included. As well as randomised controlled experiments, a range of quasi-experimental designs are eligible for inclusion. Quasi-experimental designs included in the GPD include those that minimise risk of bias and maximise comparability between treatment and comparison groups through design features, for example, designs that control the assignment of cases to treatment and control groups (e.g., regression discontinuity), match the characteristics of the treatment and control groups (e.g., matched control designs with or without preintervention baseline measures such as propensity or statistically matched), statistically account for differences between the treatment and control groups (e.g., designs using multiple regression analysis) or provide a difference-in-difference analysis (parallel cohorts with pretest and post-test measures). We also include meta-analyses, cross-over designs, cost–benefit analyses, short interrupted time-series designs with a control group and long interrupted time-series designs with or without a control group. Other quasi-experimental designs such as unmatched control group designs without preintervention measures (where the control group has face validity), raw unadjusted correlational designs (where the variation in the level of the intervention is compared to the variation in the level of the outcome) and treatment–treatment designs are all included.

Although we recognise the contested nature of how 'evidence' might be best developed over time (see Laycock and Tilley, this volume), the GPD adopts the Campbell Collaboration model of evidence development and excludes any research design that does not use a control or comparison condition. We acknowledge that the GPD epistemologically privileges quantitative impact evaluations because these designs provide counterfactual, and therefore qualitative, modes of knowledge, including in-depth case studies, ethnographic research, documentary analysis and observational studies, so these will all be excluded from the GPD. These ways of knowing can provide a deep and nuanced understanding of the experiences and processes of policing interventions, and can therefore speak to the experience of what *is*; however, they cannot speak to the counterfactual, what *might have been*, in the absence of the intervention. It is for this reason that these studies are excluded from the evidence base of the GPD.

Screening, coding and quality assurance

The GPD is created through a series of systematic screening stages. We begin by exporting the full search results from EndNote (reference management software), after removing duplicates, into a computer program called SysReview, a Microsoft Access database for screening and coding research (Higginson and Neville, 2014). The title and abstract of each document is screened by trained research staff to identify potentially eligible research that satisfies the following criteria: the document contains research material dated after 1949, the document is not a duplicate, the document is about police or policing and the document is an eligible document type (e.g., not a book review). Records classified as potentially eligible progress to the next stages: full-text literature retrieval and then full-text eligibility screening. After the abstract and title screening stage, the full text of each document is screened to identify studies that satisfy the following criteria: document contains research material dated after 1949, the document is not a duplicate, the document reports a quantitative statistical comparison, the document reports on a police or policing evaluation, the document reports on a quantitative impact evaluation of a policing intervention and the impact evaluation uses an eligible research design (see Higginson et al., 2015 for further detail).

Documents screened as eligible at the full-text screening stage then progress to full-text coding. Documents are coded according to publication date of the document, language of the document, country location of the intervention, type of problem targeted by the intervention, type of outcome measure(s) used to evaluate the intervention, type of participants used to evaluate the intervention and type of policing intervention evaluated. The coding uses predominantly fixed categories which then map onto the search fields available in the online GPD.

To ensure consistency in screening decisions, each screener who works across the GPD stages undergoes standardised training. Prior to working within the SysReview database, interns and staff members each complete a simulated test set for each stage to assess their understanding of the training. The results of these tests determine where staff work within the GPD process: inter-rater agreement of 95 percent or higher is required to work within any of the screening and coding stages. Furthermore, 15 percent of each screener's work within each session is cross-checked, with a focus on records or documents that have been excluded, to identify screener drift and adherence to protocols. We implement further training and rescreen the group of documents where issues have been identified, and disagreements regarding eligibility are resolved by a discussion between the coders and review managers.

Consistent with systematic review and meta-analysis standards (see Moher et al., 2009), we provide a Preferred Reporting Items of Systematic Reviews and Meta-Analyses (PRISMA) flow diagram in Figure 8.2 to show the attrition of cases to create the beta version of the GPD.

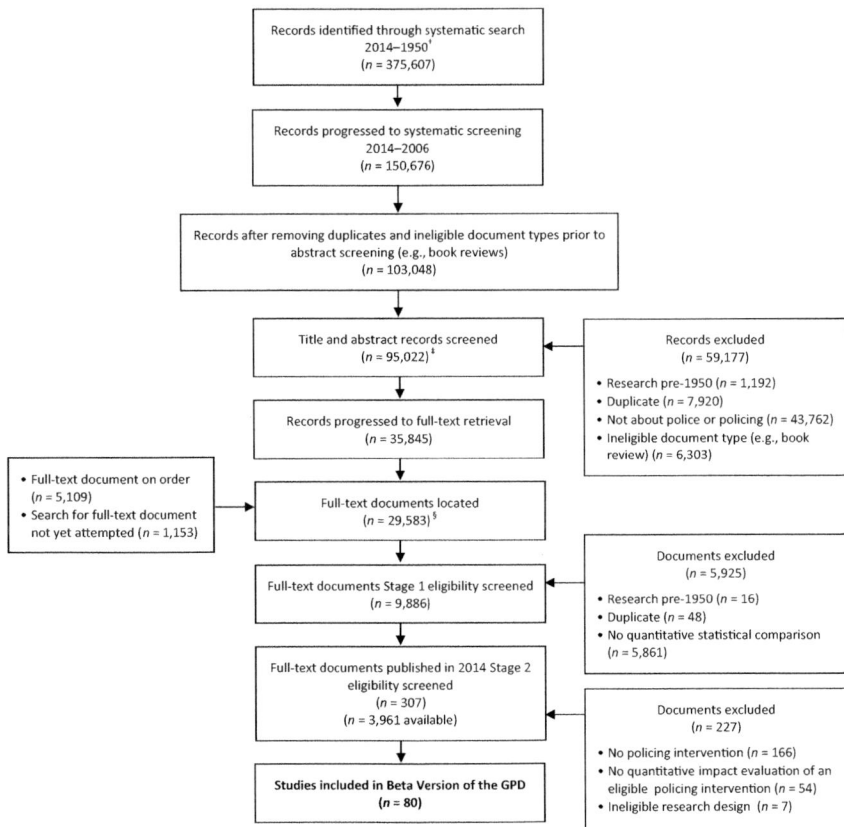

†Search conducted in Jul 2014. Search period June 2014–January 1950.
‡Represents 2014–2007 and portion of 2006 records (≈40% of all records identied in systematic search).
§Includes 504 documents in languages other than English.

Figure 8.2 PRISMA flowchart

† Search conducted in July 7, 2014. Search period June 2014–January 1950.

‡ Represents 2014–2007 and portion of 2006 records (≈40% of all records identied in systematic search).

§ Includes 504 documents in languages other than English.

As Figure 8.2 shows, the systematic search undertaken in July 2014 for the search period January 1950 to June 2014 (inclusive) identified 375,607 records. Of these, 150,676 records were identified as being for the period January 2006 to June 2014 (inclusive), the time period where the title and abstract screening has been conducted as of March 2016. After removing duplicate documents and ineligible document types, we commenced abstract screening on 103,048 unique records from this timeframe, and to date we have screened 95,022 titles and abstracts. Over 59,000 records were excluded at this stage of screening for three reasons: they were duplicate records, ineligible document types or deemed to be not about police or policing.

Of the 29,583 full-text documents located (as of March 2016), including 504 documents in languages other than English, 9,886 documents have been deemed eligible on Stage 1 full-text screening as of March 2016. At Stage 1 screening we excluded 5,925 documents because the study did not include a quantitative comparison group. The final stage of full-text document screening on the 2014 records (January to June 2014 only) produced the 80 documents included in the GPD beta version of 2014 and excluded documents that were not policing interventions ($n = 166$), reported studies with ineligible research designs ($n = 7$) or included no quantitative impact evaluation of an eligible policing intervention ($n = 54$). We provide an analysis next of both the included 80 GPD beta version studies, the 54 documents excluded because they did not provide an eligible impact evaluation and the 7 studies that were excluded because they did not utilise an eligible research design to evaluate the reported policing evaluation.

Beta version inclusions

The beta version of the GPD demonstrates that the eligible studies published in 2014 utilise a wide range of research designs and participant types, and are indeed drawn from a global population of evidence. Further, the broad scope of the GPD has successfully captured evidence across a wide range of problems, interventions and outcomes. The GPD goes well beyond providing evidence for the impact of policing strategies on crime control and captures valuable evidence of the impact of policing on police themselves, including perceptions of police, police health and well-being and police culture. For the 80 studies included in the GPD beta version (www.gpd.uq.edu.au), we present an analysis of the types of research design, country of study, types of participant, types of problem targeted, types of intervention and the primary outcome measure collected.

Figure 8.3 presents the types of research designs in the eligible corpus of studies. As Figure 8.3 shows, 30 percent of the included studies used multivariate controls, unmatched control group designs comprised 20 percent, 18 percent were matched control group designs, and a further 14 percent used regression discontinuity, cost–benefit analysis (CBA) or cross-over designs. Just 16 percent ($n = 13$) of the 80 eligible studies were randomised controlled trials.

Table 8.1 shows the number of studies in the beta GPD version by type of research design and country of intervention. The United States contributes the vast

Systematic review
with meta-analysis
2%

Other (e.g.,
regression
discontinuity, cross-
over, CBA)
14%

RCT
16%

Design with
multivariate controls
not captured by
other categories
30%

Matched control
group designs
18%

Unmatched control
group designs
20%

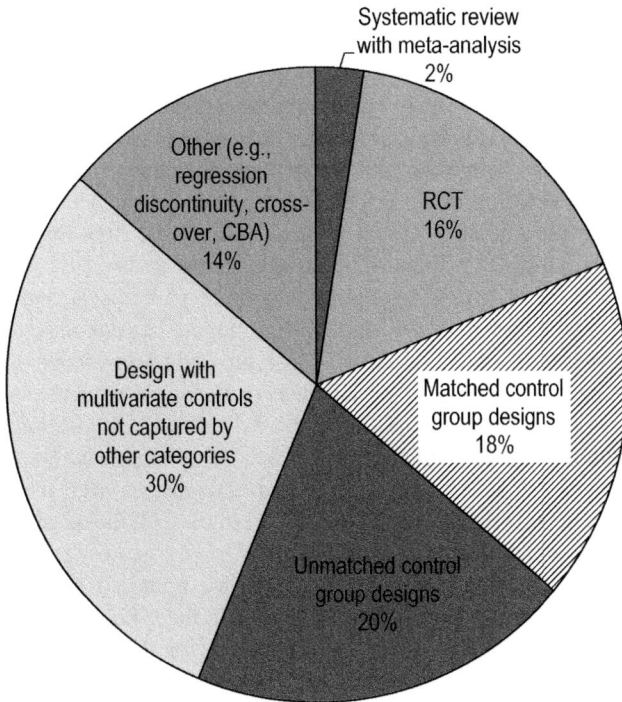

Figure 8.3 Types of research designs

Table 8.1 Distribution of research design by country of intervention

Country	Randomised Experiment	Matched Control Group	Unmatched Control Group	Multivariate Controls	Other	Total
United States	10	6	6	15	4	41
Canada	0	1	1	2	2	6
United Kingdom	1	1	2	0	2	6
Australia	1	2	0	1	1	5
Brazil	0	1	1	1	0	3
Bosnia	0	0	2	0	0	2
Czech Republic	0	1	0	0	1	2
Germany	0	0	2	0	0	2
Mexico	0	0	1	0	1	2
Finland	0	1	0	0	0	1
Ghana	0	0	0	1	0	1
India	0	1	0	0	0	1
Japan	0	0	1	0	0	1
Netherlands	1	0	0	0	0	1
New Zealand	0	0	0	0	1	1
Slovenia	0	0	0	1	0	1
Sweden	0	0	0	1	0	1
Thailand	0	0	0	1	0	1

Note: Due to the two meta-analyses which contain studies from multiple countries, the 'Total' column does not sum to 80.

majority of eligible studies (*n* = 41), including 10 randomised experiments and 32 quasi-experiments. As a truly global database of policing evidence, Table 8.1 shows that the English-speaking countries of Canada (*n* = 6), the United Kingdom (*n* = 6), Australia (*n* = 5) and the non–English-speaking countries of Brazil (*n* = 3), Bosnia (*n* = 2), Czech Republic (*n* = 2), Germany (*n* = 2) and Mexico (*n* = 2) each contribute multiple studies to the GPD beta version, with non–English-speaking countries contributing 24 percent of the evidence base to date (*n* = 20).

Figure 8.4 presents the distribution of research participants and shows that although the vast majority of the studies were impact evaluations evaluating the effect of interventions on individuals (*n* = 56), the GPD beta version also includes studies utilising a broad range of participants. These included micro places (*n* = 6), macro places (*n* = 8), cases or specimens (*n* = 5), police organisations (*n* = 3) or studies themselves as the unit of analysis (such as the two meta-analyses included in the GPD). Of these studies, randomised experimental designs were used in 10 individual participant and 10 place (micro or macro) studies. Of the quasi-experimental studies, 46 used individuals as the participants, 5 used cases or specimens, 6 used macro places, 5 used micro places, and 3 used police organisations.

Figure 8.5 presents the distribution of studies in the GPD beta version for the types of problems targeted by the intervention, showing that the GPD can provide robust evidence for more than crime and disorder. The most common types of problems addressed in the GPD are police investigative practices, such as interviewing and line-ups (*n* = 15). The GPD beta version also includes 11 studies that target police well-being, 7 that target violent crime, 6 that target driver behaviour, and 2 that focus on police values.

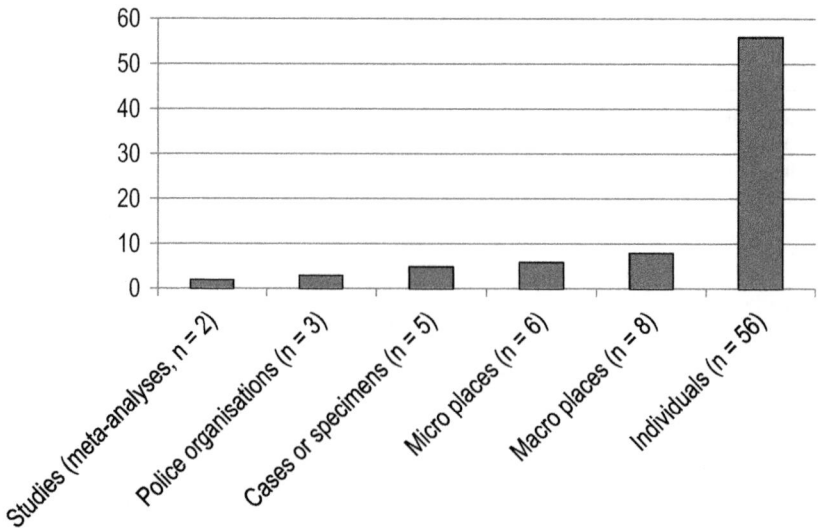

Figure 8.4 Distribution of research participants

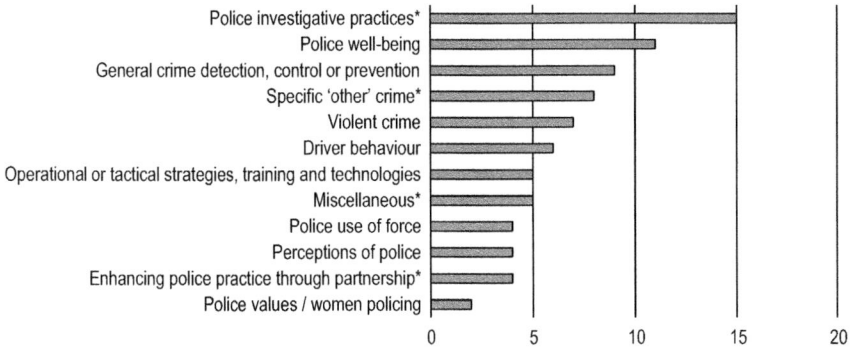

*Examples of police investigative practices targeted: interviewing practices, line-ups. Examples of 'other' crime targeted: illicit drugs, human trafficking. Examples of miscellaneous: racialisation, border control, citizen perceptions of crime, victim well-being. Police partnerships may be with citizens or other agencies.

Figure 8.5 Distribution of problem targeted

Table 8.2 provides a rank order distribution of a broad and general catego-risation of intervention categories (more detail is used in coding for the online GPD). Over a quarter ($n = 22$) of the 80 eligible studies are about police inves-tigative techniques, particularly diagnostic testing and interviewing techniques. Thirteen studies report the impact results of legislative or policy change, and 10 report results from police training interventions. When we examined the strength of research design by type of intervention, we found that interventions focusing on police investigative techniques comprise half of the randomised experiments ($n = 6$) and the other half consist of a range of interventions from hot spots to policing interventions focusing on procedural or restorative justice. For the quasi-experiments, interventions are distributed somewhat evenly across the categories, with most falling into the category of police investigative techniques ($n = 16$); police training interventions ($n = 10$); and legislative, policy or organisation struc-ture interventions ($n = 13$).

Figure 8.6 provides a summary of the types of outcome measures used in the corpus of 80 studies in the GPD beta version. Once again, we see that the corpus of impact evaluation evidence on police and policing evaluates more than crime and disorder, with 44 percent of the included studies to date examining outcomes beyond criminality. Over a quarter (26 percent) of the studies use case- or judicial-level measures of crime, such as rate of clearance or conviction, as the primary outcome measure, and one-fifth use official measures of crime such as incidents, arrests or calls for police service. Interestingly, 19 percent use psychological or physiological outcomes; perceptions of police and police-level outcomes make up 8 percent and 16 percent, respectively, and we identify 4 percent of studies that report multiple types of outcome measures.

Table 8.2 Distribution of intervention categories

Intervention Category	Randomised Experiment[*]	Quasi-Experiment	Total
Police investigative techniques (e.g., diagnostic testing, interview techniques)	6	16	22
Legislative, policy or organisational structure change	0	13	13
Other police practices (e.g., general arrest, traffic enforcement)	0	10	10
Police training (e.g., fitness, dealing with special populations)	0	10	10
Police tools or technologies (e.g., Tasers, geographic information systems [GIS], CCTV)	2	4	6
Proactive or innovative policing (e.g., pulling levers, hot spots)	4	4	8
Miscellaneous (e.g., hotlines, early intervention)	0	6	6
Procedural justice, restorative justice or other change in police–citizen interaction	3	2	5

* Includes systematic reviews with meta-analyses.

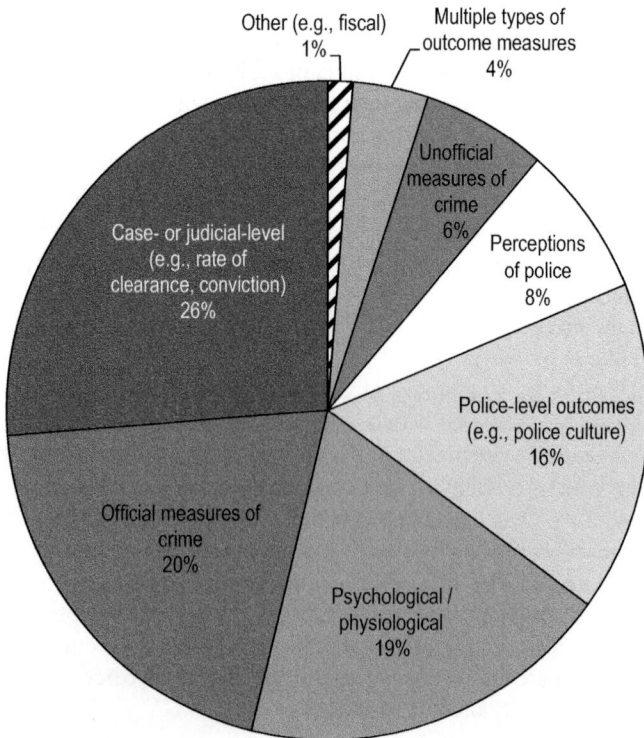

Figure 8.6 Distribution by type of outcome measures

Beta version exclusions

One of the key tenets of the theory of disruptive innovation is that consumers are not willing to switch to the new offering until they perceive that the quality of the new product has improved enough to satisfy them (see Christensen et al., 2015). We argue, therefore, that open-access provision of police scientific evidence needs to be of sufficient quality if EBP is going to disrupt the incumbent mode of policing. Where to draw the line on 'quality' provision of scientific evidence is, of course, debatable. The GPD is very clear about where the quality line is drawn and focuses on studies that provide a counterfactual, to eliminate confounding sources of impact (see earlier). As such, we would expect the GPD to build a reputation of being a quality source of policing evidence. But which subject areas may have been excluded from the GPD to date by including only robust quantitative impact evaluations?

The PRISMA flow chart presented in Figure 8.2 identifies two sets of studies excluded from the 2014 GPD beta version. The first set of 54 records represents documents that have been full-text screened and contain some report of an eligible police or policing intervention. However, these 54 studies were not included in the GPD because they did not include an eligible quantitative impact evaluation of that policing intervention. The second smaller set of records includes those that were excluded because the quantitative impact evaluation of an eligible policing intervention did not utilise an eligible research design. In the following sections, we examine these two sets of excluded studies to assess what the GPD might miss from the wider corpus of policing studies in drawing the line at including only robust quantitative impact evaluations.

Policing interventions without a quantitative impact evaluation

Figures 8.7 and 8.8 provide a Leximancer text analysis of the content of the 54 excluded studies. Leximancer is a text analytics tool that uses visual maps to summarise the themes and conceptual structure of text documents and how these themes and concepts interrelate (Stockwell et al., 2009; Leximancer Manual, 2011). Leximancer provides one method for analysing the content of the excluded studies, without the labor-intensive exercise of coding studies that would not find their way into the GPD. It allows for an independent investigation and extraction of major themes and concepts and removes researcher subjectivity and bias in textual analysis (Palmer, 2013).

Figure 8.7 provides the thematic summary of the 54 documents, showing the dominant themes within the excluded studies ranked by relevance (importance of the themes) and a connectivity score that summarises the degree of connection between lower-level concepts that comprise each theme (expressed as a percentage of all 54 studies).

The thematic summary in Figure 8.7 identifies the top eight themes emerging from the corpus of 54 studies excluded from the GPD. Unsurprisingly, *crime* was the most important theme and frequently utilised concept in the text documents

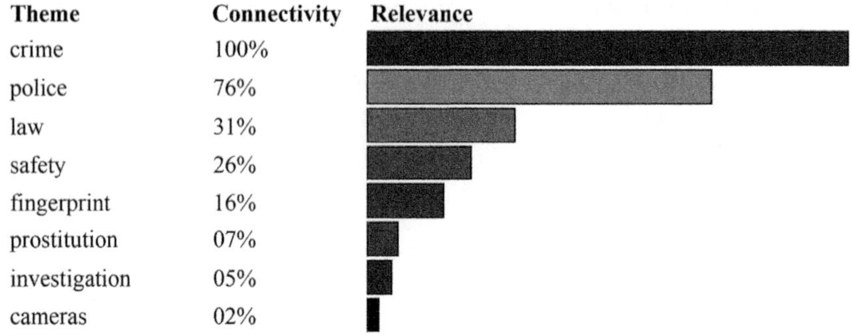

Theme	Connectivity	Relevance
crime	100%	
police	76%	
law	31%	
safety	26%	
fingerprint	16%	
prostitution	07%	
investigation	05%	
cameras	02%	

Figure 8.7 Themes by connectivity and relevance

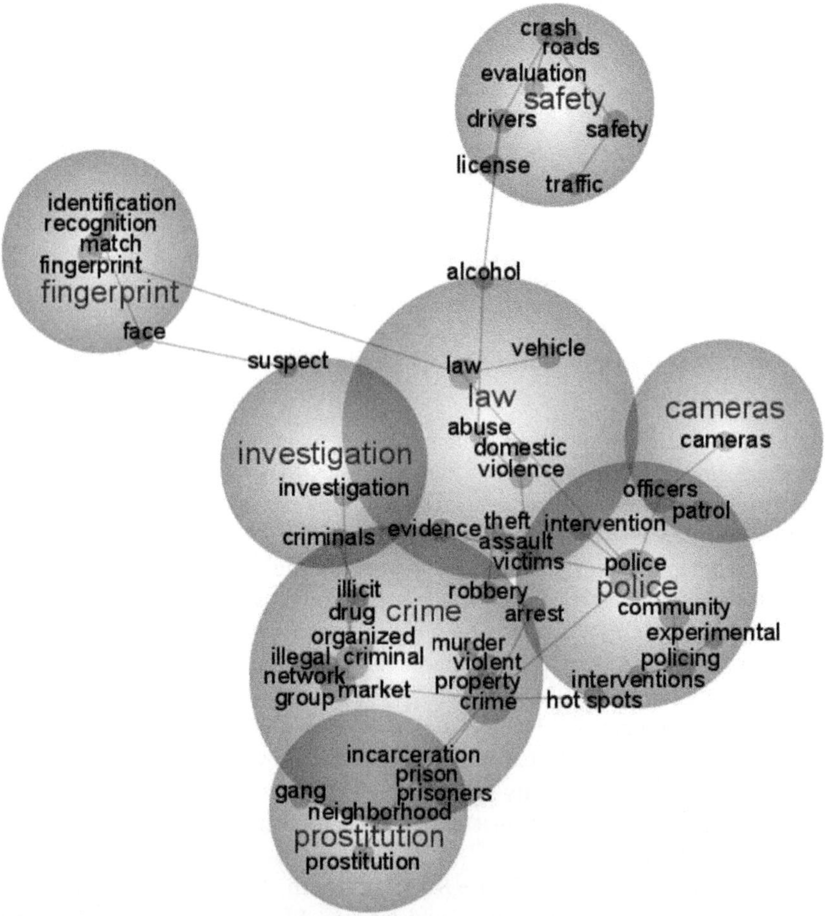

Figure 8.8 Conceptual map of the 54 documents excluded from the GPD beta version

(with 100 percent of all 54 articles identifying a dominant theme of crime), followed by the themes *police* (75 percent of all articles identified police as the most important theme), *law* (31 percent), *safety (*26 percent), *fingerprint* (16 percent), *prostitution* (7 percent), *investigation* (5 percent) and *cameras* (2 percent). In addition to the thematic summary table, the Leximancer concept ranking table (not displayed) includes further quantitative information on how often concepts are used in the text documents. An exploration of the ranked concepts found that the concept *police* was utilised 1,741 times, followed by *crime* with 1,282 counts, *officers* with 731 counts, *law* with 716 counts and *fingerprint* with 685 counts.

Figure 8.8 displays a map of the conceptual structure and displays the themes for the 54 excluded studies. The key themes are presented by circles, which provide a 'quick high-level summary' (Palmer, 2013: 226) of the text documents and are composed of clusters of concepts. The concepts in the map are indicative of co-occurring words in the text documents such that the more frequently concepts co-occur in the text documents, the closer they will be clustered together on the Leximancer map (Fisk et al., 2012). The size of the thematic circles represents the number of concepts encapsulated by the theme and a grey scale to determine their importance (Leximancer uses heat mapping based on the colour wheel to determine key themes emerging from the documents, from red being most important to blue being least important.)[1] (see Leximancer Manual, 2011) and spatial separation of themes, with themes in the centre of the map emerging more frequently and themes in close proximity linked more closely.

Figure 8.8 reveals that the most dominant and frequently used theme in these 54 text documents is *crime*, which is most frequently linked to concepts such as *group, criminal, drug, illegal, network, market, violent, neighbourhood* and *property*. The text documents, for example, refer to criminal or offending groups or groups under study, criminal markets or opportunities. The terms 'criminal justice' and 'criminal individuals' are also closely linked to the main theme of *crime*. Text documents reveal that the concepts *drug, illicit, illegal, market* and *network* in terms of drug crimes, the war on drugs and illicit drugs, as well as the illegal drug market and crime networks, are part of the dominant theme. This first dominant theme also includes studies about property and violent crimes.

The second theme, *police*, is most closely linked to the concepts *officers, policing, community, victims, arrest* and *hot spots*. The concept *policing*, for example, often refers to policing scholarship, policing powers and roles, as well as community and experimental policing and policing interventions. The third theme identified in the concept map is *law*, which includes concepts such as *vehicle, violence* and *evidence*. The concept *vehicle* is used, for example, in relation to speed limit policies, equipping vehicles with dash cameras and licence plate recognition. The concept *violence* is connected to domestic violence and abuse, and the concept *evidence* is connected to victims (e.g., of assault, robbery or abuse), hot spots and investigation.

Theme number four is *safety*, which is connected to concepts such as *crash, drivers, traffic* and *roads*. As Figure 8.8 shows, this theme is spatially separated from the other themes and is also conceptually distinct from the other themes in the map, suggesting that there is likely a group of studies in the excluded corpus that bear little relationship to the other studies. This theme most prominently revolves around road and driver safety, as well as traffic crashes, and is not conceptually linked with the studies that are strongly focused on crime and crime problems. The fifth theme is *fingerprint*, closely linked to the concept *match*, as well as connected to *identification* and *recognition*. This theme indicates a focus on fingerprint matching and the identification of fingerprints and is also conceptually distinct from the other themes on the map. The sixth theme is *prostitution*, which is linked to *neighbourhood* and *arrest*, and theme seven, *investigation*, refers to criminal and police investigations. Theme eight, *cameras*, refers to speed cameras, CCTV cameras and surveillance cameras, as well as dash and body-worn cameras.

The overlapping clusters of concepts in the middle of the map around the dominant themes of *crime*, *police* and *law* indicate a close connectivity amongst these themes. For example, the themes *crime*, *law* and *investigation* are interrelated, and the themes *police*, *law* and *cameras* display close connectivity. An exploration of the concept nodes (the grey circles) shows that the most relevant concepts to the text creators included *crime*, *police*, *group*, *criminal*, *officers*, *drug* and *policing*.

Quantitative evaluations of policing interventions without an eligible research design

Of the 307 documents screened at Stage 2 eligibility screening, only 7 have been excluded from the GPD BETA VERSION due to utilising a research design that does not meet our inclusion thresholds. Two of these documents were excluded because they only qualitatively reported on the results of other eligible studies and did not conduct their own secondary analysis (e.g., meta-analysis). Upon examining these documents, we found that the studies reported have all been captured by the GPD systematic search and will eventually enter the GPD in their own right. Of the five remaining documents, three examined quite focused aspects of police practice: the impact of Tasers on cognitive functioning, training to increase the use of open questions in investigative interviewing and electronic tracking devices in stationary unmarked police vehicles to apprehend property offenders. The remaining two documents examine more complex policing interventions. One of these examines community interventions that integrate media, education and law enforcement to prevent motor vehicle crashes and increase seatbelt use. The other examines the impact of a blended emotional regulation and resilience intervention using iPad apps and mentoring for improving personal well-being and perceptions of the organisational environment. Of the five original intervention studies, three used simple single-group pre–post designs without any control of confounding factors, and the other two provided time-series data, but with <25 observations and no comparison group. These studies report on important areas of policing; however, the research designs employed to evaluate the interventions minimise the ability to reliably attribute the observed effects to the intervention. Although informative studies, we contend that including such studies potentially reduces the importance of relying on the methodologically robust intervention research that is required to advance EBP.

Comparing the included and excluded GPD beta studies

When comparing the thematic and conceptual analysis of the excluded studies to the descriptive analysis on the coded included studies, we observe some similarities and important differences. First, the Leximancer analysis shows that concepts such as *intervention, evaluation, impact, research, empirical* and other concepts generally used to describe quantitative evaluation studies are not commonly co-occurring concepts in the collection of the 54 excluded studies. This suggests that although the excluded studies are 'on topic' in that they cover a range of policing problems and issues, they are not the types of studies that help inform evidence-based practice, if one adopts the Campbell Collaboration model of evidence development. Second, there are some similarities in the topics covered in both the excluded and included collections of studies. For example, both the Leximancer analysis (Figures 8.7 and 8.8) and Table 8.2 show that investigative techniques, law/legislation and tools/technologies (such as cameras) and traffic/road safety policing are common areas of study. This is also true of the smaller set of seven studies excluded because the evaluation of the policing intervention did not utilise a sufficiently robust research design. However, the collection of included studies and the smaller set of studies excluded because they did not employ a sufficiently robust research design appear to be more closely aligned than the larger set of 54 studies excluded because they did not contain a quantitative impact evaluation of a policing intervention. For example, the 80 included studies and the 7 studies excluded due to a less robust research design cover topics such as police training, restorative/procedural justice, early intervention and partnership policing, whereas our analysis of the excluded studies has not identified these topics as being prominent. Conversely, we find that the excluded corpus seems to include studies on topics such as drug law enforcement and organised crime that are not reflected in the included corpus of studies in the GPD so far.

This analysis only covers a fraction of what will ultimately become the final GPD, with only a six-month period of evidence production having been fully screened and coded for the GPD beta version. We anticipate that the overlap of subject matter between the included and excluded studies will become even greater once a larger number are fully screened and coded. However, there may be subject areas that are less amenable to quantitative impact evaluations that may end up being underrepresented in the final GPD. We do recognise the value of research methodologies beyond our inclusion thresholds (e.g., qualitative research) and how these excluded research methodologies may augment the quantitative evidence included in the GPD.

Discussion and conclusions

The worldwide diffusion and upward innovation trajectory of the EBP movement offer an opportunity to consider the shift from the craft to science approach to policing through the lens of a disruptive innovation. EBP, we argue, is characterised by a number of initiatives that are transforming policing from a craft-based occupation into a profession that generates and uses its own science to guide professional practice. One of these enabling initiatives is quality, web-based information tools, such as the Crime Reduction Toolkit, the Lum-Koper Matrix, the Center for Problem-Oriented Policing resources, CrimeSolutions and the Global Policing Database. We discuss how the EBP movement is dependent on police accessing open, freely available and useable research evidence. As one of a half-dozen websites offering police access to extensive collections of the international policing evidence base, the GPD aims to provide police with access to the largest corpus of published and unpublished experimental and quasi-experimental evaluations of policing interventions conducted globally since 1950.

Far from a finished product, considerable investments are still needed to further develop the GPD and fully populate the database with all eligible studies dating back to 1950. Yet what is already available in the beta version of the GPD is instructive: first, the search methods are clearly identifying studies from all over the world, albeit dominated by U.S. studies. Nevertheless, the fact that 24 percent of the GPD studies come from non–English-speaking countries suggests that the GPD is, and will be, truly a global evidence source of information. Second, the GPD demonstrates that evidence exists across a relatively wide range of policing topics, including wellness, training, violent crime and police use of force – all of which should inform better management of staff as well as crime tactics. Third, most of the policing evidence so far is focused on interventions that target individuals, whether they are individual police attending innovative training programs or offenders/suspects being targeted in a variety of different policing operations. This suggests that although the search and screening filters used by the GPD create a robust corpus of evaluation studies, it also highlights the intrinsic preferences in the GPD that are different and distinct from the preferences in all of the other policing web-based tools. The GPD protocol, for example, uses some 30-plus search terms (see Higginson et al., 2015) to identify quantitative evaluation studies, which sets up a selective filter that excludes studies that might explore the mechanisms of change using nonquantitative methods. The What Works Toolkit, by contrast, only includes results filtered from systematic reviews. Indeed, all six of the web-based evidence-based policing tools use different search, inclusion and exclusion filters generating their own intrinsic preferences. Yet as a family of web-based evidence tools, they collectively offer policing search options which, we argue, is a critical step in policing using their science to guide practice.

Our chapter also compared and contrasted the studies that were excluded and included in the GPD beta version. Although the excluded studies have not been coded in the same manner as the included studies, we were able to conduct a Leximancer concept analysis using the full-text of studies excluded due to there being no quantitative impact evaluation of a policing intervention. We also provided a brief thematic overview of the smaller set of excluded studies that did report a quantitative impact evaluation of a policing intervention but did not implement a sufficiently robust research design (according to our thresholds). This analysis provided some insight into the different topics covered in the excluded studies and revealed that a theme around evaluation/intervention was noticeably missing from the set used in the Leximancer analysis, which was why these studies were not included in the GPD beta version. Given that the GPD search and screening filters favour robust quantitative methods, it is likely that evaluations of complex, transnational crime problems found within the population of excluded studies are less amenable to quantitative impact evaluations (e.g., organised crime). This suggests that the continued establishment and proliferation of the family of web-based evidence tools, rather than just one access tool alone, will ultimately be the catalyst for change.

Upon completion, the GPD is expected to contain over 5,000 quantitative impact evaluations of policing interventions. Yet to move from the beta version to the fully populated site raises many challenges. The first challenge is to develop a sustainable approach to completing and then routinely updating the GPD. At present, the team based at the University of Queensland, with funding from the UK College of Policing and London's Mayor's Office for Policing and Crime (MOPAC), is working to identify a cloud-based system to enable teams of interns all over the world to contribute screening and coding time to populate the GPD. Realising this goal will provide the capacity to quickly complete the backlog of studies, begin populating the GPD with translated studies from non–English-speaking countries and update the GPD on a regular basis.

The second challenge of the GPD is securing open access to the original research material and/or resources to translate the findings from the original research into plain English summaries along the lines of the UK Crime Reduction Toolkit. This is a barrier at the present time that is likely to be surmounted in the not-too-distant future. For example, funding agencies around the world are now moving to demand all funded research outputs be made open access (see www. arc.gov.au/arc-open-access-policy; www.esrc.ac.uk/funding/guidance-for-grant-holders/open-access-to-research-outputs/), and researchers are disrupting regular publishing patterns by publishing in open-access journals such as *PLOS One* and creating websites that make available for download author copies of publications (e.g., ResearchGate).

The evidence-based policing movement has all the hallmarks of a paradigm shift in policing. The use of evidence, and the availability of evidence in the form of websites like the GPD, is fundamental to whether or not the movement can actually move from rhetoric to reality. It is possible, therefore, to view repositories like the GPD to be a form of disruptive innovation, a term first coined by Clayton Christensen (1997) of the Harvard Business School in his book titled *The Innovator's Dilemma*. Christensen described how improvements in a product or service turn out to dominate in a way that is not expected by other market participants when first launched. In the early years of the evidence-based policing movement, the synthesis of evidence was seen as the foundation product for advancing evidence-based practice. Sherman and colleagues' (1997) report *What Works, What Doesn't and What's Promising* is an early example of how evidence resided in the hands of academics, where it could be synthesised and summarised for uptake in the practitioner world. Similarly, the establishment and growth of the Campbell Collaboration around the turn of the century focused on mostly academic-based researchers accessing and synthesising research and offering insights on best practice interventions. Websites like the GPD, however, offer something a little different: the capacity to synthesise the research evidence remains, yet a synthesis on any given police topic using the GPD can be completed by practitioners and academics alike, in about one-tenth of the time and with far fewer resources.

At this point in time it is unknown whether or not the GPD (along with the family of online tools) are able to facilitate the capacity of the EBP movement to gain a foothold in the policing marketplace as a disruptive innovation. Christensen, Raynor and McDonald (2015) have revisited the original disruptive innovation theory and suggest that several characteristics distinguish disruptive innovations from industry shake-ups or innovations in general. First, disruption is viewed as a process of moving from the fringe to the mainstream over a period of time. EBP has clearly been on the fringe for some 20 years, slowly gaining momentum over time. Second, the business models of disruptive innovations are very different from the incumbent model. In policing, we are already seeing changes in the funding models of policing, where police leaders need to produce evidence to secure new or ongoing funding for initiatives. This trend towards a dependence on evaluation evidence in business modelling is likely to spill over into how police will be performance evaluated and required to show due diligence in implementing those practices that show promise and do no harm. Third, Christensen and colleagues (2015) argue that the disruptive innovation needs to be of sufficient quality for it to disrupt the mainstream marketplace. We argue that the provision of evidence-based practice, sourced from quality online tools that allow police direct access to the evaluation evidence, will reach a tipping point under the following conditions: when the majority of police access online tools to guide policy and practice as a matter of routine, when the online tools are widely and freely available, when the content of the tools reaches a threshold of quality such that consumers are satisfied with the product, and when the content of the tools reaches a threshold of coverage of topics that are seen as useful to police.

The challenge for all of the EBP web-based tools is to consider how the policing profession can institutionalise the use of these tools on the job, in parallel with the craft approach to policing. Infusing available EBP material with recruit training modules, as well as other craft-based training opportunities, is a critical next step. Similarly, creating performance frameworks that require police to generate, harvest and effectively use the best available evidence to guide practical decision-making will also help institutionalise the EBP approach in policing practice. Regardless of the pace of change, policing as a profession is in a watershed moment. Mass access to police science through online tools like the GPD, therefore, marks a significant turning point in the history of policing.

Note

1 The size of the circles is not indicative of the importance of the themes; rather it indicates that more concepts are encircled in the theme.

References

Christensen, C.M. (1997). *The Innovator's Dilemma: When New Technologies Cause Great Firms to Fail*, Boston: Harvard Business School Press.

Christensen, C.M., Raynor, M. and McDonald, R. (2015). 'What is disruptive innovation?', *Harvard Business Review*, 93(12): 44–53.

Dunham, R.G. and Alpert, G.P. (2015). *Critical Issues in Policing: Contemporary Readings*, Long Grove, IL: Waveland Press.

Fisk, K., Cherney, A., Hornsey, M. and Smith, A. (2012). 'Using computer-aided content analysis to map a research domain: A case study of institutional legitimacy in postconflict East Timor', *SAGE Open*, 2(4): 1–16, doi: 10.1177/2158244012467788

Helbing, D. (2015). *Thinking Ahead-Essays on Big Data, Digital Revolution, and Participatory Market Society*, Cham, Switzerland: Springer.

Higginson, A., Eggins, E., Mazerolle, L. and Stanko, E. (2015). *The Global Policing Database Protocol*, Official Report to Mayor's Office of Policing and Crime, Brisbane, Australia: University of Queensland. Retrieved from www.gpd.uq.edu.au/faq.php

Higginson, A. and Neville, R. (2014). *SysReview* [Computer software], Brisbane, Australia: University of Queensland, Institute for Social Science Research.

Johnson, S.D., Tilley, N. and Bowers, K.J. (2015). 'Introducing EMMIE: An evidence rating scale to encourage mixed-method crime prevention synthesis reviews', *Journal of Experimental Criminology*, 11(3): 459–73.

Kelling, G.L. and Moore, M.H. (1989). *The Evolving Strategy of Policing*. Washington, DC: US Department of Justice, Office of Justice Programs, National Institute of Justice.

Leximancer Manual. (2011). *Leximancer Manual Version 4*. Retrieved from www.leximancer.com/site-media/lm/science/Leximancer_Manual_Version_4_0.pdf

Lum, C. and Koper, C. (2015) 'Evidence Based Policing', in R.G Dunham and G.P. Alpert (eds) *Critical Issues in Policing: Contemporary Readings*, pp. 260–274, Long Grove, IL: Waveland Press.

Moher, D., Liberati, A., Tetzlaff, J., Altman, D.G. and The PRISMA Group. (2009). 'Preferred reporting items for systematic reviews and meta-analyses: The PRISMA statement', *PLoS Med*, 6(7): e1000097, doi: 10.1371/journal.pmed1000097

Neyroud, P. and Weisburd, D. (2014). 'Transforming the police through science: The challenge of ownership', *Policing: A Journal of Policy and Practice*, 8(4): 287–93.

Palmer, P.D. (2013). 'Exploring attitudes to financial reporting in the Australian not-for-profit sector', *Accounting & Finance*, 53(1): 217–41.

Queensland Police Service. (2014). *Strategic Plan 2014–2018*. Retrieved from www.police.qld.gov.au/corporatedocs/reportsPublications/Documents/QPS%20Strategic%20Plan%202014-2018.pdf

Sherman, L.W., Gottredson, D.C., MacKenzie, D.L., Eck, J.E., Reuter, P. and Bushway, S. (1997). *Preventing Crime: What Works, What Doesn't, What's Promising. A Report to the United States Congress*, College Park, MD: University of Maryland, Department of Criminology and Criminal Justice. Retrieved from www.ncjrs.gov/App/AbstractDB/AbstractDBSearchResults.aspx?Title=PREVENTING+CRIME%3a+WHAT+WORKS%2c+WHAT+DOESN%27T%2c+WHAT%27S+PROMISING&Author=&Journal=&NCJNum=&General=&StartDate=&EndDate=&SearchMode=All&SortBy=4&Offset=0

Stockwell, P., Colomb, R.M., Smith, A.E. and Wiles, J. (2009). 'Use of an automatic content analysis tool: A technique for seeing both local and global scope', *International Journal of Human – Computer Studies*, 67(5): 424–36, doi: 10.1016/j.ijhcs.2008.12.001

Telep, C.W. and Lum, C. (2014). 'The receptivity of officers to empirical research and evidence-based policing: An examination of survey data from three agencies', *Police Quarterly*, 17(4): 359–85.

Weisburd, D. and Neyroud, P. (2011, January). 'Police Science: Toward a New Paradigm', New Perspectives in Policing. Retrieved from www.hks.harvard.edu/content/down load/67528/1242922/version/1/file/NPIP-Police+Science-TowardaNewParadigm.pdf

9   The long and winding road

Embedding evidence-based policing principles

Tiggey May, Gillian Hunter and Mike Hough

In March 2013 the UK government launched the 'What Works Network', a nationally coordinated initiative aimed at positioning research evidence on 'what works' at the centre of public policy decision-making. The 'what works' philosophy is that good decision-making should be informed by the best available research evidence. If relevant or adequate evidence is unavailable, decision-makers should be encouraged to use high-quality methods to find out what works. Currently there are seven What Works research centres[1] in the UK focusing on key areas of public policy, including health, education, early intervention, well-being, ageing, local economic growth and crime reduction. These 'research hubs' are intended to build on existing models of delivering evidence-based policy – such as the well-established and well-funded National Institute for Health and Clinical Excellence (NICE). This provides independent evidence-based guidance to the National Health Service (NHS) and health professionals about the targeting of funding and the most effective ways to prevent, diagnose and treat disease and ill health. The newer centres follow a similar pattern of synthesising available experimental research and making it readily accessible to professionals. For example, the Educational Endowment Foundation has developed a toolkit to appraise interventions in education in terms of their cost and impact, whilst also commissioning primary research to fill in gaps in research knowledge. The What Works Centre for Crime Reduction is following the same pattern: synthesising the research evidence and making it available for the police and others in a readily digestible form. However, one feature sets it apart from the other six centres: it is situated within policing's professional body, the College of Policing (hereafter, the College). Such an arrangement should present the perfect opportunity for both the producers and consumers of evidence to work in partnership.

Since its inception in 2012, the College and indeed its predecessor, the National Policing Improvement Agency (NPIA), have promoted the importance of research evidence to inform practice in policing and crime reduction. An NPIA action plan for improving knowledge use in policing (NPIA, 2010) presented a vision of 'a police service that routinely uses good quality knowledge to decide what to target, what action to take and what resource to deploy' and cited a range of targets to be achieved by 2013, over which the What Works Centre now takes ownership. These include:

- Investing in research and developing research partnerships.
- Quality assuring research evidence.
- Sharing and embedding that knowledge in professional practice.

The College is now making a clear push for evidence-based decision-making to become the norm rather than the exception for police officers. As part of the College's professionalisation agenda, officers are being encouraged to move away from policing by 'custom and convention' and towards evidence-based decision-making. As Sherman has stated: 'This body [the College] has tremendous potential to follow the pathway to innovation' (Sherman, 2013: 380). The College has stated that by 2020:

- There will be more effective policing based on a research and evidence base which is informed by members, forces and the public.
- There will be a measurable increase in policing practice based on research.
- Members will be routinely assessed in their annual performance development review (PDR) and for selection for promotion or specialisms, on their application and development of evidence-based practice.[2]

The core of the What Works Centre consists of an academic consortium grant-funded by the College and the Economic and Social Research Council to synthesise and summarise research on crime reduction. Our institute – The Institute for Criminal Policy Research, Birkbeck, University of London – is part of the consortium, but our role is to mount an independent evaluation of the What Works Centre. This chapter presents some of the findings that have emerged by the end of the second year. Its structure is as follows. We start by summarising the activities of the What Works Centre and some of its achievements to date. We then present findings that give a sense of the extent to which the police have adopted principles of evidence-based policing (EBP).[3] We present findings from two case studies of potential 'opinion leaders' or 'opinion changers' working within the police. In addition to the case studies, we detail the views on progress of the various groups involved in the What Works Centre. To anticipate our findings, the evaluation suggests a large gap between the College's aspirations for evidence-based policing and the status quo. We end with an analysis of our findings and present thoughts about future developments, including suggestions for bridging the gap between aspiration and the reality.

The case study findings presented here are drawn from interviews with 19 'evidence champions', and with seven officers who had been selected for, and mostly completed, the High Potential Development Scheme (HPDS). Evidence champions are individuals within a police force, usually police officers below the rank of chief inspector (middle manager) who act as mediators between producers of research and police practitioners; they are expected to promote awareness of research evidence and ensure that it is taken into account in policy and practice.

HPDS officers are those who have demonstrated that they have the potential to be future leaders. At the start of their course they will usually be a police constable or sergeant, and most would expect to be promoted whilst participating in the scheme, which lasts five years and includes presentations on the relevance and importance of EBP. Both groups of officers should be well placed within their organisations to disseminate knowledge and promote EBP practices. In addition to these two groups we present views of College staff, the academics involved in producing and refining the evidence base and other well-informed stakeholders about the centre's evolution. More details about the methods and wider findings can be found in our evaluation reports.[4]

Work to date: the What Works Centre's Products

The What Works Centre coordinates and manages a number of initiatives, which range from housing the National Police Library and hosting 'The Research Map' (or directory of research) to coordinating a £10 million Police Knowledge Fund.[5] Given how tightly professional knowledge is interrelated with other features of the College's professionalisation process, the boundaries of the What Works Centre within and beyond the College are inevitably porous. The What Works Centre is, however, committed to delivering various 'core products' that relate to the provision of research evidence on policing. These include:

- Identifying pre-existing systematic reviews of research into crime reduction.
- Carrying out additional systematic reviews where there is scope for doing so.
- Providing web-based summaries of pre-existing and new systematic reviews in terms of the quality, cost and impact of interventions; the mechanisms by which the impact is achieved; and the ways in which contexts determine impact and implementation issues.
- Providing police officers, Police Crime Commissioners[6] (PCCs) and others with a remit to tackle crime, with the knowledge, tools and guidance to help them target their resources more effectively.

Figure 9.1 illustrates some of the key mechanisms which ultimately deliver the College's core products.

The products and the mechanisms delivering these products are the main elements of what we have described as a 'push strategy', aimed at getting the police to adopt principles of evidence-based policing (Hunter et al., 2016). The idea is that organisations will automatically make use of evidence on effectiveness if this evidence is 'pushed' towards them in attractive and accessible ways. Increasingly, however, the College of Policing has recognised the need for 'pull strategies' that create an organisational appetite for research evidence. These strategies involve the creation of organisational incentives to adopt EBP principles (cf Langer et al., 2016). Thus work is in hand to make EBP principles more prominent in police training and to ensure that staff selection and promotion procedures attach greater weight to the adoption of these principles as core criteria. It is becoming

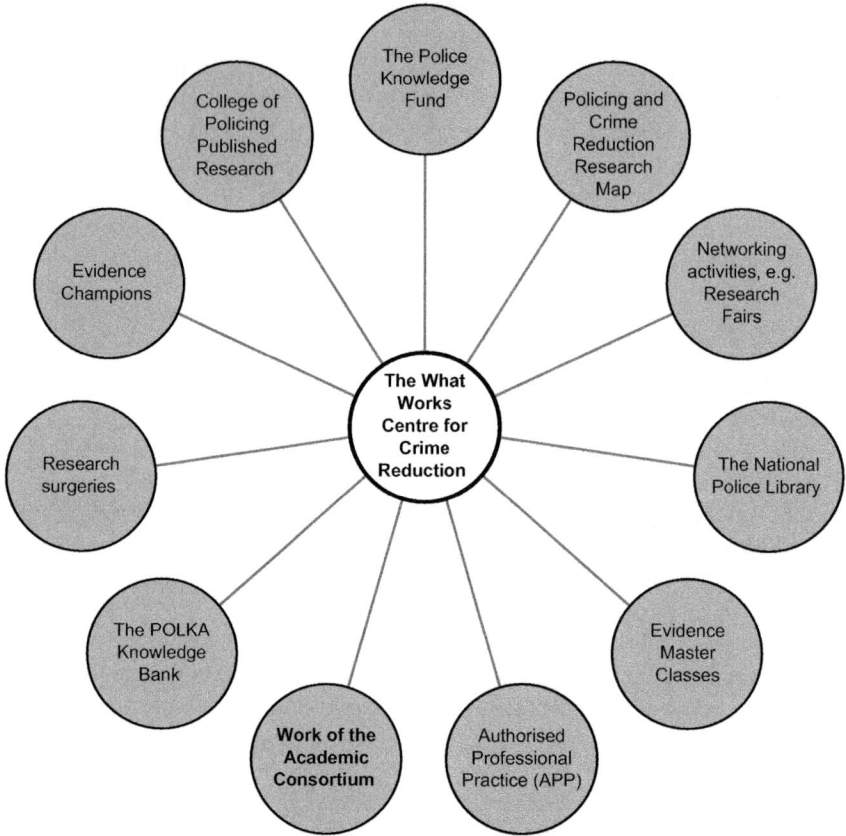

Figure 9.1   Key evidence mechanisms of the WWCCR

increasingly clear to all those involved in the What Works Centre that there needs
to be a better and more detailed understanding of the influence of 'push' and the
'pull' strategies and how these influence the adoption of EBP principles throughout an organisation and the extent to which such principles are accepted and valued within the professional culture (cf Ritter and Lancaster, 2013).

Progress in embedding EBP principles

Our report on the first year of the What Works Centre (Hunter et al., 2015) painted
a picture of slow progress down the road towards the adoption of EBP principles.
We found that from inspectors to chief constables:

- Research evidence is one factor among many that affects decision-making.
- Professional judgement and advice from colleagues are key influences on
  decision-making.

- A common complaint about research from academics and researchers was that it is long winded, full of jargon and lacking clear messages.
- Time is limited, and a Google search is the go-to information source.

This picture should not, however, be viewed as an indicator of the willingness of police officers to adopt EBP principles, but should be seen as a gauge of the types of evidence currently sought and used by police officers and an indicator of the perceived barriers to the greater take-up of research. It should also be highlighted that traditionally, the police have been measured and judged by their arrest and conviction rates; only recently, in the last five or so years, has the over-reliance on the performance culture been questioned, challenged and gradually replaced. Encouraging officers to move from a culture of measurement and targets to one of critically appraising the available evidence and problem-solving will undoubtedly take time, especially given the structure of policing and the unpredictable nature and immediacy of the problems that need solving. It is clear that research evidence is only one factor that enters into the decision-making process in policing; it is still a relatively small factor in comparison to the legal requirements and organisational regulations, professional judgement, craft traditions, performance management systems and the less formal features of the organisational culture that determines which people get rewarded in policing. EBP is still very much in competition with these daily pressures faced by both operational and senior police officers. It is unsurprising therefore that the uptake of adopting the principles of EBP has, to date, been slow. Awareness of the What Works Centre products was (unsurprisingly) very limited, and there was considerable scepticism about the aspirations of evidence-based policing. Over the second year there has been substantial progress in populating the toolkit and in developing a more sophisticated set of push and pull strategies to promote EBP principles. However, it is also becoming clear that it will take considerable time to achieve the cultural shift towards valuing evidence and attaching importance to a professional knowledge base. Findings from our case studies of evidence champions and officers selected to take part in a High Potential Development Scheme (HPDS) illustrate this only too clearly.

Evidence and frontline champions

Evidence champions are individuals within a police force who act as mediators between the researcher/research organisation and other police practitioners, helping to promote and filter evidence into viable policy and practice. The 'champion' as an essential component of knowledge mobilisation or knowledge to action strategy is well established in the literature (e.g. Nutley et al., 2007). Their role is variously described as 'intermediary', 'broker', 'messenger', 'opinion leader' or 'role model', but essentially, these are individuals who will act as a mediator between the researcher and other practitioners, helping to promote and filter evidence into viable policy and practice (Cherney and Head, 2011). There are various examples of such roles, including the Student Champions Scheme run by NICE which recruits and trains students to disseminate information about the organisation to fellow students, or Project Oracle Evidence Champions – commissioners and funders of programmes for young people whose role is to 'promote an understanding of the significance of embedding evidence and evaluation in the commissioning process'.

Two types of champions are endorsed by the College: frontline champions, who are operational officers recruited and paid for by the College for a period of six months to raise awareness of the College and its programmes and services and to act as a point of liaison between the College and force; this initiative preceded the What Works Centre. The network of Evidence Champions was an initiative developed as part of the What Works Centre in 2013 to encourage discussion and collaboration amongst peers about evidence-informed practice both within and across forces. This was a voluntary role and open to anyone with an interest in research.

Most of our interviewees described the aims of the role in terms of being a 'mediator' or 'go-between' for the College and force, and in the words of one champion as doing the 'PR for research' but also to embed or normalise the use of research evidence in everyday work by identifying evidence for good practice or encouraging and developing capacity for evaluative research within the force in order to adapt or develop crime reduction initiatives. Champions were of varying police rank, comprising Police Community Support Officers[7] (PCSOs) to chief inspector but also civilian staff linked to analytic or corporate departments and the Police and Crime Commissioners' offices. Sixteen of the 19 were educated to at least the degree level and two had (or were working towards) a doctorate. A personal interest in research or academic study was often cited as a reason why they had been suggested for the role; sometimes it was considered to fit well with their existing activities, and others were self-nominated rather than selected by their force or they became involved after having some contact with staff at the College.

We found no standard model of how a champion was deployed; although, as noted, frontline champions were operationally based, there was sometimes a clear structure in which the champion role was positioned, for example, in departments focused on organisational learning or evaluation and improvement, or within the office of Police and Crime Commissioner, with clarity about line management (and link to chief officer team) and roles and tasks to be undertaken. But sometimes, the role was less formalised or integrated and therefore much more influenced by an individual's personal interest and enthusiasm for research:

> It's not really [line managed.] It kind of happened organically just through the work I do, the academic stuff I do and the contact with the College of Policing, you start getting invited to things. They do have an actual evidence-based policing lead in the force who is a superintendent but I don't report to them. I don't have any contact with them.
>
> [C9]

Additionally, the role was rarely full-time and tended to be fitted in alongside other responsibilities. The priority it was given is illustrated, in part, by the time allowed to undertake 'champion' activity. However, most champions discussed the impact of having limited resources and how this lack of resource impeded the championing of research:

> I went from probably spending 15% of my time doing this down to about 5% at the moment, and I do a lot of my own time on it . . . it's very piecemeal.
>
> [C11]

Champions reported a wide range of activities with some tasks – listed next – such as overseeing academic partnerships or creating inventories of force research activity or offering information to other officers about research. More commonly mentioned tasks included:

- Developing or managing partnerships with universities.
- Reviewing knowledge gaps and the research needs of the force.
- Developing systems for feeding learning from research into practice.
- Auditing or cataloguing research undertaken within the force to ensure greater knowledge about what work had already been done to avoid duplication.
- Coordinating force involvement in the Knowledge Fund bids.[8]
- Raising awareness of the evidence base in strategic or leadership meetings or in particular areas or using evidence to challenge 'received wisdom'.
- Developing or quality-assuring in-house evaluations for assessing force policy and practice.
- Organising seminars to promote research evidence for a range of ranks.
- Promoting the work of the College of Policing and the What Works Centre (including the Crime Reduction Toolkit).

On this last point, most of the Champions we interviewed were aware of the toolkit, but a majority said that they had either given it only a cursory glance or not looked at it at all. Only a minority had reviewed its content in detail, and their comments were not especially positive. In part this simply reflected the fact that the toolkit was still being developed and limited the amount of available information – a problem that can be solved only over time. But criticisms also included the fact that much of the research was North American, what was available was dated and it failed to address the specific questions on which they were seeking answers. Although the academics developed EMMIE to provide research-based insights to *support* decision-making, some users failed to understand this and simply wanted a system that removed professional judgement and uncertainty from decision-making and told them what to do in any given situation. This desire for simplicity and certainty was not universal, however, and some thought the toolkit oversimplified:

> I like the EMMIE framework. I think that's quite good. My initial view was I like the layers of information, but I think there needs to be another layer, of more complex information . . . There are pockets of individuals who do

understand research and have a background in research. We've got quite a number of people who are in the service doing PhDs.

[C1]

Other comments included unhappiness at a perceived lack of practitioner consultation[9] about its content and design and a view that the multiplicity of tasks undertaken by police – and the limited research available that met the evidence standard for the toolkit – demanded a forum for dissemination of 'good enough research' of observational studies or exploratory research into emerging problems:

I know what the What Works Centre funding is about, but policing is so multidisciplinary, it's got so many tasks and bits to deal with, and partners and everything else . . . public order policing tactics, for example . . . I wouldn't say I'm underwhelmed by the Toolkit. I think it's useful. I just think we need to go beyond that.

[C2]

The champions we interviewed were generally cautious about discussing impacts of their role on the status of evidence-informed practice in their force, often stressing their work was a long-term rather than a short-term endeavour. The activities they reported ranged from raising awareness to 'laying the groundwork' or 'setting up the framework' for promoting and embedding evidence-informed practice.

It's certainly not embedded at a force-level. If you went and asked 100 Chief Inspectors about EBP, you would probably get two or three who had heard of it. I sit and wax lyrical about it quite a lot of the time and people find it really interesting. I've done lots of presentations in the force around Hot Spot and the evidence regarding it, and people generally find it quite interesting . . . They use me to go and promote it because I present the case quite well, I guess. I'm quite passionate about it.

[C11]

High-potential development scheme (HPDS) Officers

The HPDS ran from 2002 until 2016 and was a national scheme. Its aim was to prepare for future leadership roles those officers who demonstrated potential. In the current policing climate this meant preparing officers who had excelled in an operational capacity, were astute, were academically able and were innovative thinkers. Successful HPDS officers were expected to understand new ideas and track the development and relative merits of new initiatives. The overriding objective of HPDS was to increase the quantity and quality of future chief officers. In terms of embedding evidence-informed practice, these officers are crucial to future strategic development and thus constitute key opinion leaders. Our interviews with HPDS officers provided some useful insights into levels of progress in adopting EBP principles. Most of them recalled a methods course which had included an introduction to the academic world, essay writing, research methodologies and the appropriateness of quantitative and qualitative approaches. All remembered the module on the usefulness of evidence-informed practice. Some responses on research aspects of the scheme are detailed next:

> I remember we did quite a big module on evidence based policing and spent quite a bit of time on it . . . We had our eyes opened to what gold standard research looks like i.e., what the medical profession looks like. We all realised that police research, so-called police research doesn't meet any standard at all because we just do an operation and something happened . . . Now we realise that it might have been due to the weather or a good film on telly or anything like that going on.
>
> [HPDS 2]

None of the HPDS officers reported very extensive use of the toolkit. One thought a Google search was easier to use, and another preferred to call colleagues if he had a 'research' question. The following comments detail some of their views:

> Yes, I've been on the website, I've looked at EMMIE. I think it's basic, it's quite simple, it's straightforward to use.
>
> [HPDS 4]

> It's interesting, I think the challenge is – how do we make it so that some of the What Works information is really relevant to people and actually feasible for people to start to use in their own force.
>
> [HPDS 6]

Only two officers, although not personally involved, were aware of collaborations between their home force and local universities; one had previously held the position of university liaison officer, and another noted his force and local university was also in receipt of a Home Office Innovation grant.[10]

We asked the officers how 'research savvy' they considered their home force to be. Their various responses highlighted commonly raised problems, including a perceived disconnect between having an awareness of research and its value and knowing how to apply this to strategic and operational decision-making:

> I think we are becoming more open to it [EBP]. We've got a couple of examples now where we've seen evidence-based projects, and we've actually incorporated them into our workings. That's possibly because we've now got a new Chief Officer team. I would say that senior officers and strategic posts may be more research savvy, as opposed to operational. I don't think EBP has filtered down as far as operational staff. Certainly, between senior and middle management ranks, I think we're seeing more, and we're more open to that idea of 'Actually, it worked there, so rather than making something up, let's use that'.
>
> [HPDS 3]

And there was a wariness or cynicism among senior staff about research which may prevent change or innovation:

> We continually do the same things over and over and over again, which aren't bad; we do deliver a really good service to members of the public, but we never really look at how we can take that next step and make things more efficient. Research would drive that, but research isn't really trusted . . . it just isn't really accepted at a high level within the organisation.
>
> [HPDS 1]

Being able to challenge and engage in healthy debate is viewed as an essential ingredient of a culture which critically evaluates evidence. The traditional command-and-control structure of policing was viewed as an impediment to this type of interaction:

> There are a lot of people in the organisation that would not challenge me as a superintendent because I am a superintendent. Even if the thing I said was the most absolutely ludicrous, ridiculous thing in the world – yes, there might be some grumbles, but it's surprising how much people will do and not push back just because it's a rank talking. That's not how to deliver a service.
>
> [HPDS 6]

Although all the HPDS officers felt that they had benefitted academically and all had excelled at the course work and assignments, none had engaged with the toolkit in any more than a superficial way. The skills they had learned appeared to enhance their career progression prospects but had not been exploited. HPDS officers were not universally viewed by their forces as an invaluable conduit for evidence-informed practice to reach operational ranks. There appeared to be a disconnect between the scheme, individual learning and dissemination at the force level.

The What Works agenda as a long-term project

What has become increasingly clear to all of those involved in the What Works Centre is that infusing the police service with EBP principles is a much more ambitious project than originally appreciated. The way in which the What Works Centre is intertwined with the College of Policing's agenda for professionalising the police makes it much harder to assess than would be the case if it were a free-standing evidence warehouse. Some interviewees felt they had grossly overestimated the ability of the What Works Centre to effect rapid change at the outset of the venture:

> There is no parallel whatsoever between evidence-based medicine and evidence-based policing. Evidence-based policing is a small group of enthusiasts. It is not embraced by large quantities of the police, and it's not understood by senior people in policing. The size of the task is way, way, way greater than that which I had thought . . . When I'm asked, "Has the What

Works Centre met your expectations in its first two years?" my expectations were seriously inappropriate at the beginning . . . We've got 'EMMIE'. Great. We can talk about what we've done. Has it made a difference to policing? I don't believe it has yet. I don't think that should necessarily be seen as a failure, because of the scale of the task.

[S1]

There was a strong consensus amongst most interviewees that the impact of the work would only become evident in the longer term as illustrated by the following quote:

It's not sensible to expect any measurable change within a three-year time-scale. It's ridiculous. Given the size of the tanker that they are trying to turn around, the base from which the police had started in terms of their views of research, their knowledge of What Works and their experience on just about anything to do with what we might regard as academic.

[AC3]

Presentation and communication

A small number of respondents were critical of the way in which the 'What Works agenda' had been presented by the College of Policing. In particular, the use of the terminology 'evidence-based policing' – rather than, for example, evidence-informed policing – was seen to be problematic. This was so for two reasons. First, there was concern that the terminology had conceptualised the evidence agenda as replacing professional judgement, rather than supplementing it, which risked research being viewed as a threat. Second, such language was seen to create unrealistic expectations that research evidence can tell someone what to do in response to a specific problem, whereas the reality is more complex:

'Evidence-based policing' as a phrase is very simplistic and it kind of implies there is a bucket full of evidence here and all you have got to do is dip into it and you will have the answer. That's totally wrong and it always will be.

[AC3]

I just think the evidence-based kind of thing is misleading . . . They ought to take into account the evidence that is available to them but that doesn't mean that their decision should be defined on the evidence.

[AC5]

In this context, it was also highlighted that there are many research gaps remaining in crime reduction, meaning that in some areas there is no evidence for 'what works'. There was consequent apprehension that the credibility of the What Works

Centre – and the success of the wider evidence agenda – might be undermined if it was unable to meet the expectations that it had created:

> The college, the What Works Centre is heading for a massive great embarrassing crash on its face . . . they're going to say 'what's the evidence for that?' and most of the time the answer is going to be 'there isn't any'.
>
> [AC3].

Resistance to change

There was no underestimating the challenge for the College of Policing and for the What Works Centre in changing the thinking and attitudes of police, and the way in which practitioners were involved in this process was considered crucial:

> People will be resistant for a long time, and it's about how you manage that, and how you explain what you're trying to do to people and with people. What we know about any kind of successful change is you have to do change with people, not to people.
>
> [CP1]

As highlighted earlier by our interviewees, affecting change in any large-scale organisation takes time. Unlike other professions, decisions taken by operational police officers are rarely guided by evidence. If an arrest needs to be made, the decision is guided by law; if a situation needs to be managed, the decision is often guided by good judgement and discretion. Very little of an officer's early policing career (to date) involves assessing the evidence of what works and implementing change in accordance with this evidence. It is unsurprising, therefore, that operational officers and middle management have been cautious about engaging with the What Works agenda. Police culture, which has been extensively observed, analysed and documented, has tended to frown upon and mistrust academics and academic outputs (Green and Gates, 2014; Flynn and Herrington, 2015; Rojek et al., 2015). Academics and stakeholders all spoke about the resistance from officers to evidence-informed practice, concluding that the lack of engagement between academics and police officers provided a partial explanation for officers' mistrust of academia and all that it has to offer.

> I think it's right that the police get extremely irritated at the idea of a bunch of academics telling them what to do, it is unacceptable. That's why we should be at pains to tell the police, categorically, that is not what this is about. This is about trying to help you make better decisions, not tell you what those decisions should be.
>
> [AC3]

One of the stakeholder interviewees highlighted the importance of engaging with the entire workforce for evidence-informed practice to be accepted and not viewed as yet another passing fad:

> That culture is not there in policing, and until it is, it will be very difficult to get evidence-based policing accepted more widely than by a group of enthusiasts . . . The real challenge is to get everybody in policing to understand how it's got to change.
>
> [S1]

Finally, interviewees discussed how resistance from rank-and-file officers and their representative body, the Police Federation, to the introduction of a minimum academic entry requirement is hindering the development of policing. Resistance to the professionalisation of the police is holding officers back and failing to equip them with the necessary skills that policing in the twenty-first century demands. The complexity of the situations police officers now face demand that they are equipped with more than just an understanding of the 'craft of policing'; officers now need to understand what works, in what situations and why, as highlighted here:

> Until we crack the 'cultural' thing about accepting that there should be some national standards which are done consistently, we won't get professionalism in policing.
>
> [S1]

The future

This chapter has sought to describe the evolution of the What Works Centre. Our 'headline finding' is that progress has been slow. However, this 'front-page news' masks a substantial amount of work undertaken by the What Works Centre over the past two years, including the systematic reviews of crime reduction interventions and their translation for practitioners, the design of the EMMIE system and the toolkit, and bespoke training for officers in appraising the research evidence. After two and a half years, the basic structures and outputs of the centre are in place. This is a significant achievement, even if the original ambitions for the centre were both ambitious and narrow. By this we mean that the College had large ambitions for getting an evidence warehouse off the ground, but narrow ambitions in not initially seeing (or at least not articulating) how this would contribute to, and be a central part of, its wider professionalisation agenda.

Furthermore, as we have stressed earlier, there have been additional developments, for example, to police training and professional practice, initiated or managed by the College of Policing which may fall outside any exacting remit of the What Works Centre but which all contribute to the solid base on which to build and sustain the What Works Centre.

A central and ambitious aim of the What Works Centre, however, is to change the organisational culture of police and other crime reduction practitioners, to increase their use of evidence for policy and strategic decision-making and, in essence, to make evidence use a 'professional norm'. This is no easy feat when other more traditional approaches to decision-making based on professional judgement are deeply ingrained, prompting one of our interviewees to describe the project as 'turning around a tanker'.

In achieving this change, we suggest that there would be considerable value in the College articulating a theory of change more fully. This might include:

- The rationale for moving to an 'evidence-informed' style of decision-making.
- The key groups (ranks of officers, particular departments, etc.) whose decision-making style is being targeted.
- The mix of strategies that is being deployed to achieve this change in decision-making style.
- How these are linked and coordinated.

Adopting EBP is tightly intertwined with ambitions to professionalise policing: a central criterion for regarding an occupation as a profession is that best practice is defined by a body of well-established knowledge. There is a strong case to be made for policing reform that shifts policy and practice toward the professional end of the spectrum. However, as the policing environment becomes more complex and less predictable, we can see good arguments in favour of some form of professional accountability over traditional 'command and control' management. In our view, this form of accountability might involve providing frontline staff with more autonomy, on the one hand, and, on the other, giving them the knowledge tools needed to exercise this autonomy effectively.

The previous paragraph has briefly illustrated what a rationale for professionalisation might look like. This may not be the best or only way of setting out the aims of professionalisation, but it would be helpful for the service to have *some* clear articulation of what professionalisation involves and why it is important for the future of policing. We appreciate, however, that setting out clear and precise aims is not always the best way of building a consensus for change. However, the value of making such a statement has to be judged against the context of a lack of understanding about what professionalisation and evidence-informed decision-making actually involve and the scepticism that many police officers feel about what they regard as a fad of evidence-informed decision-making.

A theory of change would also need to identify the target groups for change and what sort of change is needed for each target group. Target groups will depend on the model of professionalisation that is being proposed, but if the aim is to provide frontline staff with more professional autonomy, it is clear that they must form an essential target group.

There is increasing evidence about the best mix of strategies to achieve a shift in the direction of evidence-informed decision-making. At the start of their lives, What Works Centres have tended to focus effort on 'push strategies' that make evidence available to decision-makers. We would argue that the College's push strategies are taking shape well, with the Crime Reduction Toolkit at their heart. However, there is still room for creating a more balanced economy of push and pull strategies. In examining the scope for broadening the range of strategies for stimulating evidence use, we have used as our starting point some of the categories of evidence-use mechanisms defined by the Alliance for Useful Evidence (2016); in so doing we can highlight where headway is being made and where adjustments or further work are vital.

Building awareness, understanding and support towards using evidence

We found limited engagement with the What Works Centre, or more specifically with the Crime Reduction Toolkit, at the time of our interviews, including amongst those who are intended to help 'push' or embed the evidence agenda such as the Evidence Champions or HPDS officers. Reasons offered included doubts about the relevance of the toolkit to most police decisions. In time, there is clearly a need to broaden the scope of the toolkit beyond crime reduction and to find a means of including nonexperimental research, especially in areas of emerging interest for the police, such as cybercrime. If academics and researchers actively seek to meet the needs of policing, it is likely that the curiosity of officers regarding how research is generated will be stimulated. In essence there needs to be a move towards 'focusing on what people care about' if we want to improve the chances of officers seeking out evidence when attempting to problem-solve or look for new ways to tackle old problems.

Care still needs to be taken with the format and content of the material that is 'pushed out'. In particular, it would be worth considering finding an alternative to the label of 'evidence based decision-making', which many perceive as giving insufficient recognition to the role of professional judgement. In our view, the approach taken by the Alliance for Useful Evidence, which talks about 'evidence-informed decision-making', is preferable.

Building agreement on the relevant questions to seek answers to

We have noted the limitations of the current evidence base and how this will likely impede any large-scale conversion of police officers to the utility of using evidence to inform practice. However, at a force level and through the work of the Evidence Champions there is scope to initiate a conversation about the kinds of research questions that the police service need answered and how to support officers who are undertaking academic study to better match dissertation or doctorate research to knowledge gaps.

The co-production of research and building sustainable partnerships between police forces and academic institutions in England and Wales is the aim of the Knowledge Fund, and the process and outcomes of those various collaborations will be hugely important in cementing future relationships and matching research to knowledge needs.

Access and communication: providing communication of, and access to, evidence

A great deal of work and thought has gone into the 'packaging' of evidence for crime reduction practitioners. The toolkit and the EMMIE system were designed in response to common practitioner criticisms about the unnecessary complexity or long-windedness of academic research and the failure of academics to translate findings usefully for a practice audience. One area of difficulty has been communicating the uncertainty of the research evidence on crime reduction interventions – rarely does it provide unequivocal answers to the 'what works' question, and thus toolkit users need to think about how interventions would be applied in their local context. Building capacity to critically appraise research findings in this way is another important task for the College of Policing and the What Works Centre (discussed next).

Promote interaction between decision-makers and researchers

The Police Knowledge Fund, coordinated by the College of Policing, is a key mechanism for bringing together police and academic researchers. Cultivating academic partnerships was also a common activity reported by the evidence champions we interviewed and was being prioritised by many forces.

The network of evidence and frontline champions is another structure through which researchers and decision-makers are intended to interact, and there is considerable scope to develop the current network initiated by the College. Such roles naturally attract the research enthusiasts within forces – we have shown the range of activities they have been involved in – and with some clarity of purpose and a more defined place within force strategic organisation, one can envisage how their positive attitude towards research could be 'infectious'.

Support skill development

Most of those we interviewed for our evaluation were educated to the degree level (Hunter et al., 2015, 2016), and often this had been done as part of career development, with some proportion of fees funded by the police, although it was noted that there is much less resource for this now. There is a strategy in place for enhancing skills in appraising and making use of the research evidence – this includes specific activities run by the College of Policing and academics to increase engagement with the evidence such as Evidence Base Camp or toolkit training, but there are also wider curriculum changes to embed an understanding of research into basic recruitment training for police constables and in the National Policing Curriculum. Again consistency in content and aims and some clear framework for continuous development of skills in this area will be important across these various curriculum and training initiatives.

Promote a culture of experimentation among senior police managers

The police service is accustomed to facing challenges; indeed it has always moved with the times to keep abreast of new and evolving criminal behaviours and legislation. However, although many senior officers actively promote experimentation and innovation, it is perhaps the exception rather than the norm in some force areas. Encouraging and nurturing a culture of experimentation has the potential to become a significant 'pull' factor to embedding EBP principles, as inventive and creative ideas need to be informed and supported by both policing colleagues and the available evidence. A healthy police force is one where innovation is encouraged, nurtured and supported. Organisational change in any large institution, however, can take time and is likely to require architects and champions. There is no doubt in our minds that these architects and champions already exist across the forces and ranks in policing.

By way of conclusion we should stress a theme that some interviewees developed. Retreating from the project of developing a professional evidence base for policing would have very heavy costs for the College of Policing and for the police service more generally. Because this project is so tightly entwined with the broader professionalisation agenda, a retreat from EBP principles could destabilise the latter. This would be a seriously retrograde step for UK policing.

Notes

1 National Institute for Health and Care Excellence (NICE), Sutton Trust/Educational Endowment Foundation, College of Policing What Works Centre for Crime Reduction, Early Intervention Foundation, What Works for Local Economic Growth, the Centre for Ageing Better and the What Works Centre for Wellbeing.
2 Taken from the College of Policing 'Our Functions file:///C:/Users/tiggey%20may/Downloads/CoP_Guide_2016%20(1).pdf.
3 Evidence-informed and evidence-based policing are often used interchangeably, even though there are subtle but important differences between the two terms. Ostensibly, however, they refer to imbuing evidence into the world of police practice.
4 Hunter, G., Wigzell, A., Bhardwa, B., May, T. and Hough, M. (2016). *An Evaluation of the 'What Works Centre for Crime Reduction': Year 2: Progress*, London: ICPR. Retrieved from http://whatworks.college.police.uk/About/Documents/ICPREvaluation WHAT WORKS CENTRE.pdf.
5 This particular initiative was jointly resourced in 2015 by the Home Office and the Higher Education Funding Council for England (HEFCE). Fifteen bids were funded involving 39 (of the 43) forces, 30 universities, the British Transport Police, the Police Service of Northern Ireland and the National Crime Agency. All the successful bids are partnerships involving police forces and universities; some are in the process of developing regional evidence-based hubs, whereas others are collaborating on research in areas such as cybercrime and mental health issues.
6 Police and Crime Commissioners (PCCs) replaced Police Authorities in 2012; every force area is represented by a PCC, except Greater Manchester and London, where PCC responsibilities lie with the mayor. The role of the PCC is to be the voice of the people and hold the police to account; they are responsible for the totality of policing. The aim of PCCs is to cut crime and deliver an effective and efficient police service within their force area. PCCs have been elected by the public to hold Chief Constables and the force to account, effectively making the police answerable to the communities they serve.
7 'PCSO's are uniformed staff whose role is to support the work of police officers within the community. Their role is to assist the police in certain areas, acting as the eyes and ears on the streets. PCSOs particularly work to reassure the public and to tackle the social menace of anti-social behaviour'. www.cambs.police.uk/recruitment/pcso/role.asp.

8 'The Police Knowledge Fund provides opportunities for officers and staff to get involved in innovative approaches to policing and crime reduction. The fund is a joint initiative between the College of Policing and HEFCE. It is resourced by the Home Office and HEFCE, who are also administering the fund'. www.college.police.uk/News/College-news/Pages/Police-Knowledge-Fund.aspx.

9 Although there was a perceived lack of consultation, the College of Policing did conduct an extensive consultation process with a range of stakeholders, which included the police.

10 The Home Office Innovation fund is available to all police forces in England and Wales. Applicants are encouraged to submit projects aimed at transforming policing through innovation and collaboration.

References

Breckon, J. and Dodson, J. (2016). *Using Evidence: What Works*. A Discussion Paper, Alliance for Useful Evidence, London file, Retrieved from :///R:/ESRC%20What%20Works%20College%20of%20Policing/Kongsvinger/Alliance-Policy-Using-evidence-v4.pdf

Cherney, A. and Head, B. (2011). 'Supporting the knowledge-to-action process: A systems-thinking approach, *Evidence and Policy'*, 7(4): 471–88.

Flynn, E.A. and Herrington, V. (2015). 'Toward a Profession of Police Leadership', *New Perspectives in Policing Bulletin*, Washington, DC: US Department of Justice, National Institute of Justice, NCJ 248573.

Green, T. and Gates, A. (2014). 'Understanding the process of professionalisation in the police organisation', *Police Journal Theory, Practice and Principles*, 87: 75–91.

Hunter, G., Wigzell, A., Bhardwa, B., May, T. and Hough, M. (2016). *An Evaluation of the What Works Centre for Crime Reduction Year 2: Progress*, London: ICPR.

Hunter, G., Wigzell, A., May, T. and McSweeney, T. (2015). *An Evaluation of the What Works Centre for Crime Reduction Year 1: Baseline*, London: ICPR.

Langer, L., Tripney, J. and Gough, D. (2016). *The Science of Using Science: Researching the Use of Research Evidence in Decision-Making*, London: Institute of Education.

NPIA. (2010). *Policing Knowledge: Sharing What We Know, Learning What We Don't: An Action Plan for Improving Knowledge Use in Policing 2010–2012*, London: National Policing Improvement Agency.

Nutley, S., Walter, I. and Davis, H. (2007). *Using Evidence. How Research Informs Public Services*, Bristol: Policy Press.

Ritter, A. and Lancaster, K. (2013). 'Policy Models and Influences on Policy Processes', in A. Ritter, T. King and M. Hamilton (eds) *Drug Use in Australian Society*, pp. 99–132, Oxford: University Press, Australia, Retrieved from www.oup.com.au/titles/higher_ed/health_sciences/9780195518863

Rojek, J., Martin, P. and Alpert, G.P. (2015). *Developing and Maintaining Police-Researcher Partnerships to Facilitate Research Use: A Comparative Analysis*, New York: Springer-Verlag.

Sherman, L.W. (2013). 'The rise of evidence-based policing: Targeting, testing, and tracking', *Crime and Justice*, 42(1): 377–451.

10 Advancing policing by using, producing and diffusing evidence

Johannes Knutsson

This chapter is about how an innovative police scheme to support management of protest events – dialogue policing – was established by the Swedish police. The scheme has become an integrated function in the new national tactic for crowd management and control. How dialogue policing originated, its principles, its implementation process, how it fared over a longer time perspective, transmission to other countries, and how it was researched will be accounted for. During the process, research evidence[1] played distinct roles. It was used, produced, and diffused in an iterative process over a prolonged period and in multiple countries.

Commonly a paper's format is research question, earlier research, theory, data, result, and discussion. Chance factors, creative progression, idiosyncrasies, irregularities, and threats that occur along the way are usually omitted. Full accounts of implementing new policing tactics are rare,[2] and it is to this gap in the literature that I attempt to contribute to with this descriptive chapter from an insider perspective. My hope is that it might be useful for academics interested in applied police research to get an understanding of how it might be 'out there in the field', as well as for practitioners to get some insights into how researchers may act and react in these kinds of processes.

Applied research and researcher role

The intention with applied police research is to provide the police with policy-relevant research evidence. It means, to put it somewhat pointedly, research carried out for and with the police (Cockbain and Knutsson, 2015). One way for the police to increase utilisation of science is to embed researchers in the organisation (Tillyer et al., 2014; Braga and Davis, 2014). This creates an opportunity for the researcher to have long-standing relations with the police, to have more direct access to the organisation and its data, and thus to be in an advantageous position to support the police with research evidence.

I was employed by the police[3] as an embedded researcher, meaning that I had access to the police organisation, to key personnel, and could prospectively follow and study its practise for an extended period. For a time I was involved in an implementation project of a new tactic for crowd management, of which dialogue policing is an integrated part. On recognising that the scheme constituted a genuine police innovation with strong potential to improve tactics for policing crowds, I began to study and document the approach and asked police officer and researcher Stefan Holgersson[4] to be a collaborator.

Holgersson can similarly be categorised as an embedded researcher. He was one of the architects of dialogue policing, practiced it for several years, and on his own initiative authored a report about it (Holgersson, 2008). He also served as a uniformed police officer in many protest demonstrations when the traditional tactics were in use (including in Gothenburg, 2001, see later). This was a conventional crowd management tactic based primarily on police show of force and, when considered necessary, use of force. It was practiced more or less in the same fashion, irrespective of the type of crowd and the reasons for the rally. As one commander later commented on this tactic when I interviewed him, 'it was an aggressive wall of meat'.

Holgersson also possesses rich experiential knowledge of the new tactic of crowd management through serving as uniformed officer, group, and squad leader.

Eck (2015) has described the two principal approaches we employed in our research. According to one, a researcher (or practitioner) gets insights into a problem which is interpreted in light of an existing theoretical framework. This is applicable to Holgersson, whose experiences of crowd dynamics was the starting point. According to the other process, relevant to me, a researcher begins with a theoretical framework from which perceptions of a problem are selected and interpreted. My assumption was that if the new tactic was effective, situational crime preventive techniques (see, e.g., Clarke, 2007) were bound to be employed.

Our intention was to validate the tactic, its principles, and theoretical foundation. The result (Holgersson and Knutsson, 2011) underlines another of Eck's points (2015), namely that close collaboration between police officers and researchers can give rise to testable ideas and provide guidance for effective actions to reduce problems.

This research was not commissioned by the police. We did it on our own initiative motivated by a conviction that the model represented an achievement,[5] and that a study would be valuable for the police concerning a core task with implications for democratic societies' basic values. Our aim was in line with Tilley's (2015) argument: that an important function for applied police research is to assist the police, providing them with better theories than the ones usually employed.

In endeavours like this researchers primarily report to, and in this context interact with, the upper police bureaucracy. In such a relationship researchers' motivation, curiosity, ethos, and ethics must reconcile with the police organisation and its culture. Researchers highly value academic prowess and can be particularly sensitive about integrity and independence (Knutsson, 2015). Greene (2015) characterises this relationship in allegory as that between tango dancers where the ability to lead and follow, to change roles and rhythm, and to improvise are important traits. As a researcher one must be prepared for unexpected events, and within reasonable limits, to adapt.

The police can be reserved and even suspicious to external examinations they cannot control. This may prove to be problematic for researchers – namely when officials in need of control with superficial academic insights deal with research issues and are empowered to influence the decisions. Even collaborative efforts may, especially when expectations do not agree, end up with frictions, and, in the worst case, termination of the relationship (Knutsson, 2015).

Core assumption of the new scheme

Dialogue policing is ultimately about how police can support freedom of speech and right of assembly. By entering a continuous channel of communication based on trust with protesters, indicating police willingness to facilitate the fundamental democratic right to express opinions, the police desire to diminish the apparent conflict between, on the one hand, their task to protect these rights and, on the other hand, the police duty to maintain public order. An assumption is that both parties will benefit: police will get more orderly protests and protesters will get increased attention to their ideas.

Impetus for reform: the riots in Gothenburg

Like in other cities where international meetings were held (Noakes and Gillham, 2006: 97), severe riots erupted in 2001 in Gothenburg during the European Union Summit (see, e.g., SOU, 2002; Peterson and Oskarsson, 2006). Matters did not improve by a visit from President George Bush. The riots and the police failure to control the violent protesters became a national calamity – this was something unprecedented in Sweden.

A committee appointed by the government headed by two senior politicians strongly criticised the police operation in Gothenburg (SOU, 2002). Their main conclusion was that Sweden needed a new national tactic to police mass events. It was proposed to be nonconfrontational and de-escalating and to include violence preventive strategies. The dialogue that specially appointed contact police officers had established with protester representatives was mentioned positively, and the committee suggested that the new tactic should include such a function.

The birth of dialogue policing: using experiential knowledge and research evidence

In 2002 a group of police negotiators was appointed by the Stockholm police management to serve as dialogue police officers (Holgersson included). Because no time was set aside to give substance to their new task, the officers suspected that this was merely lip service. The police management informed media that they now had dialogue police officers and could thus show that they had complied with the political request. But because management's supposition was that dialogue did not work, it could later be abolished with the argument that it was ineffective. Things could then go back to normal again – on the whole a rather common practice in police organisations to neutralise politically imposed unpopular ideas.

At this point in time the traditional tactic for crowd control still was in use. Dialogue policing hence came to be added on to the traditional tactic. It is important to note that such a scheme should not be seen as an isolated function. It is highly dependent on the rest of the police organisation and its tactic (see Gorringe and Rosie, 2013).

Left by themselves, the appointed officers started to work out what dialogue policing was about. The group was resourceful: they were all trained police negotiators; some had conducted university studies in different disciplines, and a few had served as military officers in UN peace missions in the Balkans with its strong ethnic conflicts. The method developed incrementally, largely building on the officers' experiences, but as will later be pointed out, an empirically founded theory also played a significant role.

To introduce such a model challenging conventional police wisdom requires police officers with courage to stand up for their beliefs and who are willing to contest traditional decision-making within the police. In an authoritarian hierarchical organisation like the police, this is a demanding task. In order to apply the new principles, dialogue police officers occasionally had to put pressure on police management. They even threatened to go public revealing police management's resistance. It is obvious that management did not anticipate that this group of officers would take their task this seriously and on their own initiative actually put substance to dialogue policing.

Dialogue policing

During rallies dialogue police officers, in civilian clothes and yellow vests marked *Dialogue police officer*, began moving inside or proximal to the crowds of protesters. Acting as an accessible communication link, information could immediately be exchanged between commanders and protester representatives. Dialogue police officers also monitored moods among protestors and gauged how that was affected by police activities, in addition to the mood among officers. This information was communicated to the commanders.

Dialogue police officers do not act physically. If the police are attacked, or if the police resort to use of force, dialogue officers withdraw but continue to observe and remain available. They visibly show that they are not part of forceful police actions by removing their vests but continue when things have calmed down. This was one means to build trust among protesters – something that is imperative for a mutually constructive dialogue.

Dialogue policing is a continual process where, in advance of rallies, the officers act as intermediaries between protesters and police commanders, aiming to get the best possible outcomes for both parties. During protests they strive to support protesters' legitimate wishes and act as links of communication. After rallies they discuss the occurrence with commanders and protester representatives and reflect on the opportunities for organisational learning.

Functioning inside or close to crowds, the dialogue police officers got a new perspective and understanding of how protesters perceive and react to the police in these particular situations. In the days of the traditional tactic, if a minority of protesters acted violently and aggressively, the whole collective could be treated as having aggressive tendencies. Instead of decreasing the number of persons acting violently towards the police, the traditional tactic could, potentially, exacerbate the situation. Initially, when the dialogue police officers began forming the scheme, they had observed peaceful protesters become violent in response to this practice which was common in the old tactic.

The dialogue police officers doubted their observations and instincts, but found a theory – the Elaborated Social Identity Model (ESIM) – that explained the processes at play (Reicher, 1996; Stott and Reicher, 1998; Stott and Drury, 2000; Reicher et al., 2004). In essence, ESIM says that if the police treat a group of protesters as homogenous with aggressive intentions, the resulting inter- and intragroup processes will make the group more coherent and the police will be perceived as an enemy. The arising dynamic group processes may thus result in an escalation, and people who initially had no aggressive predispositions might become prone to use violence against the police. A self-fulfilling prophecy is created. The dialogue officers had observed processes that accorded with this theory and could now refer to an accepted and well-substantiated theory corroborating their experiences.

Initially, it was difficult for commanders and police officers to see their actions as part of the problem; namely that the traditional police tactic in some instances was counterproductive – increasing instead of decreasing confrontations.

In the beginning dialogue officers were thoroughly disliked by both police and protesters. The police looked upon them as some kind of traitor – they had conspired with the protesters. Activists perceived the dialogue officers as an instrument of deception, providing the police with further means of control. However, slowly but surely attitudes changed.

To be accepted by leaders, and by sceptical and even hostile uniformed officers, a police officer with background as a SWAT team leader was promoted to become spokesman for dialogue policing. The idea was that a 'tough cop' would give legitimacy. He was placed in police headquarters as leader of the dialogue officers and was a strong advocate of the concept.

A decisive reason for the gradual acceptance of the dialogue policing scheme was positive experiences among commanders and protesters. The chances of fulfilling their respective objectives were generally higher when dialogue was practiced. To begin with, some brave commanders dared to follow advice from dialogue police officers. For instance, expected outbursts of violence did not come about. When these commanders found out that dialogue had positive effects, other leaders' willingness to try it increased. Protesters, on their side, discovered that attention could shift from their acts of violence to their message.

ESIM not only helped the dialogue police officers understand reactions to police actions from protesters; its principles for minimising tensions and confrontations between police and protesters also inspired the officers in developing and fine-tuning the scheme. Principally, ESIM's core philosophy was put into practice. When the new national tactic for crowd management was introduced in the late 2000s, dialogue policing had largely found its form and could just be added on.

Principles of the Special Police Tactic for crowd management

In 2004 the National Police Board decided on the founding principles for the new concept – the Special Police Tactic – and its organisation. About 1,200 police officers were trained in the tactic (Sweden has about 20,000 police officers). It is not a full-time assignment. All officers, including the commanders, work in their ordinary positions until need arises. Only the police regions with Sweden's biggest cities – Stockholm, Gothenburg and Malmö – have tactical units. The tactic is national in the sense that all units have the same training and when dealing with large, potentially troublesome mass events, they reinforce each other and act as a single united force.

Communication is central in this tactic. Through dialogue – where dialogue police officers have a crucial role – the police wish to facilitate protesters' efforts to achieve their legitimate goals. An important aim is to stimulate self-policing among protesters. From knowledge of different protester groups' perceptions of the police, they consider group processes between the police and protestors, as well as among police and activists, and the police attempt to avoid an escalation of hostility and aggression as an effect of police actions. Through intentional and consequent use of both verbal and nonverbal signalling (e.g., choice of police formation, whether blue lights are on or not on police vehicles, or helmets are worn or not) police readiness to use force is continuously conveyed to the crowd. The desired default value signifies a relaxed and controlled situation. Differentiation, where police act to avoid affecting a whole crowd if they need to intervene, is one method to avoid escalation. For these reasons the tactic's main principles are in agreement with ESIM.

Due to the experience that was gained, the execution and practice of the new tactic evolved (see later). However, there is no guarantee that relapses to the old tactic that heavily relied on show of and use of force will not occur. There are also some extreme situations where the only option for the police is to exercise force.

The Implementation Project: stimulating use of and producing research evidence

Implementing a radically new tactic is a slow undertaking. In 2007 when the process was well under way, the Swedish National Police Board decided to run a project, *Knowledge Development within the Special Police Tactics*, to support and follow up its implementation (see Adang, 2012). The project ran for three years and had three subgroups: a steering committee, who was responsible for the project's plan, budget, and the final report to the board; the reference group that had an advisory function; and a project group[6] giving input to the organisation and who did follow-ups of how the tactic was practiced.

As part of the project a number of national and international seminars were held with police commanders, police officers, instructors, and researchers. Many of the activities occurred in workshops. Examples of themes are explanations of ESIM principles where leading international experts made presentations, experiences of dialogue policing, or feedback from observed protest demonstrations. Interviews and a survey with attending police personnel indicated that initially the practitioners had a sceptical attitude towards the researchers, which gradually shifted to an open and receptive posture (Hilton and Wessman, 2013).

Method for follow-ups

Field observations, executed by instructors and police in collaboration with researchers, served as the method of follow-up of the actual performance of the tactic during protest rallies. However, it took some trials and failures before a working model for follow-ups could be implemented. In the aftermath of the first field observation some police officers claimed that the ethical rule that data collected for scientific purposes – in this particular case observational data of instances where crimes were committed – cannot be used for other purposes conflicted with their obligation as police officers to report observed offences. They maintained that the collision between these rules made it impossible for them to be observers. As a consequence this strategy had to be abandoned.[7]

In an alternative scheme, students at the police academy who were not yet sworn officers were used as observers in conjunction with researchers and instructors. But this turned out to be problematical for a number of reasons. As observers they were not familiar enough with policing, and it was often difficult for them to leave their studies to make the observations.

Because this second approach for conducting field observations did not work, a third strategy was introduced: a peer review methodology. This can be characterised as a 'light' process evaluation method. It was practiced in the following manner: pairs of observers with one police officer, usually a leader from another police district trained in the tactic, and one researcher observed different aspects of the event, for example, interaction between protesters and uniformed police or dialogue police officers' performance. The police officers were taught fundamental principles of observation methods and field interviewing before conducting the observations. In an effort to safeguard expert competence and objectivity, leaders from other districts trained in the tactic were chosen as police observers.

Field interviews were conducted with different groups: protesters, organisers, police officers, commanders, and bystanders. The following day all observers participated in a focus group interview resulting in a protocol where observations and interviews were documented. This document was then forwarded to the observed police unit for comments. In the final report the event is described, and things that went well, that could be improved, or that went wrong were pointed out. In this manner the police received feedback on how they had practiced the tactic with an emphasis on how its principles and routines were maintained. Besides observing the events, interviews, ranging from formal to very informal, were carried out with dialogue police officers, commanders, ordinary police officers, instructors, protest organisers, protesters, and bystanders.

I participated in most of the field observations, usually focusing on dialogue policing. After my first observation I decided to utilise the presenting opportunity to write a paper about the innovative qualities of dialogue policing. This decision was not well received by the project group. One speculation was that these people wanted to be in charge and, instead of perceiving this research as a free further accomplishment, they looked upon it as some kind of undue competition, even though a focused study on dialogue policing was not planned. I persisted and stated that I would do it anyway, in the worst case using other means and channels to get access to the organisation. The end product was a paper written together with Holgersson (Holgersson and Knutsson, 2011). In this paper research evidence about dialogue policing, its principles, theoretical foundation, and how it was practised was presented, providing an opportunity for a wider dissemination of the concept.

Effectiveness of dialogue policing and the new tactic

How can the alleged effectiveness in reducing confrontations and violence by dialogue policing and the new tactic be documented in a manner that sceptical academics – or dubious police officers for that matter – accept? How can we generate strong enough evidence?

According to Sherman (1998, 2013) and Weisburd and Neyroud (2011) randomised controlled trials is *the* means – the gold standard – to establish the effectiveness of police work. However, within the implementation project, at no time was there a plan to conduct an experiment.

An intriguing question is this: Would it at all be possible to design and execute a controlled randomised experiment of dialogue policing? In this case it would mean to randomly apply it as a treatment, and the tactic without it as a control, to protest demonstrations. But performing the tactic without dialogue policing would change the performance of the whole tactic, meaning that, actually, it would not be a comparison where other influences are controlled for (see Sampson, 2010). Another problem is to get a sample big enough. Protest events are not that frequent – many of them are annual occurrences. Add to this the wide variation among rallies in violence and disturbances – one would need many rallies for a valid research sample. This implies many years of data collection, which to police management and politicians, who have to set aside resources for this venture, might be too long to wait for conclusive knowledge into the effectiveness of the new scheme. To sum up, as with many areas of police practice (see, e.g., Laycock, 2012: 104–6), it is simply unfeasible to evaluate this type of tactic with randomised controlled trials.[8]

To make statements about the new tactic's effectiveness a range of evidence can, and should, be marshalled (see, e.g., Tilley, 2006; Kennedy, 2015; Sparrow, 2016). This evidence emanates from a combination of experiential knowledge, case studies, supporting theories, and what might be described as hypotheses tests. Illustrations will be given for each type of evidence.

Experiential knowledge

Dialogue policing challenges many deeply held conventional policing ideals and, initially, police officers typically had a sceptical view of it. Over time, however, when police commanders followed its principles, saw it in action, and witnessed its positive effects on crowd management, many changed their opinion. A typical answer from commanders when I asked them about their opinions of dialogue policing was 'I can't understand how we could have been without it'. And to the follow-up question if their view always had been the same: 'To begin with I thought it was a joke'.

Case study support

In interviews with organisers after a protest march that had included violent outbursts, the organisers commended the police. A couple of years earlier, when the traditional tactic was still in use, a protest in the same city had gone awry with questionable use of force by the police – something that remained in many protesters' memories. The organisers told how they had met in advance with dialogue police officers on several occasions to discuss the rally and the conditions for it. During the eruption demonstration-stewards formed a chain to stand between the aggressive protesters – a small, extremely violent group – and the uniformed police. An organiser using a loudspeaker appealed to the protesters and called, 'The police are our friends, they are here to support us'. The police took shelter during the frenzy and advanced stepwise in guarded formations as the violence faded out. A few violent protesters were arrested, but the police remained calm and did not take forceful action.

Theoretical concordance

Another argument in favour of the new tactic's effectiveness in preventing aggression and conflict is its concordance with theory. When practiced according to its principles, it is harmonious with a strong and accepted theory of group dynamics: the ESIM. There is also a systematic application of context-specific situational crime prevention techniques (see Holgersson and Knutsson, 2011: 207–12).[9] In fact, some of these situational techniques may be perceived as actual expressions of ESIM. For example, two of the mechanisms in situational crime prevention (see, e.g., Clarke, 2007) *removing excuses* and *reducing provocations*, clearly are in line with recommendations from the ESIM literature. An example of removing excuses is *facilitate attainment of legitimate goals* and, of reducing provocations, *to focus restraining and coercive actions on misbehaving protesters, whilst avoiding affecting the whole crowd.*

Tests

The implementation of dialogue policing in other settings can be seen as practical hypotheses tests. Will other more beneficial outcomes fall out compared to the ones that usually occur? For instance, South Yorkshire Police (UK) trialled a police liaison team, and somewhat hesitant officers and commanders practiced it during a large protest demonstration. The experience confirmed the model's soundness: the expected beneficial outcomes of dialogue policing did materialise with increased legitimacy for the police and less high-profile conventional police actions (Gorringe et al., 2012 and Waddington, 2013). Indeed, the success experienced in South Yorkshire inspired other UK police forces to adapt the concept with liaison police officer teams (Stott and Gorringe, 2014).

Negative examples of the consequences of using liaison police officers in another force also exist (Gorringe and Rosie, 2013). These arise from situations where dialogue policing principles were not adhered to, such as dialogue police officers administering threats to use force or acting in a manner that was perceived as intelligence gathering. This behaviour was deemed to undermine the trustworthiness of police among the protesters (Gorringe and Rosie, 2013). However, and strikingly, when dialogue policing is performed in keeping with the set of established principles, it appears that positive outcomes like increased legitimacy for police and fewer confrontations are overwhelmingly experienced, resulting in the establishment of permanent full-time liaison police teams in a number of UK police forces (Stott et al., 2013).

Swedish reception of the research evidence

One of the goals of the implementation project was to publish reports about the new tactic. With consent from Holgersson in 2007 I proposed to the project leader that his forthcoming report about dialoguing (Holgersson, 2008) should be included as one of the project's outputs. The response was a strong no, with the argument that it had not been commissioned by the project. The story about Holgersson's report does not end here.

In a meeting in 2009 with the national police commissioner I suggested that because of dialogue policing's innovative qualities Holgersson's report ought to be translated to English and published by the Swedish National Police Board, an idea to which the commissioner agreed. However, somewhat surprisingly, some officials at the board thwarted the translation, and the report (Holgersson, 2010) was severely delayed. One might speculate that these administrators wished for the study to become outdated, and thus not worthy of publishing; they had been in touch with the Stockholm police and asked if the report was outmoded.

Further instances of obstruction to publication followed. Funded by the Norwegian Police University College I organised a small international conference in 2009 with the purpose to produce a book about policing crowds. The end product was *Preventing Crowd Violence* (Madensen and Knutsson, 2011). During the meeting the intended papers for the book (including Holgersson's and mine) were examined and discussed with the group of invited experts.

However, the national police commissioner was advised to stop the printing of a Swedish version by the obstructing officials because of alleged deficiencies in the Holgersson and Knutsson paper. The leader of the project group in the implementation support project, Otto Adang, had, though, examined and acknowledged the paper. These allegations were forwarded in a note.[10] An oddity is that the note was 'secret' and I was not supposed to have access to it. This obscurity is underlined by the fact that I at that point of time was head of an evaluation unit at the National Police Board. The book was nevertheless published by the board (Madensen and Knutsson (2011), but the officials' reaction hampered its use in Sweden. The book has for instance not been part of the literature in the training of leaders in the tactical organisation, which was the intent. It has also made it easier for sceptics to disregard dialogue policing and to stick to traditional ideas.

A third instance nonetheless indicates that the obstructing officials paradoxically had a positive view of dialogue policing. An EU project – *GODIAC: Good practice for dialogue and communication as strategic principles for policing political manifestations in Europe* – was organised and managed by the National Police Board with a focus on dialogue between police and protesters. However, in spite of the fact that the Holgersson study (2010) and the paper by Holgersson and Knutsson (2011) were in accord with the goals of the project and were well known, no references were made to them in the project report (Hilton and Wessman, 2013). Furthermore, Holgersson's report was generously handed out and wanted by many from the participating countries.[11]

A possible reason for the officials' efforts to marginalise these studies could be a sense of ownership; they wanted to be in charge and get the credit for the new tactic, including dialogue policing. The authority associated with their positions in the upper police bureaucracy made it possible for them to act in the manner they did (see Hartman, 2014).

Later Swedish developments[12]

Given, among other things, the way the studies were received at the National Police Board, it is unsurprising that dialogue policing has not fared well. The number of dialogue police coordinators at police regional headquarters in Stockholm has decreased from three to two, and the number of dialogue police officers[13] from twelve to nine.

In order to understand this development one must go back to the situation when dialogue policing was introduced. The concept constituted a break with earlier ways of policing crowds. The prior focus was on risks and threats. Intelligence with emphasis on violent protesters was provided by the intelligence unit and security police. The protesters had no voice; their perspectives and how they looked upon the police was neglected. No one within the police really knew why they protested or about their values – their intentions were mostly misinterpreted or misunderstood.

Dialogue police dared to listen to and acknowledged the dynamics of ESIM. Something the police had previously not understood became apparent, and conventional 'police thinking' was confronted. Even though it was impracticable to verify in quantitative terms, experience clearly indicated less violence and less forceful action by the police when commanders followed advice from dialogue police officers.

Since the beginning of the 2010s a shift has occurred concerning dialogue policing tasks. Large protest demonstrations have become infrequent, which means that dialogue police officers are less visible. Their work is now centred round three themes – religion, ethnicity, and politics – where in-depth knowledge can help police in mastering different problems that might emerge connected to the different affiliations.

An important reason for the decreased significance of dialogue policing is that intelligence-led policing (ILP, see, e.g., Ratcliffe, 2008) has become a leading philosophy for the police. As a consequence the intelligence unit has been strengthened, and information focused on threats and risks is given more weight.

Dialogue policing's ultimate function is to support freedom of speech and right to assemble, and, in doing so, to prevent confrontations between protesters and the police. The philosophy of dialogue policing has obvious affinities with community policing, although community is not geographically determined, but as a congregation oriented around some common opinions, beliefs, or ideology. In community policing, just as in dialogue policing, the police work together with the community to collaboratively solve problems.[14]

Intelligence-led policing has a 'here and now' focus, whereas dialogue policing is conducted through long-lasting relationships based on trust with representatives from different groups. Through this the dialogue police officers gain comprehensive insights about these groups and can provide deeper and qualitatively better information. Yet information from the intelligence unit carries more weight in an ILP paradigm and that from dialogue police is, according to dialogue police officers' experience, often downplayed. This has sometimes been paradoxical because on occasion the only source of information is from dialogue officers, but nevertheless is interpreted as threats from the perspective of the intelligence unit.

An assumption among some commanders is that apprehending and punishing offenders is the key to successful crowd control. In contrast, dialogue policing fundamentally has prevention as its goal, even if the necessity to act towards offenders is recognised. However, coercive measures should be balanced, where enactment of the law should preferably be performed in such a way that a whole collective is not affected.

A few commanders have not followed the tactic's basic conflict-reducing principles during protest events. For example, they did not include dialogue police in the operative command centre during a critical protest rally, thereby missing the vital real-time information from dialogue police officers on the field. Because the police could not adequately adapt and act on this type of information, as stated by dialogue police officers, it created mistrust among protesters amenable to dialogue.

There is also the continual shift of commanders. Those active when dialogue policing was introduced had firsthand experiences of the benefits. However, newly recruited commanders are in another situation and may not understand its significance or may even question the dialogue policing scheme.

More troublesome is how the dialogue function is integrated or, more pointedly, not integrated in the police organisation. Dialogue police officers feel that for years they have been doubted by, and lack support from, management. The situation worsened after a large-scale organisational reform in 2015: the officers believed that the management does not care for their function, how it is organised, and where it fits within the organisation. To express their concerns, all dialogue police officers (including the coordinators) wrote a letter to police management which they ended by 'making their positions available'. Besides being told off by a leader and asked to explain their requests and reasons for them, not much changed as a result of their action.

Even if experienced commanders support dialogue policing, they remain silent. An explanation could be that some influential senior police administrators disregard dialogue policing. It would then not serve the careers of these commanders to raise their voices and speak up for dialogue policing. Taken together this means that the prospects for dialogue policing are rather gloomy in its country of origin.

International transmission: diffusion, use and production of evidence

If Swedish police have downplayed the dialogue policing tactic, the reverse can be said for some other countries. Among those expressing a strong interest are South Korea, Hungary, and Jordan,[15] who join early adopting police agencies in the UK.

Clifford Stott, an expert on crowd psychology, was in 2009 a member of the group examining the Metropolitan Police Service's failure to police the G20 summit in London in an acceptable manner. Through his participation in a collaborative book about policing crowds (Madensen and Knutsson, 2011) he had seen the draft version of the Holgersson and Knutsson paper about dialogue policing and brought the strategy to the group's attention. Dialogue policing was mentioned as exemplary in their report (HMCI, 2009b: 24, 74–77). In a follow-up report, the extent to which dialogue policing had been implemented was investigated (HMIC, 2011).

It is somewhat odd that Swedish police seem to disregard the scheme when it has become a model in other countries.

Conclusion

During the process, from creating and implementing the scheme, to its diffusion and implementation in the UK, research evidence has been crucial. As exemplified by the Swedish experience, existence of strong research evidence is by no means a guarantee that a new strategy will become a mainstream practice, even if it is created and developed by police officers within the police organisation.

Thus, even though dialogue policing had been borne out of a request from senior politicians for improved dialogue between police and protesters and was supported by strong research evidence, this has not precluded the model from being disregarded by the Swedish police. The experiences described in this chapter indicate that, in spite of these favourable factors, the process of producing and utilising research evidence in order to establish a new tactic in policing is not necessarily a rational straightforward progression, as is assumed in the original

EBP model (Sherman, 1998, 2013). Irregularities, politics, chance, and other factors intervene. There are in fact similarities to the experiences Kennedy (2011) documented when introducing the 'pulling lever'–focused deterrence strategy. Rather, the process is probably better understood as an incoherent and largely unpredictable progression. In this case what might be described as malfunctions in the upper Swedish police bureaucracy reinforced processes deemphasising dialogue policing.

The notion that applied police research would thrive if police have ownership of the research (Weisburd and Neyroud, 2011) is not supported by Swedish experiences. The National Swedish Police Board acted contrary to its own mission – that of being required by the government to establish an independent, and hence impartial, evaluation function (Knutsson, 2015). A necessary prerequisite is for the police management to have a genuine understanding of research, the conditions under which evidence is produced, and how such evidence may contribute to practice. In order for police research to flourish, we must strive to foster contexts where the police and academia can establish long-standing collaborative arrangements, both of whom benefit according to their different needs and perspectives (Madensen and Sousa, 2015). This is the real challenge.

Acknowledgments

I am indebted to the dialogue police officers for generously sharing their experiences with me. During the Kongsvinger meeting Michael Scott made constructive comments to help me improve the paper. I am also grateful to Lisa Tompson for language check, careful reading, and helpful remarks.

Notes

1 Here evidence primarily refers to printed research reports or papers available in journals.
2 An exception is the book *Don't Shoot: One Man, a Street Fellowship, and the End of Violence in Inner-City America* by David Kennedy (2011) which inspired this paper's format.
3 I had a part-time employment at the Swedish Police Academy and later on at the Swedish National Police Board in addition to my position at the Norwegian Police University College.
4 Holgersson has a PhD in Information Systems Development.
5 Due to my opinion I am in the risk zone of a confirmation bias, that is, that I selectively have looked for supporting evidence. On the other hand, there are researchers who have ended up with similar conclusions when studying the approach. See, e.g., Waddington (2013), Adang (2012), and the following quotation: 'For many years academics and others – including HMIC (2009a, 2009b) – have looked to Swedish Dialogue units for inspiration on proactive, consensual policing' (Gorringe et al., 2012: 18).
6 Otto Adang from the Netherlands, whose expertise is in crowd behaviour, was project leader. I was a member of the steering committee, chairman of the reference group, and participated in the project group's work
7 As chairman of the reference group I invited a qualified lawyer to clarify the rules at a reference group meeting. He explained that, by being sensible, it is possible to handle

the police officers' obligation and that science's ethical rule does not mean that data under no conditions can be used for other purposes than scientific. Both requirements are unsustainable if taken to their extremes.

8 However, although not a controlled experiment, an interesting opportunity occurred in Portugal during the European Football Championships in 2004 with two organisationally and geographically separated police forces where one (Polícia de Segurança Pública) used a graded tactic based on conflict reducing principles, and the other a conventional 'high profile' tactic (Guarda Nacional Republicana). This situation provided a kind of natural experiment. The result was in favour of the graded tactic with less confrontation and violence (Reicher et al., 2007; Stott et al., 2007).

9 See Holgersson and Knutsson (2011: 207–12). We identified 38 specific techniques that were used in the tactic. For effects of situational prevention in general, see, e.g., Guerette (2009), and for prevention of crowd violence and crowd hazards see Madensen and Eck (2011), Plant and Scott (2011), and Sousa and Madensen (2011).

10 NPB note November 23, 2010.

11 Personal communication from project manager Helène Lööw, who was charge during the later stages of the project.

12 This subsection, covering the period from 2010 and on, draws upon a number of interviews and conversations with dialogue police officers (former and still active) from the Stockholm region in the period 2014 to 2016.

13 Dialogue police officers use 80 percent of their time on their ordinary duties as police officers and are thus free to spend 20 percent on dialogue policing activities. However, one section leader responsible for the function somewhat puzzlingly questioned this order, with the consequence that it has become difficult to call up dialogue officers when they are needed.

14 See Ratcliffe (2008: 66–76) for differences between intelligence-led policing and community policing.

15 In 2010 I organised a crash course in dialogue policing for commanders from South Korea during a visit in Stockholm, including observations of a rather confrontational protest demonstration where they could experience the tactic in practice. In Hungary a police commander made a short version of Holgersson's report from 2010 available in Hungarian (Ferenc, 2012), and dialogue policing is looked upon as a model in efforts to introduce a low-profile consensual and communicative tactic (Hajas, 2013). The dialogue police coordinator in Stockholm has trained police in Jordan.

References

Adang, O.M.J. (2012). 'Reforming the policing of public order in Sweden: Combining research and practice', *Policing*, 7(3): 326–35.

Braga, A.A. and Davis, E.F. (2014). 'Implementing science in police agencies: The embedded research model, *Policing*, 8(4): 294–306.

Clarke, R.V. (2007). 'Situational Crime Prevention', in R. Wortley and L. Mazzerolle (eds) *Environmental Criminology and Crime Analysis*, pp. 178–220. Collumpton: Willan Publishing.

Cockbain, E. and Knutsson, J. (2015). 'Introduction', in E. Cockbain and J. Knutsson (eds) *Applied Police Research*, Abingdon, Oxon: Routledge.

Eck, J.E. (2015). 'There Is Nothing so Theoretical as Good Practice: Police-Researcher Coproduction of Place Theory', in E. Cockbain and J. Knutsson (eds) *Applied Police Research: Challenges and Opportunities*, pp. 129–40, London: Routledge.

Ferenc, L. (2012). A svéd rendőrség tárgyalás központú tömegkezelési stratégiája, paper.

Gorringe, H. and Rosie, M. (2013). '"We will facilitate your protest": Experiments with Liaison Policing', *Policing*, 7(2): 204–11, doi: 10.1093/police/pat001

Gorringe, H., Stott, C. and Rosie, M. (2012). 'Dialogue police, decision making, and the management of public order during protest crowd events', *Journal of Investigative Psychology and Offender Profiling*, 9(2): 111–25, doi: 10.1002/jip.1359

Greene, J.R. (2015). 'Police Research as Mastering the Tango: The Dance and Its Meanings', in E. Cockbain and J. Knutsson (eds) *Applied Police Research: Challenges and opportunities*, pp. 117–28, London: Routledge.

Guerette, R.T. (2009). 'The Pull, Push, and Expansion of Situational Crime Prevention Evaluation: An Appraisal of Thirty-Seven Years of Research', in J. Knutsson and N. Tilley (eds) *Evaluating Crime Prevention Initiatives*, pp. 29–58, Crime Prevention Studies, vol. 24, Monsey, NY: Criminal Justice Press.

Hajas, B. (2013). 'Does the GODIAC Project have any Impact on the Keeping of Public Order in Hungary? Trends in the Policing of Mass Events in Hungary, 2008–2012', in *The Anthology, GODIAC – Good practice for dialogue and communication as strategic principles for policing political manifestations in Europe*, pp. 60–71, Polisen.

Hartmann, M.R.K. (2014). *In the Gray Zone: With Police in Making Space for Creativity*, Dissertation, Copenhagen Business School.

Hilton, M. and Wessman, C. (2013). 'The Influence of Knowledge-Based Learning on the Development of Special Police Tactics in Sweden', in *The Anthology, GODIAC – Good Practice for Dialogue and Communication as Strategic Principles for Policing Political Manifestations in Europe*, pp. 8–42, Polisen.

HMIC. (2009a). *Adapting to protest*, London: Her Majesty's Chief Inspector of Constabulary. Retrieved from www.hmic.gov.uk/SiteCollectionDocuments/Individually%20Referenced/PPR_20091125.pdf (accessed 30 June 2010).

HMIC. (2009b). *Adapting to Protest: Nurturing the British Model of Policing*, London: Her Majesty's Chief Inspector of Constabulary. Retrieved from www.hmic.gov.uk/Site CollectionDocuments/Individually%20Referenced/PPR_20091125.pdf (accessed 30 June 2010).

HMIC. (2011). *Policing Public Order*, London: Her Majesty's Chief Inspector of Constabulary.

Holgersson, S. (2008). *Dialogpolis* [Dialogue police], Rapport 002–2008, Växjö: Växjö universitet.

Holgersson, S. (2010). *Dialogue Police: Experiences, Observations and Possibilities*, Stockholm: The Swedish National Police Board.

Holgersson, S. and Knutsson, J. (2011). 'Dialogue Policing – a means for Less Crowd Violence?', in T.D. Madensen and J. Knutsson (eds) *Preventing Crowd Violence*, pp. 191–215, Crime Prevention Studies, vol. 26, Colorado: Lynne Rienner Publishers.

Kennedy, D. (2011). *Don't Shoot: One Man, a Street Fellowship, and the End of Violence in Inner-City America*, New York: Bloomsbury.

Kennedy, D. (2015). 'Working in the Field: Police Research in Theory and in Practice', in E. Cockbain and J. Knutsson (eds) *Applied Police Research: Challenges and Opportunities*, pp. 9–20, London: Routledge.

Knutsson, J. (2015). 'Politics, promises and problems: The rise and fall of the Swedish police evaluation unit', in E. Cockbain and J. Knutsson (eds) *Applied police research: Challenges and opportunities*, pp. 95–105, Crime Science Series no. 16, London: Routledge.

Knutsson, J. and Madenson, T. (eds) (2010). *Att förebygga brott i folksamling* [To prevent crimes in crowds], Rikspolisstyrelsens utvärderingsfunktion, Rapport 2010:1, Stockholm: Rikspolisstyrelsen.

Laycock, G. (2012). 'Happy Birthday', *Policing*, 6(2): 101–7.

Madensen, T.D. and Eck, J.E. (2011). 'Crowd-Related Crime from an Environmental Crimi-nological Perspective', in T.D. Madensen and J. Knutsson (eds) *Preventing Crowd Violence*, pp. 115–38, Crime Prevention Studies, vol. 26, Colorado: Lynne Rienner Publishers.

Madensen, T.D. and Knutsson, J. (eds). (2011). *Preventing Crowd Violence*, Crime Preven-tion Studies, vol. 26, Colorado: Lynne Rienner Publishers.

Madensen, T.D. and Sousa, W.H. (2015). 'Practical Academics: Positive Outcomes of Police-Researcher Collaborations', in E. Cockbain and J. Knutsson (eds) *Applied Police Research: Challenges and Opportunities*, pp. 139–58, London: Routledge.

Noakes, J. and Gillham, P.F. (2006). 'Aspects of the New Penology in the Police Response to Major Political Protests in the United States, 1999–2000', in D. della Porta and A. Peterson, *The Policing of Transnational Protest*, pp. 97–115, Chippenham: Ashgate.

Peterson, A. and Oskarsson, M. (2006). 'The Police Riots in Gothenburg: The European Union Summit in Gothenburg, June 2001', in A. Peterson and M. Björk (eds) *Policing Contentious Politics in Sweden and Denmark*, Maastricht: Shaker Publishing.

Plant, J.B. and Scott, M.S. (2011). 'Trick or Treat? Policing Halloween in Madison, Wis-consin', in T.D. Madensen and J. Knutsson (eds) *Preventing Crowd Violence*, pp. 159–90, Crime Prevention Studies, vol. 26, Colorado: Lynne Rienner Publishers.

Ratcliffe, J. (2008). *Intelligence-Led Policing*, Cullompton: Willan Publishing.

Reicher, S. (1996). ' "The battle of Westminster": Developing the social identity model of crowd behavior in order to explain the initiation and development of collective conflict', *European Journal of Social Psychology*, 26: 115–34.

Reicher, S., Stott, C., Cronin, P. and Adang, O. (2004). 'An integrated approach to crowd psychology and public order policing', *Policing: An international Journal of Police Strategies & Management*, 27: 558–72.

Reicher, S., Stott, C., Cronin, P., Drury, J., Adang, O., Cronin, P. and Livingstone, A. (2007). 'Knowledge-based public order policing: Principles and practice', *Policing*, 1(4): 403–15.

Sampson, R. J. (2010). 'Gold standard myths: Observations on the experimental turn in quantitative criminology', *Journal of Quantitative Criminology*, 25: 489–500.

Sherman, L.W. (1998). 'Evidence Based Policing', in *Ideas in American Policing*, Wash-ington, DC: Police Foundation.

Sherman, L.W. (2013). 'The rise of evidence-based policing: Targeting, testing, and track-ing', *Crime and Justice*, 42(1): 377–451.

SOU 2002. (2002). *Göteborg 2001. Betänkande från Göteborgskommittén*, [Gothenburg 2001. Report from the Gothenburgcommittee], Statens offentliga utredningar, 2002:122, Stockholm: Fritzes förlag.

Sousa, W.H. and Madensen, T.D. (2011). 'The Police and Major Event Planning: A Case Study in Las Vegas, Nevada', in T.D. Madensen and J. Knutsson (eds) *Preventing Crowd Violence*, pp. 139–58, Crime Prevention Studies, vol. 26, Colorado: Lynne Rienner Publishers.

Sparrow, M. (2016). *Handcuffed*, Washington, DC: Brookings Institution Press.

Stott, C. and Drury, J. (2000). 'Crowds, context and identity: Dynamic categorization pro-cesses in the "poll tax riot" ', *Human Relations*, 53: 359–84.

Stott, C. and Gorringe, H. (2014). 'From Sir Robert Peel to PLTs: Adapting to Liaison-Based Public Order Policing in England and Wales', in J.M. Brown (ed) *The Future of Policing*, pp. 239–51, London: Routledge.

Stott, C. and Reicher, S. (1998). 'Crowd action as intergroup process: Introducing the police perspective', *European Journal of Social Psychology*, 28: 509–29.

Stott, C.J., Adang, O.M.J., Livingstone, A. and Schreiber, M. (2007). 'Variability in the collective behaviour of England fans at Euro2004: "Hooliganism", public order policing and social change', *European Journal of Social Psychology*, 37: 75–100.

Stott, C.J., Adang, O.M.J., Livingstone, A. and Schreiber, M. (2008). 'Tackling football hooliganism: A quantitative study of public order, policing and crowd psychology', *Psychology Public Policy and Law*, 14(2): 115–41.

Stott, C., Scothern, M. and Gorringe, H. (2013). 'Advances in Liaison based public order policing in England: Human rights and negotiating the management of protest?', *Policing: An International Journal of Research and Practice*, 7 (2): 212–26, doi: 10.1093/police/pat007

Tilley, N. (2006). 'Knowing and Doing: Guidance and Good Practice in Crime Prevention', in J. Knutsson and R.V. Clarke (eds) *Putting Theory to Work: Implementing Situational Prevention and Problem-Oriented Policing*, pp. 217–52, Crime Prevention Studies, vol. 20, Monsey, NY: Criminal Justice Press.

Tilley, N. (2015). 'There Is Nothing so Practical as a Good Theory: Teacher-Learner Relationships in Applied Research for Policing', in E. Cockbain and J. Knutsson (eds) *Applied Police Research: Challenges and Opportunities*, pp. 141–52, London: Routledge.

Tillyer, R., Skubak Tillyer, M., McCluskey, J., Cancino, J., Todaro, J. and McKinnon, L. (2014). 'Researcher – practitioner partnerships and crime analysis: A case study in action research', *Police Practice and Research: An International Journal*, (15)5: 404–18, doi: 10.1080/15614263.2013.829321

Waddington, D. (2013). 'A "kinder blue": Analysing the police management of the Sheffield anti-"Lib Dem" protest of March 2011', *Policing and Society: An International Journal of Research and Policy*, 23(1): 46–64.

Weisburd, D. and Neyroud, P. (2011). *Police Science: Toward a New Paradigm*, Paper of the Harvard Executive Session on Policing and Public Safety 2010, Washington, DC: National Institute of Justice.

11 How to make police–researcher partnerships mutually effective

Lisa Tompson, Jyoti Belur, Julia Morris and Rachel Tuffin

Evidence-based policing is grounded in the notion that practitioners use the best available evidence to inform their decision-making; the implicit assumption being that practitioners are open to new ideas stemming from research evidence. Such receptivity in operational policing circles has, however, been documented as being stubbornly low (Kennedy, 2010; Weisburd and Neyroud, 2011). This is not unique to policing and has been observed across other professions that are generally assumed to be research driven (see Guillaume, Sidebottom and Tilley, 2012 for examples).

Police resistance to research evidence, when it exists, has been attributed to a myriad of factors, not least the legacy of the critical police research era, during which the police were 'the subject of research and the unwitting recipient of researcher's attentions' (Rojek, Martin and Alpert, 2015). That is, research in the mid-twentieth century was typically 'on' the police, rather than 'with' or 'for' the police (Cockbain and Knutsson, 2015). The result was a body of research largely (but somewhat justly) critical of the police, often without adequate appreciation of the practical challenges faced by the service. In the decades that followed, many scholars have documented disconnect between what academics study and what matters to different tiers of police practitioners (e.g., see Willis and Mastrofski, 2016). In light of this, the police's disinclination to embrace research findings is hardly surprising.

Police receptivity to research is influenced by many factors (Telep, 2016). Thus a multipronged approach is required to engender an attitudinal change in the police at an organisational level so that they are open to research findings. The challenge for proponents of evidence-based policing is to make research evidence less 'academic' – that is, esoteric and marginal – but more 'practical' and of operational relevance.

Echoing others (e.g., see Lum et al., 2012), in this chapter we argue that police involvement in research partnerships, from defining the problem through to the implementation of an intervention, can increase the practical relevance of the findings. Moreover, police 'ownership' of research has the potential to secure support for the findings to be accepted and integrated into practice (Weisburd and Neyroud, 2011). As an after-effect, the 'co-production' of research (see Crawford, this volume) may bring the philosophy of the scientific process into sharp focus for police practitioners and, through this experiential learning, elevate their receptivity to research evidence.

Being open to evidence is, of course, the first step. Credible evidence should lead to an adaption of police practice, which in turn ought to result in better performance. However, translating research findings to implementable changes in police practice is much more challenging and complex than many academics appreciate (Engel and Whalen, 2010; Rojek et al., 2015). The traditional model of the police as 'research customers' and the academics as 'research providers' is thus outdated and unproductive in influencing practice. A 'coalition for a common purpose' might be more fruitful (Strang, 2012), although this is not neccesarily an organic process. Hence, both police practitioners and researchers need to change how they do their business – which could be conceived of as organisational change – if they want to collaborate in partnerships.

With austerity budgets forcing police agencies to rethink the efficiency and effectiveness of their responses (Huey and Mitchell, 2016), and the prevailing political climate favouring evidence-based policing, effective police–researcher partnerships have never been so sorely needed. The aim of this chapter is to present a logic model of an idealised effective police–researcher partnership. In other words, we propose a plausible and sensible model of how an initiative (police–researcher partnerships) will work under certain conditions. In doing so, the intention is to provide a road map for those embarking on a partnership endeavour. In particular, this narrative is for researchers who wish to engage with practitioner communities, to encourage them to think about their demeanour and the interpersonal skills they deploy when building relationships. Receptivity to craft-based[1] police practice by researchers is of equal importance to receptivity to research by police practitioners. We hope the model will stimulate thinking and provide a means of evaluating existing partnerships by offering a way of structuring (perhaps tactic) knowledge on how partnerships work.

The chapter begins by considering the links between receptivity to research and the professionalisation agenda before summarising the UK College of Policing's activities to promote a cultural shift towards an evidence-based policing profession. Next, we review the documented barriers to police–researcher partnerships. We then describe our approach to conceptualising police–researcher partnerships, before presenting a logic model that traces the process of setting up police–researcher partnerships, focusing on four essential stages that support effective partnerships.

Moving towards being an evidence-based police profession

Police receptivity to research findings is largely confined to individual officers in individual police forces. The penetration of evidence-based policing in a police operating model is thus variable across countries, across forces within a country, across ranks within an organisation, and is not particularly joined up amongst early adopter officers (Telep, 2016). One of the main reasons for police lack of receptivity to research findings more generally (Weisburd and Neyroud, 2011) and amongst specific forces and ranks in particular (Cordner and Biebel, 2005) can be attributed to the strength and omnipresence of a police subculture that revers skills and experience. Three notable features of this subculture need highlighting. First, it is not monolithic, but consists of several subcultures specific to different levels and ranks within the service (Reuss Ianni and Ianni, 1983; Manning, 1993; Chan, 1996). Second, individual police officers are not passive receptors of the occupational subculture, but actively interpret and absorb or resist it (Fielding, 1988; Reiner, 1992; Chan, 1996). Finally, occupational subculture does not exist in a vacuum but is influenced by the external social, political, legal, and organisational context (Chan, 1996).

Thus, measures to increase police receptivity to becoming more evidence based (implicitly increasing receptivity to research) need to be addressed at the individual, operational, and organisational levels, accompanied by changes in the wider sociopolitical context to provide the impetus for such change. Chan (1996) uses Bourdieu's relational theory concepts of 'field' and 'habitus' (Bourdieu and Wacquant, 1992) to explain the process of engendering change as a dynamic interaction, whereby police actors use 'their habitus (cultural knowledge) to interpret and react to their structural conditions (field) to produce and to modify practice' (O'Neill, 2016: 477). Thus, there is a strong argument made for refashioning the role of police through a change in social expectations; in other words, a change in the structural conditions in which they operate and in the expectations from the police, in order to bring about desired receptivity to change within the occupational subculture (Loftus, 2010).

Arguably, transforming policing from a craft into a profession would be the necessary precursor to police officers welcoming research evidence into their decision-making (Kennedy, 2015). Efforts to induce this transition are currently underway at the UK College of Policing, with a number of incentives being offered to practitioners and researchers to support such a sea change. These might usefully be conceptualised as the external influences of the field modifying the policing habitus.

The UK's College of Policing

The College of Policing (CoP) was established in 2013 as the professional body for the police in England and Wales. At the heart of the college's activity is a strong drive to ensure that policing becomes an evidence-based profession, supported by standards, guidance, and training that are built upon evidence. The end goal is to foster a profession that produces reflective and enquiring practitioners, who make decisions by integrating evidence into their professional experience, and who are active participants in developing the profession. Research receptivity is an intermediary stage in this journey.

To embed this scale of change in any complex system is not straightforward or undemanding. The college uses a number of different (explicit and implicit) levers to encourage a shift in professional practice. Explicit and implicit levers include the selection and assessment of officers and staff (e.g., for promotion); the design and delivery of evidence-based policing modules throughout the national policing curriculum; the delivery of national policing guidance, standards, and associated training curricula; the development of an evidence-based career pathway; and capacity-building exercises such as the Evidence Base Camp courses which are designed to teach research methods with real-world examples. Importantly, the college also oversees the provision of grants for police–researcher partnerships through schemes such as the 2015 £10m Police Knowledge Fund. This emphasises building practitioner research capability over the longer term and the genuine co-production of knowledge.

The active involvement of police in conducting research is thought to be vital in building an evidence-based profession for two reasons. The first is a logistical issue – the dearth of good quality studies in policing means that academics working alone simply cannot supply the volume of studies demanded to fill the current evidence gaps. The second reason is more fundamental. Palmer's (2011) research documented that police officers tended to rely on and prefer professional experience over research evidence. Yet the more those officers knew about research, the less they believed the police had sufficient knowledge within their organisation to respond to crime. Palmer (2011) further revealed that the more police officers are exposed to research, the more willing they are to do research; and finally, when research is part of their professional experience, the more likely they are to use it. Actively involving practitioners in research is thus not only important to increase the output of quality studies in policing and plug key knowledge gaps, but also as a lever for getting evidence into practice.

Practitioners with a positive experience of a research partnership are subsequently ideally placed within their organisations to become 'opinion leaders' on evidence-based policing principles. Given the powerful nature of peer influence in a 'closed' culture like policing (Reiner, 1992) and that practitioners privilege information from institutional sources (Palmer, 2011; Lum et al., 2012), we suggest that this is an effective mechanism through which to galvanise a cultural change towards receptivity of research. Our assumption is that a cultural revolution might best begin internally, with these key individuals promulgating an appetite for evidence to be ingrained into practice. The first step to realising these aims, however, is the positive experience of a research partnership, which is by no means guaranteed, for reasons that we now unpack.

Organisational culture as a barrier to partnership harmony

Police officers and academics lead vastly different working lives. Each hails from a distinct organisational culture with divergent values, different reward systems, and conflicting languages (Rojek et al., 2015). Historically the exchanges between the police and researchers have been wryly dubbed 'the dialogue of the deaf' (MacDonald, 1986: 1), which captures the lack of communication and lingering mutual mistrust from the critical police research era (Engel and Whalen, 2010; Wilkinson, 2010). The differences in the two working cultures are frequently cited as the main barriers to collaborative working (e.g., see Bradley and Nixon, 2009).

The police are said to be action oriented and decisive (Foster, 2003). They operate in an ever-changing political and organisational environment and are regularly exposed to the very worst of human nature. 'Street smarts' are often a presumed requisite for the countless situations a police officer might face, to the denigration of intellectual or 'book smarts' (Kennedy, 2015). In stark contrast, researchers are trained to be critical and reflective thinkers. In terms of research interests, the police seek clear and unambiguous findings that translate into operational changes to local problems (Lum et al., 2012; Rojek et al., 2015). Academics have traditionally been more concerned with testing and developing criminological theories (Madensen and Sousa, 2015) and are comfortable with uncertainty (Strang, 2012). As a consequence, both parties hold a different world view on what type of knowledge is valuable and worth investing time and resources in (Buerger, 2010). Hence, the lack of a natural overlap between each partner's objectives makes the practical relevance of much research questionable for the police (Rojek et al., 2015).

These dissimilar philosophical positions are compounded by the timescales and the reward systems in which both parties tend to work (Lum et al., 2012). Policing is characterised by dynamic operational circumstances, requiring real-time solutions to be administered as situations and problems unfold. Practitioners are consequently rewarded for producing concrete results that satisfy their various stakeholders (e.g., the media, the public, and politicians) (Rojek et al., 2015). Researchers, on the other hand, are rewarded for scholarly productivity. Prestigious publications that advance academic careers require high-quality methods that take considerable time to execute and require reflective and slow deliberation throughout the research process. This timing mismatch can consequently compromise the relevance of the research to practitioners (Weisburd and Neyroud, 2011).

Two dominant themes are recurrent in the literature on the barriers to effective partnership working: *trust* and *communication*. These are somewhat interdependent and can either reinforce or undermine each other. As in all human relationships, trust is paramount. The police culture is one that is necessarily secretive (Kennedy, 2015) and, at the same time, is closely scrutinised by the media, the public, and politicians. Whereas scientific communication is a public affair, the police prefer to deflect critical media attention (Fleming, 2010). Police sensitivity to negative press coverage is formative in the development of trust between partners.

The researcher's motives for engaging in a partnership are also central to trust. The police are all too aware that the research community needs them more than they need the researchers to do their work (Engel and Whalen, 2010). Any sense of the partnership being one-sided or exploited by the researcher will not gain traction; 'data robbers' will not be tolerated.

A recurrent criticism from the police is that researchers do not appreciate the 'daily rigours' of police work and, consequently, can neglect to work to the police's objectives (Fleming, 2011: 141). In reality few researchers have practical experience of policing and are likely unaware of the idiosyncratic operational and political constraints under which the police often work. A lack of operational exposure for the researcher can result in research findings that are not sensitive to implementation practicalities, which will fail to be seen as credible by the police (Engel and Whalen, 2010).

Police and academic cultures are then manifestly different or, as Laycock (2014: 397) remarks, 'the cultural equivalents of oil and water spring to mind'. An effective partnership, defined here as mutually beneficial and producing reciprocated knowledge, requires partners to transcend these differences in pursuit of a common objective. As we expand on later, this can be achieved by all partners valuing each other's strengths and acknowledging the weaknesses so that there is mutual respect for the breadth of knowledge and skills across the spectrum of the partnership which can be put to the best use (Fleming, 2011).

Conceptualising police–researcher partnerships

The literature on encouraging police–researcher partnerships has identified a number of factors that facilitate or hinder a partnership working (e.g., see Fleming, 2011, 2012; Rojek et al., 2015). However, this knowledge remains prescriptive rather than processual. Here we attempt to synthesise this information into a logic model that traces the process of how effective partnerships should operate.

The model presented here is the result of a thought experiment, but one that is underpinned by a synthesis of the literature on partnership working and extensive individual, and collective, experience of working with, and as, police researchers. We additionally gathered survey data from practitioners and academics with experience of partnership work to test some of our suppositions generated from the literature and our practical experience. This survey was administered and promoted in various practitioner-oriented events.[2,3] Because we sought participants with experience of partnership working in the previous five years, the response rate was low,[4] with 44 responses overall, and 22 respondents with previous partnership experience (see results in Appendix 11.1). The survey data are hence used to support our contentions, but fall short of acting in the capacity of 'evidence'. In addition a working version of our partnership model was presented to a group of practitioners at an evidence-based policing event in the UK, with the objective of testing and validating our nascent model. This exercise generated valuable feedback that helped refine the model.

Effective partnership working

Partnerships can take many forms and degrees of formality. Central to all are some basic requirements that contribute towards a partnership being effective, namely 1) mutual areas of interest, 2) trust, 3) communication, and 4) feedback to and from police practitioners. Although prerequisites for all police–researcher partnerships, the intensity and depth of these individual 'ingredients' differs depending on the maturity of any particular partnership and the scale of the research objectives.

To elaborate, Rojek and colleagues (2015: 31), borrowing from the International Association of Chiefs of Police, outline three categories of partnerships, which differ in their level of commitment:

1) *Cooperation* – short-term and informal partnerships that may involve such efforts as the agency seeking advice from a researcher or simply providing the research partner data for analysis.
2) *Coordination* – more formal partnerships that centre on a specific project or goal, such as contracting a researcher to conduct a specific analysis or jointly securing grant funding with a researcher to evaluate a specific initiative. The partnership ends with the conclusion of the project.
3) *Collaboration* – formalized long-term partnerships where police agencies and researchers work together on multiple projects over time. An example of such a partnership could involve a 'memorandum of understanding' or contract between an agency and university or researcher for engaging in ongoing and multiple research efforts.

Cooperation partnerships represent a fledgling, but not established, relationship between the partners. It is likely that these partnerships involve ad hoc unfunded projects that commonly occur between individuals, rather than institutions. Many variations of these partnerships exist. Sometimes, in a more traditional setup, the terms will be agreed to at the outset and the researcher will be provided data to analyse off-site. Other times this partnership will pivot around the researcher providing technical support or advice to the practitioner. Problem-oriented policing partnerships and researchers embedded in police agencies (e.g., see Braga and Davis, 2014) take yet other forms.

A deepening of the four components outlined earlier will move a cooperation partnership into a coordination, or even collaboration, partnership. (We should stress at this point that although these partnership styles are presented in a somewhat sequential fashion, collaboration partnerships are the only style that require pre-existing partner relationships.) Real life is often messy, and partnerships may fall within the margins of different models rather than neatly into any one category. What may begin as a professional acquaintance in a cooperation partnership can evolve into a personal relationship through the cementing of trust and mutual understanding of each partner's professional worlds.

We assert that regular partner interaction is the mechanism through which trust and communication are established and relationships between partners develop. The frequency and intensity of interaction also directly influence the nature of knowledge dissemination between the practitioner and researcher, because each interactive occasion provides an opportunity for learning more about the other partner's organisational culture and constraints. Collaboration partnerships involve extensive interaction, strong levels of trust, and personal relationships and result in the authentic two-way exchange of knowledge (Rojek et al., 2015). Cooperation partnerships, in contrast, usually result in one-way knowledge transfer from the researcher to the police practitioner. Coordination partnerships fall somewhere in between the other two partnership styles on the continuum of knowledge flow direction (Rojek et al., 2015).

If our assumptions about how partnerships might elevate receptivity to research have merit, then positive experiences of partnership working are vital to promulgating the principles and influence of evidence-based policing. In our opinion, collaboration partnerships represent the pinnacle of co-produced research and embody crystallised trust and sustainable research agendas. Arguably, one of the chief precursors to collaboration partnerships are coordination partnerships, and it is on these latter partnerships which we specifically focus in this chapter.

Our model portrays an idealised version of the essential ingredients needed to make effective partnerships work. This draws from our collective experience of the relationship dynamics required in applied police research and is supplemented by feedback garnered from practitioners. In essence the model seeks to invert the barriers identified in the literature, because 'barriers and facilitators to partnerships are not separate issues, but two sides of the same coin' (Rojek et al., 2015: 41). We do though fully acknowledge that our model is a crude representation of how things work on the ground. (To accurately model the complexity and diversity of partnership processes would result in an incomprehensible schematic with an excess of divergent paths and feedback loops.) For example, we are assuming here that pre-existing relationships are not necessary in a partnership and there is a blank slate for building interpersonal relations. In practice, researchers embarking on these kinds of endeavours have either established networks of police contacts or are connected with police practitioners through a third party. Reputations and first impressions may, therefore, influence both partners' initial opinions of the other.

Coordination-style partnerships

Coordination partnerships are purposeful; they involve explicit objectives and people working together in pursuit of a shared agenda. They may be new in terms of the relationships between partners, and the stimulus for these partnerships may be conditions for funding which stipulate co-production of research. This model presented in Figure 11.1 comprises four stages: 1) initiation, 2) planning, 3) building trust, and 4) applying knowledge. In this we pay particular attention to the practical aspects of initiating and maintaining such partnerships, which are sorely neglected in the academic literature (Cockbain, 2015).

Stage 1: initiation

Identifying the beginning step of a partnership is harder than it sounds. The first (working) version of the model proposed that coordination partnerships could be initiated by either of the partners and that a mutual area of interest would precede the pursuit of grant funding. The practitioners in our validation exercise, however, challenged this assumed sequence. Several participants stated that the identification of a funding source was the impetus to liaise with researchers over mutual

STAGE 1 - INITIATION

Project initiated by either partner → Mutual area of interest identified → Funding secured → Senior officer buy-in

STAGE 2 - PLANNING

Outcomes, timescales and obstacles discussed → Flexible research plan devised → Adequate resource allocation

STAGE 3 - BUILDING TRUST

Confidentiality and discretion assured   Each partner's skills and experience is valued ← Commitment to research by the police practitioner

Police culture valued by the researcher

Trust established ↔ Frank and frequent communication

STAGE 4 - APPLYING KNOWLEDGE

Interim findings presented → Findings operationalised by partners → Findings implemented

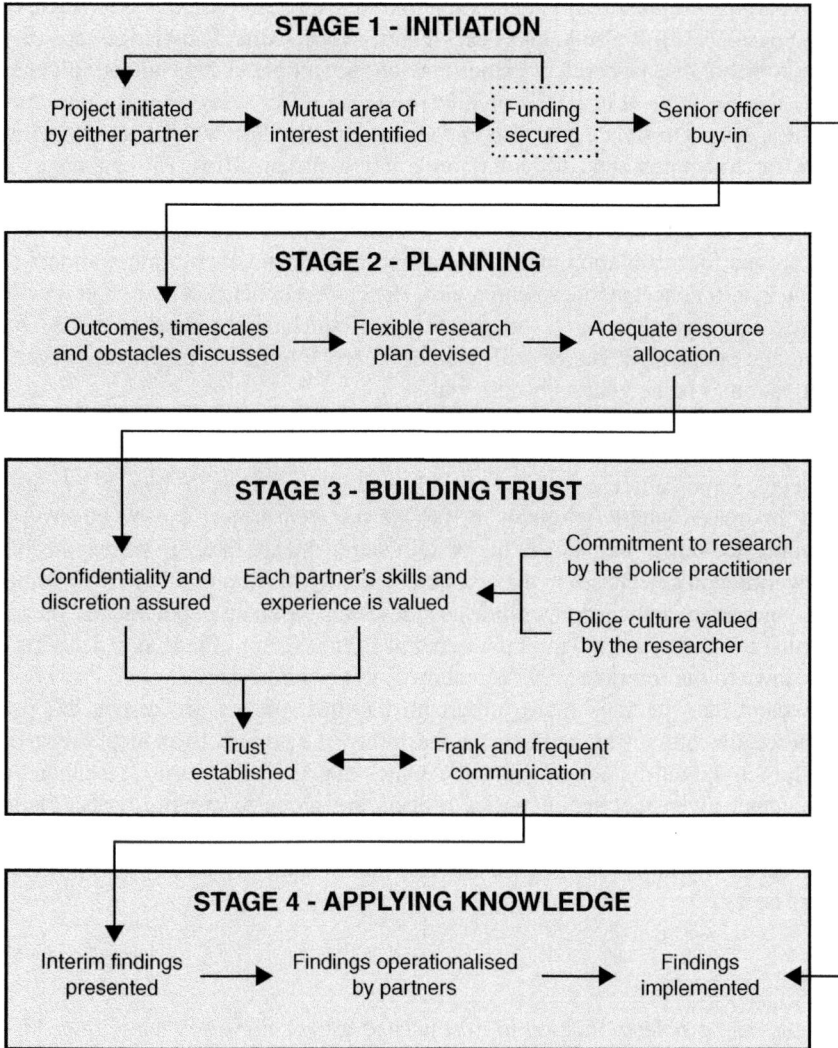

Figure 11.1 Logic model of an effective coordination partnership

areas of interest. Another participant was confident that a funding source could always be found for a well-formulated research proposal. The model was thus refined to reflect these two scenarios. Other entry points are equally possible. The responsibility for securing funding is more likely to fall to the research partner because, generally speaking, researchers are familiar with the procedures for writing grant proposals and identifying funding bodies sympathetic to a research topic (see questions 1 and 2 in Appendix 11.1).

Identifying reciprocally beneficial research goals requires dialogue to explore each partner's rationale and negotiation to find compatible objectives (Madensen and Sousa, 2015). It also helps if each partner knows what knowledge gaps they wish to fill. Police research priorities may be susceptible to stakeholder influence (e.g., the government or public opinion) and may differ across the rank structure of the agency. The police may also find articulating their knowledge gaps, in terms of research requirements, difficult (Goode and Lumsden, 2016). The challenge for the researcher is to work with the practitioner to identify what the research objective is, its context and influences, and, crucially, the desired outcome. This may require tactful negotiation and some degree of adjustments by both partners to arrive at a joint acceptable research aim. Hence researchers need to learn how to share the process of research with practitioners, which takes time and patience. An open and cooperative stance will facilitate a first impression of the researcher's motivation as being genuinely collegial.

The final step of stage 1 is that 'buy-in' from senior officers is obtained. This is important for two main reasons: first, due to the hierarchical rank structure in policing, senior officers wield great influence over their subordinates. Enthusiasm, or indeed simple pragmatism, for the research project can be effectively promulgated down the ranks to the practitioners who are likely to be responsible for working on key phases in the research. Although, as Strang (2012: 216) points out, 'agreement at the top can dilute as it descends the chain of command', meaning that the endorsement (for a partnership) from a senior officer may not percolate down to the frontline staff. We return to this point in stage 3.

Second, and perhaps more importantly, senior officers are responsible for resource allocation, which affects the feasibility of a project. In an ideal scenario, the buy-in should be sought from the senior management team, rather than an individual, given that senior police officers are prone to moving posts (Fleming, 2010). Practitioner feedback in the validation exercise also emphasised the importance of senior buy-in at the *implementation* stage of a research project (see more later).

Stage 2: planning

To alleviate problems relating to mismatched expectations of what partnerships can deliver, and when, the next logical step in the model is the discussion of outcomes, timescales, and obstacles. Acknowledging that unfavourable results are still important sources of evidence can help to temper perceptions of 'success' and 'failure'. Setting out clear terms of reference and a project plan can further reconcile any conflicting expectations across partners of how the partnership project is to run, what outcomes might be produced, whose intellectual property they are, and how and where they might be communicated or published. Fleming (2011) notes that these issues commonly generate misunderstandings and can undermine relations between partners. Documenting collective decisions can therefore be a useful means of maintaining commitment from all partners and can help to protect against misconceptions of what each partner's role is in the project. The survey results from question eight in Appendix 11.1 lend weight to this recommendation: 'clear communication and negotiation at the outset of the projects' and 'better management of police expectations' were purported to be good solutions to the issue of timeliness by participants in open-ended questions (not shown).

Policing is founded on shifting political and operational sands. Partnership research thus requires the adoption of a plan which includes flexibility regarding the allocation of resources (Rojek et al., 2015). Resourcing demands for, say, a critical incident or public outcry can naturally take precedence over partnership working (Foster and Bailey, 2010; Stephens, 2010). Relatedly, research often encounters unforeseen delays. Research that wishes to retain 'currency' (Wilkinson, 2010) needs to adapt to changing circumstances and recognise that police practitioners face internal pressures (Fleming, 2012). Sometimes this may require revising the research plan entirely; other times it may necessitate a recalibration of resources and timescales.

Having practitioner input at the planning stage is thus crucial, as practitioners are more familiar with the types of abstractions and hurdles likely to be encountered during the research. The 'co-production' (see Crawford, this volume) of the research plan is hence very important (see question 6 in Appendix 11.1). However, Wilkinson (2010) observes that researchers are not always comfortable with 'interference' in their professional habits. The same might be said of the police – the participants in the validation exercise said that although the police like to ask questions, they do not like to be questioned by others.

It would seem that both partners might benefit from suspending their usual customs and being accommodating to the shared goal. In this vein, Madensen and Sousa (2015: 76) recommend that 'researchers should not cling to form at the expense of substance'. By this they mean that research methods should be appropriately tailored to the presenting situation, and the researcher, or 'pracademic' (see Huey and Mitchell, 2016), should take care to translate relevant theoretical concepts into insights that can feed into practice. Understanding how the research findings will be used is essential for the researcher when explaining the research design and the robustness of the findings to the practitioner. At times, less rigorous methods (from an academic perspective) are arguably a better fit for many policing circumstances and can yield useful insights for the police, but might then have to be cautiously used by practitioners to make causal inferences or definitive arguments.

Stage 3: building trust

Building trust is embedded into the whole partnership lifecycle, but intensifies as the research is executed. Two fundamental requirements: 'confidentiality and discretion assured' and 'each partner's skills and experience is valued', are precursors to the establishment of trust in stage 3. The first can be achieved through careful and transparent agreements for the provision of data sharing and intellectual property rights, but may also be augmented by a researcher's reputation. The second is more challenging. In part it is dependent on the 'right' people being involved in the partnership (Goode and Lumsden, 2016), who possess personality traits – such as open-mindedness and good communication skills – to engender reciprocated understanding and respect (Fleming, 2012).

Two key mechanisms enable this mutual respect: a 'commitment to the research by the police practitioner' and 'police culture valued by the researcher' (Rojek et al., 2015). The former requires buy-in from the partnership team, which is different than buy-in from senior officers. Although senior officers may hold sway over subordinates, it is critical that the police practitioners in charge of executing the research understand the rationale behind the project and what constitutes fidelity to the research plan (Strang, 2012). Being able to communicate the real-world application of the research findings to the police is a distinct advantage at this stage of the process (Fleming, 2010).

The literature suggests that researchers ought to value police culture (Rojek et al., 2015). Sometimes the researcher will be 'embedded' within the police department in which the project is being done (Braga and Davis, 2014) in order to immerse them in the culture. If this is not feasible, a researcher must convey a readiness to understand, and be respectful of, police heritage, processes, and operational constraints (Stanko, 2007). To gain legitimacy in the eyes of the police, researchers must be prepared to be repeatedly tested (Engel and Whalen, 2010), to prove they are motivated and that their behaviour is trustworthy. Visibility, approachability, availability, and willingness to work on tasks outside the scope of the project all contribute to achieve this goal (Rojek et al., 2015).

Many police practitioners might determine that personality dynamics are fundamental to this stage of the process; however, in reality researchers can hone their emotional intelligence to gain social acceptance within the police organisation. This includes cultivating softer skills such as carefully listening and observing, showing interest in the views of others, asking pertinent neutral questions, using straightforward language, and being courteous and respectful of police traditions and processes (Brown, 2015). Such intelligence can be developed through 'self-awareness and self-reflection' (Cockbain, 2015: 31). It is hence helpful for the researcher 'to be carefully attuned to organisational politics and to be able to navigate them smoothly' (Holgersson, 2015: 111). It is worth noting, however, that police culture is not homogenous or 'unitary' (Reiner, 1992; Kennedy, 2015), but differs subtly both within and between police agencies, and researchers need to be aware of these differences.

It is also critical for the researcher to acknowledge the craft- or practice-based knowledge held by the police. Failure to do so can impede the development of trust, limit access to research subjects, and undermine the willingness of the police practitioner to cooperate (Engel and Whalen, 2010; Lum et al., 2012). The police's practical wisdom can contribute insights to the project and refine the research plan, and thus should be an integral component to the co-produced research.

That each partner's skills and experience are valued rests on a mutual appreciation that neither partner holds the monopoly of knowledge, or experience, on the research topic. It requires an acknowledgement that each partner brings complementary strengths and contributions to the partnership (Fleming, 2011; Willis, 2016). If these factors are in place then a reciprocal relationship based on trust can flourish, but in recognition that it is fragile and may need constant renegotiation.

Continual communication between partners both influences and strengthens trust; hence these are interdependent in Figure 11.1. This ameliorates police concerns about feeling detached from developments in the research (Fleming, 2011) and, in particular, nasty surprises. Frequent and frank communication also speaks to the police practitioner's need for timely results (Rojek et al., 2015) and keeps the researcher abreast of organisational changes that might (negatively or positively) affect the research (Fleming, 2011). Communication is especially vital in the face of controversial findings being broadcasted by the media (which may happen towards the end of a project). When this happens, senior police managers need to be fully informed about the nature of the research and the factors that might have influenced the findings – or compromised the effectiveness of an initiative. In doing so, they are poised to handle questions from the media in a constructive manner.

Conflict is somewhat inevitable in partnerships due to the different priorities and personalities involved. A partnership with a custom of effective communication will be well placed to recognise and acknowledge conflict when it arises and to agree a position that satisfies the partnership's objectives. Face-to-face interaction is generally assumed to be preferred by practitioners (Cockbain, 2015). This facilitates sensitive interpretation of the research process and findings and encourages clarification questions (Huberman, 1994). However, written updates, in the form of emails and interim reports, can augment these meetings (see question 10 in Appendix 11.1).

Stage 4: applying knowledge

Interim findings feature strongly in the cycle of continuous communication in Figure 11.1. Police practitioners can feel uneasy if they are not kept informed of how the research is developing, particularly if there is a perception that the researcher is working independently of the policing agency (Fleming, 2011). Provisional interim findings also stimulate debate on whether refinements to the methods or data collection are required and forewarn partnership members if the findings are looking unfavourable. They are particularly useful vehicles for softening the impact of challenging findings (Laycock, 2015). Such reports can also be used to anticipate potential implementation problems.

Interim findings need not follow a traditional report structure, but may be more influential when delivered as practitioner-friendly briefings, practical 'toolkits', executive summaries, and/or technical applications (Telep, 2016; Holgersson, 2015). Engel and Whalen (2010: 108) advise researchers to write clearly and take care not to use language that 'implies intellectual superiority'. Relatedly, different strata of the police (e.g., frontline officers and managerial officers) will have different knowledge needs and therefore multiple written communication styles may be required (Stephens, 2010).

The penultimate step in the model of coordination partnerships is the operationalisation of the findings by all partners. This counters the historic tendency for research findings to be divorced from the operational context in which they are forged (Engel and Whalen, 2010). Involving all partners in the translation of the research findings draws on the collective strengths across the partnership; researchers can advise on the strength and reliability of the findings, and police practitioners can advise on the practical reality of the implementation plan. Doing so has the potential to result in a greater acceptance of the final outcomes of the research project and increase the likelihood of inducing organisational change (Guillaume et al., 2012).

Arguably the final stage in a coordination partnership is the implementation of the research findings – the change in practice. This is no easy task. Delivering organisational change is challenging, and especially so if it comes off the back of research that identifies a deficiency in police practice (Rojek et al., 2015). The political and organisational environment may not support such change (e.g., see Mastrofski, 2002), and change agents may feel apprehensive of delivering innovations, particularly if there is a strong culture of blame in their particular police agency. Maintaining communication and good interpersonal relations between the partners is crucial here, as is support from senior officers. Participants in the validation exercise raised the issue that practitioners who had helped generate the research findings often have to go up the chain of command for approval for resources to implement those findings. Having a senior officer who is convinced of the merits of the research, and who values the findings, is more likely to grant approval rather than someone removed from the partnership.

Although we present the model as somewhat linear, in reality it is likely that there are countless feedback loops; the building of trust pervades the entire process but has a particular role in building relationships (Madensen and Sousa, 2015). However, it is also possible that all of these steps are somewhat interdependent. Each of the stages in the model is reliant on human factors, and the people involved have to be of a certain disposition to patiently deal with the myriad of interpersonal exchanges that might be needed to overcome barriers to the partnership. Partnerships are undoubtedly an ongoing process rather than a series of one-off events, and hence key participants need to be committed to a journey, as well as a destination.

Discussion and conclusion

If the aspirations of evidence-based policing (EBP) are to be realised, research needs to become an integral part of the dialogue in police decision-making. To make this happen, police practitioners need to understand, and value, the nature of research evidence and engage critically with the findings so that they might translate them into their operational contexts. Equally, researchers need to respect and value the craft-based practice that has been built over the history of policing.

In this chapter we have argued that police–researcher partnerships are the linchpin to a cultural shift towards evidence-based policing. When effective, partnerships have the potential to elevate receptivity to research evidence. We suggest that partnerships do this via three mechanisms: 1) by giving the police (joint) ownership of police research, which is hypothesised to secure investment into the evidence-generation process and the findings (Weisburd and Neyroud, 2011); 2) by increasing the relevance of police research, through influencing the research questions studied and by injecting practical wisdom into the implementation of the findings (Rojek et al., 2015); and 3) through the inherent experiential learning within the partnership process that demystifies and humanises the scientific process (Palmer, 2011).

Partnership harmony is not a given, however, and requires organisational change from both research and police partners. In Figure 11.2 we use force field analysis to summarise the fundamental obstacles that might crop up in a partnership working process and how these might be neutralised. These are represented as 'forces against' partnerships on the right and 'forces in support' on the left. The strongest barrier – absence of trust – is positioned at the top right, because this underpins the entire partnership process. As discussed previously, communication is closely intertwined with trust, but is deserving of its own category. The police chain of command (i.e., management style) and organisational stability (i.e., the tendency of human and other resources to be in flux) comes next in the list of forces against, with the barrier of obscure operational relevance of operational findings being in the bottom right. The left-hand side of Figure 11.2 reflects the strategies we have proposed that might counterbalance these forces against.

Figure 11.2 might serve as a risk assessment tool for someone embarking on a new partnership. It prompts thinking about the setup of a partnership in terms of relationship building, communication, and governance. It forces the researcher to consider how to make the research (or other output) operationally relevant and how to maintain buy-in from senior officers.

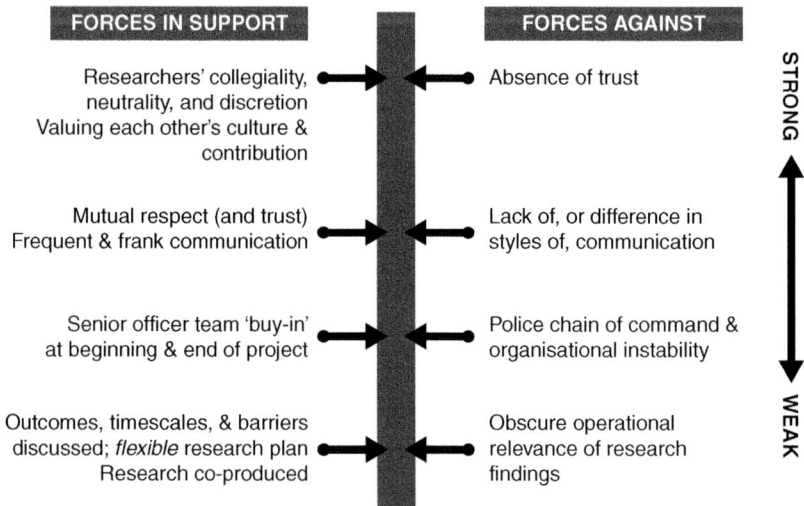

Figure 11.2 Force field analysis for police–researcher partnerships

To anyone who has worked in partnerships, the model we present in this chapter will seem rather obvious. It is, however, the first attempt (of which we are aware) to bring together all of the crucial partnership ingredients and loosely order them in sequence. We have proposed four stages in a typified cooperation partnership process: 1) initiation, 2) planning, 3) building trust, and 4) applying knowledge. Throughout each phase there needs to be trust, communication, a conjoining of motives to undertake research, and feedback to police partners. With most (if not all) of the essential ingredients in place, it is possible that a mutually beneficial partnership that produces reciprocated knowledge might flourish. We hope this model stimulates thinking on how to test whether the processes we have outlined are operating as suggested, perhaps through the participatory action research favoured by applied researchers (Wood, Fleming and Marks, 2008; Bradley and Nixon, 2009).

In conclusion, there is mounting impetus – from external and internal sources – for policing to move towards being an evidence-based profession. In contribution to this goal, in this chapter we contend that police–researcher partnerships are an important mechanism through which police receptivity to research, and researcher receptivity to craft-based practice, might be elevated. Truly effective partnerships are those that surpass organisational agendas and evolve into symbiotic and personal alliances. These have the potential to cement the value of research into police consciousness and put evidence at the heart of decision-making.

Acknowledgments

We are grateful to all of the practitioners who took part in our validation exercise and to Nicky Miller from the College of Policing for facilitating the session. The chapter was strengthened by constructive feedback from the Kongsvinger workshop participants and, in particular, Betsy Stanko.

Notes

1 Police *craft* refers to the knowledge, skill, and judgment officers acquire through their daily experiences.
2 These included the International Crime and Intelligence Analysis conference, a College of Policing–sponsored event on evidence-based policing, and the survey was promoted on POLKA (Police Online Knowledge Area), which is accessible to all police practitioners in the UK.
3 Interested parties may contact the corresponding author for a copy of this survey.
4 Several participants at the events attended said that they didn't have this experience and therefore did not fill in the survey.

References

Bourdieu, P. and Wacquant, L. J. D. (1992). *An Invitation to Reflexive Sociology*, Cambridge: Polity Press.
Bradley, D. and Nixon, C. (2009). 'Ending the "dialogue of the deaf": Evidence and policing policies and practices. An Australian case study', *Police Practice and Research*, 10(5): 423–35.

Brown, R. (2015). 'Tip-Toeing through the Credibility Mine Field: Gaining Social Accept-ance in Policing Research', in E. Cockbain and J. Knutsson (eds) *Applied Police Research*, pp. 34–44, Abingdon, Oxon: Routledge.

Buerger, M.E. (2010). 'Police and research: Two cultures separated by an almost-common language', *Police Practice and Research: An International Journal*, 11(2): 135–43.

Chan, J. (1996). 'Changing police culture', *British Journal of Criminology*, 36(1): 109–34.

Cockbain, E. (2015). 'Getting a Foot in the Closed Door: Practical Advice for Starting Out in Research into Crime and Policing Issues', in E. Cockbain and J. Knutsson (eds) *Applied Police Research*, pp. 21–33, Abingdon, Oxon: Routledge.

Cockbain, E. and Knutsson, J. (2015). 'Introduction', in E. Cockbain and J. Knutsson (eds) *Applied Police Research*, Abingdon, Oxon: Routledge.

Cordner, G. and Biebel, E.P. (2005). 'Problem-oriented policing in practice', *Criminology and Public Policy*, 4: 155–80.

Engel, R. and Whalen, J. (2010). 'Police-academic partnerships: Ending the dialogue of the deaf, the Cincinnati experience', *Police Practice and Research*, 11(2): 105–16.

Fielding, N. (1988). *Joining Forces: Police Training, Socialization, and Occupational Competence*, London and New York: Routledge.

Fleming, J. (2010). 'Learning to work together: Police and academics', *Policing: A Journal of Policy and Practice*, 4(2): 139–45.

Fleming, J. (2011). 'Learning to work together: Police and academics', *Australasian Polic-ing*, 3(2): 139–45.

Fleming, J. (2012). 'Changing the way we do business: Reflecting on collaborative prac-tice', *Police Practice and Research*, 13(4): 375–88.

Foster, J. (2003). 'Police Cultures', in T. Newburn (ed) *Handbook of Policing*, pp. 196–227, Devon, UK: Willan.

Foster, J. and Bailey, S. (2010). 'Joining forces: Maximizing ways of making a difference in policing', *Policing: A Journal of Policy and Practice*, 4(2): 95–103.

Goode, J. and Lumsden, K. (2016). 'The McDonaldisation of police – academic partner-ships: Organisational and cultural barriers encountered in moving from research on police to research with police', *Policing and Society*, 9463(February): 1–15.

Guillaume, P., Sidebottom, A. and Tilley, N. (2012). 'On police and university collabora-tions: A problem-oriented policing case study', *Police Practice and Research*, 13(4): 389–401.

Holgersson, S. (2015). 'An Inside Job: Managing Mismatched Expectations and Unwanted Findings When Conducting Police Research as a Police Officer', in E. Cockbain and J. Knutsson (eds) *Applied Police Research*, pp. 106–16, Abingdon, Oxon: Routledge.

Huberman, M. (1994). 'Research utilization: The state of the art', *Knowledge and Policy*, 7(4): 13–33.

Huey, L. and Mitchell, R.J. (2016). 'Unearthing hidden keys: Why pracademics are an invaluable (if underutilized) resource in policing research', *Policing*, doi: 10.1093/police/paw029

Kennedy, D. (2010). 'Hope and despair', *Police Practice and Research*, 11(2): 166–70.

Kennedy, D. (2015). 'Working in the Field: Police Research in Theory and in Practice', in E. Cockbain and J. Knutsson (eds) *Applied Police Research*, pp. 9–20, Abingdon, Oxon: Routledge.

Laycock, G. (2014). 'Crime science and policing: Lessons of translation', *Policing*, 8(4): 393–401.

Laycock, G. (2015). 'Trust me, I'm a researcher', in E. Cockbain and J. Knutsson (eds) *Applied Police Research*, pp. 45–66, Abingdon, Oxon: Routledge.

Loftus, B. (2010). 'Police occupational culture: Classic themes, altered times', *Policing and Society*, 20(1): 1–20.

Lum, C., Telep, C.W., Koper, C.S. and Grieco, J. (2012). 'Receptivity to research in policing', *Justice Research and Policy*, 14(1): 61–96.

MacDonald, B. (1986). 'Research and Action in the Context of Policing: An Analysis of the Problem and a Programme Proposal', unpublished document of the Police Foundation of England and Wales.

Madensen, T.D. and Sousa, W.H. (2015). 'Practical Academics: Positive Outcomes of Police-Researcher Collaborations', in E. Cockbain and J. Knutsson (eds) *Applied Police Research*, pp. 68–81, Abingdon, Oxon: Routledge.

Manning, P. (1993). 'Toward a Theory of Police Organization: Polarities and Change', paper given to the International Conference on Social Change in Policing, Taipei, 3–5 August 1993.

Mastrofski, S.D. (2002). 'The Romance of Police Leadership', in E. Waring and D. Weisburd (eds) *Advances in Criminological Theory: Crime and Social Organization*, pp. 153–95, vol. 10, New Brunswick, NJ: Transaction Publishers.

O'Neill, M. (2016). 'Revisiting the classics: Janet Chan and the legacy of 'changing police culture', *Policing and Society*. Retrieved from http://dx.doi.org/10.1080/10439463.2016.1165997.

Palmer, I. (2011). *Is the United Kingdom Police Service Receptive to Evidence – based Policing? Testing Attitudes towards Experimentation*, MSt. Thesis, Cambridge University, UK.

Reiner, R. (1992). *The Politics of the Police*, 2nd edition, Hemel Hempstead: Harvester Wheatsheaf.

Reuss Ianni, E. and Ianni, F. (1983). 'Street Cops and Management Cops: The Two Cultures of Policing', in M. Punch (ed.) *Control in the Police Organization*, pp. 251–74, Cambridge, MA: MIT Press.

Rojek, J., Martin, P. and Alpert, G.P. (2015). *Developing and Maintaining Police-Researcher Partnerships to Facilitate Research Use: A Comparative Analysis*, New York: Springer-Verlag.

Stanko, B. (2007). 'From academia to policy making: Changing police responses to violence against women', *Theoretical Criminology*, 11(2): 209–20.

Stephens, D.W. (2010). 'Enhancing the impact of research on police practice', *Police Practice and Research*, 11(2): 150–4.

Strang, H. (2012). 'Coalitions for a common purpose: Managing relationships in experiments', *Journal of Experimental Criminology*, 8(3): 211–25.

Telep, C. (2016). 'Police Officer Receptivity to Research and Evidence-Based Policing: Examining Variability Within and Across Agencies', *Crime and Delinquency*, doi: 10.1177/0011128716642253

Weisburd, D. and Neyroud, P. (2011). *New Perspectives in Policing: Police Science – Toward a New Paradigm*, Harvard Executive Session on Policing and Public Safety, Washington, DC: National Institute of Justice.

Wilkinson, S. (2010). 'Research and policing – looking to the future', *Policing*, 4(2): 146–8.

Willis, J.J. (2016). 'The romance of police pracademics', *Policing*, 10(3): 315–321, doi: 10.1093/police/paw030

Willis, J.J. and Mastrofski, S.D. (2016). 'Improving policing by integrating craft and science: What can patrol officers teach us about good police work?', *Policing and Society*, doi: 10.1080/10439463.2015.1135921

Wood, J., Fleming, J. and Marks, M. (2008). 'Building the capacity of police change agents: The nexus policing project', *Policing and Society*, 18(1): 72–87.

Appendix 11.1 Partnership working survey answers

	Police	Researcher
Who initiated your most recent partnership?		
Co-initiated by police practitioner and researcher	2	1
The police practitioner	3	1
The researcher	0	3
Other (please specify)	1	0
TOTAL	6	5
Who was responsible for obtaining the funding for your most recent partnership?		
All partners	1	0
No funding/work done 'in kind'	0	1
The police practitioner	3	0
The researcher	2	4
TOTAL	6	5
How was the partnership funded? Please choose all options that apply.		
Research council/EU commission	2	1
Charity/third-sector organisation	1	0
Government (e.g., home office, local authority)	2	3
University	1	0
Police agency	1	2
No funding	0	1
TOTAL	7	7
In your opinion was this police–researcher partnership:		
More beneficial to the police practitioner than the researcher	2	1
More beneficial to the researcher than the police practitioner	1	0
Mutually beneficial	3	4
TOTAL	6	5
Based on your most recent experience, would you consider continuing another project with the same partner?		
No	1	0
Unsure	0	1
Yes	5	4
TOTAL	6	5
How important is practitioner experience in shaping the research plan?		
Very important	6	3
Somewhat important	0	2
Not very important	0	0
TOTAL	6	5
Does the time required to conduct research inhibit its relevance to operational decision-making?		
No	4	1
Somewhat	2	2
Yes	0	2
TOTAL	6	5
How do you think this [timeliness] issue could be overcome? Please select up to three options.		
Clear communication and negotiation at the outset of the project	3	1
Better management of police expectations	2	3
Interim findings reported regularly	1	2
Flexible research plan to suit police requirements	1	0
Other (please specify)	4	3
TOTAL	11	9

(*Continued*)

	Police	Researcher
In your experience, is there effective communication between police and research partners?		
No	1	0
Somewhat	2	2
Yes	3	3
TOTAL	6	5
How can communication between partners be strengthened? (Please select up to two options)		
Co-location of partners	1	1
Regular face-to-face interaction	5	3
Regular email correspondence	2	2
Regular telephone calls	0	1
Regular interim progress reports	2	2
TOTAL	10	9
How important is trust between the police and the researcher to the success of the partnership?		
Somewhat important	0	1
Very important	6	4
TOTAL	6	5
What factors can strengthen trust between practitioners and researchers? (Please select up to three options)		
Previous experience of successful partnerships with other partners	2	2
Previous experience of successful partnerships with the same partner	1	3
Exposure to research	3	3
Exposure to police culture	4	1
Good interpersonal relationships	5	3
Reputation of partners	0	1
Minimal change in personnel during the partnership	3	2
TOTAL	18	15
Based on your overall experience of research partnerships, what is the most useful outcome that you value?		
A solution to a problem/actionable information	1	2
Access to new information or resources	1	0
Knowledge exchange	0	0
Learning new perspectives	1	1
Strong interpersonal relationships	1	1
Understanding the other partner's working culture	0	1
Other (please specify)	2	0
TOTAL	6	5

12 Research co-production and knowledge mobilisation in policing

Adam Crawford

Calls for evidence-based policing as a major plank in the professionalisation of the police have reached something of a crescendo in recent years, in the UK in particular. Against a background of fiscal restraint in the public sector, these calls have taken a decidedly prominent place in justifying continued public investment in the police organisation. In the process, social science is heralded as promising to transform and modernise the use of police discretion (Sherman, 1998, 2013). Science is thereby invested with the potency of providing the basis for contemporary police legitimacy and delivering a transformed frontline. Yet the goal of realising an evidence-based profession remains as stubbornly elusive and as complex as ever.

The existing relationship between research (in universities) and policing practice has been evocatively portrayed by Bradley and Nixon (2009) as a 'dialogue of the deaf'. In this chapter, I argue that this entrenched state of affairs is not helped by the manner in which the 'dialogue' has been conceived and conducted within certain models of evidence-based policing (EBP). My aim is to advance a distinctly different vision that is structured around the 'independent interdependence' of researchers and practitioners in the co-production of research, knowledge generation, and the mobilisation and application of evidence in policing. This demands a transformation in both the way researchers engage with policing partners and the place and value of knowledge, data, and evidence within policing. It also raises questions about the appropriate division of labour, the nature of power relations between partners, and the dangers of collusion. Although the context and experiences outlined in the chapter are distinctly British, my contention is that the implications for police–academic relations extend beyond these islands, especially to the English-speaking world in which the EBP movement has developed some considerable momentum.

In support of these arguments, I draw upon experiences and insights from leading two collaborative initiatives designed to strengthen the research evidence base and foster the mobilisation and translation of knowledge into policing practice in England. Both programmes of work were informed by a particular conceptual and philosophical approach to the need for change in the relationship between research and policing and the manner in which change might best be realised. The first was an Economic and Social Research Council (ESRC) Knowledge

Exchange Opportunities Scheme (2014–2015), a collaboration between West Yorkshire Police/Office of the Police and Crime Commissioner (PCC) for West Yorkshire and a team of researchers at the University of Leeds. This was funded as a year-long experimental pilot to explore the challenges and opportunities for different modes of knowledge exchange and research co-production. These were focused around four research themes of public order, acquisitive crime, community engagement, and policing partnerships.[1] Each brought together researchers with policing professionals working in collaborative teams overseen by a steering group incorporating senior officers. In particular, the chapter draws on evidence collected via focus group interviews conducted with members of both the research team and policing partners.[2]

The second project is the ongoing N8 Policing Research Partnership (N8 PRP) funded by a Higher Education Funding Council for England (HEFCE) Catalyst grant (2015–2020). This is a collaborative partnership between eight universities and 11 police forces in a five-year programme of activities. It constitutes a platform for collaborations between universities, PCCs, police forces, and partners across the north of England.[3] It seeks to harness the skills, capabilities, and resources across the participating police force areas, enabling multidisciplinary expertise in problem-solving. It affords opportunities to deliver research, innovation, and impact at a significant scale given the nature of cross-force participation.

The chapter draws on the design, ambitions, and practical experiences of these two initiatives to illustrate both the potential and challenges that confront a model of research–practice co-production in policing. The chapter argues for a transformation in the relation and division of labour between academic researchers and policing partners as well as the value of co-production in knowledge generation, mobilization, and application within policing. In contrast to certain dominant models of EBP (Sherman, 1998, 2013; Weisburd and Neyroud, 2011), it suggests the way forward is a judicious mixture of ambition and caution; ambitious in its transformative logic for organisational culture and working practices, but cautious in the understanding of 'evidence' which embraces a plurality of sources of data, rejects a rigid hierarchy of knowledge, and recognises that the ultimate destination is always incomplete knowledge. The attributes and challenges of co-production are explored and analysed. It argues that co-production offers opportunities to disrupt creatively existing working assumptions among both researchers and policing practitioners with a transformative potential for innovation in policing. However, it also highlights the significant hurdles that need to be negotiated to realise the necessary structural and organisational change that co-production demands.

'Dialogue of the deaf'?

Within the UK, there is a limited history of collaborative relations between research and policing. Relations are, more often than not, informed by and reflect mutual misunderstanding, suspicion, distrust, and disengagement. Undoubtedly academic researchers and police professionals both display very different organisational cultures, priorities, interests, and working practices. Not only do they embody radically different conceptions of what constitutes 'evidence of effectiveness' (Buerger, 2010) but they are also influenced by contrasting demands and driven by very distinct philosophies, values, and motivations. Although it would be wrong to become overly preoccupied with polarised stereotyping, nonetheless, caricatured misunderstandings frequently inform existing beliefs from both sides. Consequently, such perceptions need to be acknowledged, challenged, and overcome. That they exist in abundance has been apparent in both initiatives. The ESRC project provided ample examples from the focus groups. One officer, for example, commented with regard to expectations at the outset:

> I was completely unsure as to what to expect. Was it just going to be a talking shop, with lots of "academic" theory, and where nothing would have changed by the end?

Another officer suggested:

> The grant was awarded to the University of Leeds, so I was concerned that the academics might see it as a means to an end; that is to produce journal articles, rather than a useful report.

More broadly, the different time horizons of police and academics were a frequently noted source of tension. As one officer observed: 'The [police] culture of not being able to invest in something that is interesting and has longer-term benefits is a problem'. Dispelling such concerns – by producing reports in a timely manner – was therefore vital to relationship building and securing trust.

Less frequently noted are the similarities between universities and the police. They are both large bureaucratic organisations that have experienced – to greater or lesser degrees of success – recent government-imposed managerialist reforms. Both organisations exhibit traditional conservative assumptions, although different styles of management. If left to their own devices they tend to stick with what they know for as long as possible. Both are rich in 'knowledge assets' (Bastow et al., 2014) – people, data, resources, and practices – that are ripe to be deployed in and through external collaborations.

Recent changes to the UK policy environment have encouraged something of a rapprochement between universities and police practitioners, albeit sometimes more in name than in substance. As a consequence, there has been a flurry of recent police–academic partnership developments (Goode and Lumsden, 2016). Key factors propelling this trend include the inauguration of the College of Policing in 2012 with its mission to 'set standards of professional practice that draw on the best available evidence' and 'provide practical and common-sense approaches based on evidence of what works' (College of Policing, 2014: 10, 35). The college has helped push the case for an evidence-based profession to the forefront of policy debate. It has done much to stimulate the conditions for rethinking the role and operationalisation of evidence in policing. Additionally, the introduction of PCCs

as 'commissioning' bodies for crime and policing services by altering the policing governance landscape have opened up new possibilities for external dialogue
(Crawford, 2016). Since their first elections in November 2012, some PCCs have
injected new opportunities for innovation, added greater transparency, and fore-
grounded the role of 'public engagement', albeit narrowly conceived in terms of
public opinion reflected in surveys, news, and social media. However, they have
also introduced greater politicisation, shortened time horizons with regard to priorities (based on electoral timescales), fostered a certain parochialism given that
PCCs' electorate are only those within their force area, and added a new dimension
to interforce rivalries and competition. More controversially, British government
austerity measures (since 2010) – resulting in significant reductions to budgets and
police personnel – have forced senior police managers to explore ways of 'doing
more with less'. As such, they have challenged many traditional assumptions and
working practices and injected opportunities for research-informed collaborations
as a means of cost savings.

Limitations in dominant models of EBP

In their call for a 'new paradigm of police science', Weisburd and Neyroud
(2011) provide an important contribution to thinking about and reimagining the
relationship between research (universities) and practice (police). They present
a strong argument in support of the view that policing practices would be substantially improved by more systematic attention to, and application of, evidence
about the effects of policing strategies and interventions. However, it is their preferred vision for the future, the assumptions that inform their repositioning of the
police–research relationship, and their conclusion that the police take charge of
the research agenda that, for me, are problematic. They call for a 'new paradigm
that changes the relationship between science and policing', in which 'the police
adopt and advance evidence-based policy and that universities become active participants in the everyday world of police practice' (Weisburd and Neyroud, 2011:
1). They argue for a 'shift in ownership of police science from the universities to
police agencies' (Weisburd and Neyroud, 2011: 1). As Sparrow (2016: 130–1)
astutely notes, most commentators would endorse a closer, flourishing collaboration between the fields of policing and scholarship: 'However, at this time, the
relationship remains fragile, and much harm might be done if we accept a vision
for the future of the relationship that is somehow misguided, inappropriate or
off-base'. Before outlining an alternative vision, it is worth briefly summarising
deficiencies in the approach proffered by Weisburd and Neyroud.

Narrow understanding of evidence and 'elite science'

The approach they advocate advances a narrow understanding of evidence and 'science'. It posits a clear hierarchy of knowledge informed by a ranking of methodologies with random control trials (RCTs) at its apex, epitomised by the Maryland
Scale of Scientific Methods (Sherman, 2009). RCTs strip away the complexities

of reality in an effort to isolate certain factors. Such contextual factors, however, may be central to a programme's execution and impact. Although RCTs provide strong internal validity, they do not tell us much about whether we could replicate that intervention in another context (Hough, 2010). They embody a linear notion of causality. Yet for complex social phenomena, not only are causes multiple, but feedback loops may make them more circular in effect. Critically, it is important to be cognizant of the limits of our knowledge; to know what we do not know, or at least to appreciate that there are limits to what we know. Methodological pluralism is needed for such tasks. There is a palpable danger that a rigid hierarchy of knowledge – with RCTs as the 'gold standard' – simply reflects an illusory 'desire to attach certainty to police operations' (Hope, 2009: 127). In its narrowing of the frame of relevance, such an approach advances an 'elite science' (Sparrow, 2016).

This methodological elitism is unnecessarily blinkered and unrealistic in at least two senses of the word. First, it is as if 'realism' and 'realist evaluation' (Pawson and Tilley, 1997; Pawson, 2013) had not already provided a robust critique of the assumptions within and limitations of the quasi-experimental paradigm and its methodologies. As Tilley (2009: 138) summarises:

> Social programmes involve intentional inter action. Differing sub-groups interact with programme components in different ways. Stakeholders, including subjects, adapt over time, meaning not only that the intervention but also responses to it change over time. There is ineluctable complexity as programmes set off chains of action, inter action, feedback and adaptation.

Second, it is unrealistic in the sense that such experiments are costly, time consuming, and resource intensive. They are, as Eck (2002: 109) warns, 'an awkward, inefficient and unnatural way to learn about what works when we are interested in small-scale, small-claim, discrete interventions'. They do not lend themselves well to the deployment of knowledge in aid of ongoing reflection and learning.

Despite drawing heavily on evidence-based medicine (EBM) in support of a 'police science', there is less frequent acknowledgement of the nuanced debates within healthcare about what constitutes good evidence, notably the more recent shift away from evidence based on 'hierarchies' to an understanding of 'appropriateness' (Abeysinghe and Parkhurst, 2013). In place of a fixed hierarchy of evidence, the National Institute for Health and Care Excellence (NICE) in the UK has issued revised guidelines (NICE, 2012)[4] that proffer a more pluralist understanding of 'appropriate evidence'. As Michael Rawlins (a former NICE chairman) has powerfully argued, in the context of healthcare:

> The fundamental flaw with the development and use of hierarchies of evidence is that they fail to recognize that it is not the method that matters, but whether the particular method is appropriate to answer the particular question . . . practitioners . . . harm themselves, their discipline – not to mention the patients they seek to serve – by slavish adherence to hierarchies of evidence.
> (2014: 235)

Specificities of policing

Certain features of policing should not be ignored when drawing lessons from the healthcare setting. Policing entails the more routine use of coercive force over and against certain groups of people. Whilst some facets of healthcare are clearly coercive (notably mental health) and entail dimensions of control and rights, none-theless, the everyday deployment of coercion informs the fundamental relation between police and public in a distinct way to that between healthcare profes-sionals and patients. As Thacher (2001) has argued: 'Policing is not a treatment'. Arrests are not aspirins! Importantly, unlike aspirins, arrests involve coercion (either implicitly or explicitly) and can be delivered in very different ways which dramatically affect the manner in which they are received by those subject to them and their resultant impact. Simply put, there are good and bad arrests, there are ones that conform to principles of procedural justice and those that do not. Some arrests will be triggered by the manner in which suspects respond to police actions, par-ticularly in relation to public order offences. This underscores the complexities of the social world – which is neither linear nor static – and which entails 'reactance', reflexivity, and feedback on the part of practitioners charged with implementing services, as well as members of the public or 'recipients' of policing strategies. Whereas more healthcare is a good in itself, policing is contested. More security is not inevitably a social good, given the notably tense relationship with liberty.

Science alone is not enough

Even if there is agreement on the 'evidence' – be it in the context of healthcare or policing – there remain important questions about social values and deliverability. These introduce into the mix other messier dimensions in the (non)utilization of research in policy and practices. This might be interpreted as the interplay – or clash – between three very different lenses: politics (values), evidence (knowl-edge), and delivery (implementation). Evidence alone is insufficient. It has been recognised for some time that policymakers and practitioners make decisions in environments where they are subject to various, often conflicting, pressures, influ-ences, and priorities. 'Evidence' is only one (often contested) element in this com-plex mix (Nutley et al., 2007). That policing is a normative enterprise governed by key principles of respect for individual rights, due process, and equal treat-ment and, hence, intrinsically political has been long recognised (Reiner, 2010). Recently, PCCs have injected a starkly evident political dimension. Engaging with the political and normative dimensions of policing demands consideration of social value judgements, with 'the ethical principles, preferences, culture, and aspirations of society' which are themselves ultimately 'informed by the general public' (Rawlins, 2014: 233). RCTs and EBP have blind spots when it comes to politics and values. In the context of healthcare, questions of public understanding and trust in research and guidance derived from it have been identified as pivotal in transcending conflicts of interest (Lenzer, 2013). There is an important place for public understanding, deliberation, and judgement of evidence and the role of the public as agents in knowledge production. Yet the citizen and the public are conspicuously absent from the elitist 'new paradigm' in the reformulation of science in policing that some EBPs advocate. They are seen as passive recipients of a service rather than as active co-producers of security, policing, and order.

Evidence in the service of organisational legitimacy

For Weisburd and Neyroud evidence is recurrently interpreted as a means for promoting legitimacy. They argue that 'the advancement of science in policing' is 'essential to retain public support and legitimacy' (2011: 6). This appears to misunderstand that it is not science per se that enhances legitimacy but the public understanding of science wherein legitimacy resides. This implies a role for citizen engagement and public deliberation as embedded in the process of knowledge mobilization, increasingly recognised in the context of healthcare (Ocloo and Matthews, 2016).[5] What Weisburd and Neyroud construct as a bilateral relation between police and academia should rather be viewed as a multilevel relationship between policing (plurally understood), citizens, and research institutions.

Engagement that injects a judicious dimension of public purpose and social value is also important to keep in check the very powerful organisational interests that inform knowledge generation, validation, and what counts as 'science'. There is a lingering concern with Weisburd and Neyroud's arguments that evidence is to be used to legitimise policing rather than to challenge and improve it. Legitimacy from their perspective is associated with justifying large amounts of public-sector resources that are accorded to policing. They note: 'Policing is becoming increasingly expensive as a public service, and without a scientific base to legitimize the value of police, it is likely that public policing will face growing threats from other less costly alternatives, like private policing' (Weisburd and Neyroud, 2011: 10).

Evidence in the service of organisational legitimacy raises acute concerns about vested interests. It reminds us of the need for sensitivities to relations of power–knowledge and the involvement of knowledge in the maintenance of power relations. This is, of course, a significant concern in the field of medicine and healthcare where important lessons might be learnt with regard to evidence biases and the hidden hand of vested interests (Greenhalgh et al., 2014: 5). The 'dark sides' of the close relationship between 'science' and medicine are reflected in the corrosive interests of drug companies in the production and communication (as well as silencing) of scientific 'evidence' (Elliott, 2010). Research must be mindful of the interests and organisational priorities of the police or others. Knowledge needs to remain the basis of critical reflection. Hence, there is a need for research to maintain a critical independence and 'detached stance' that constitutes a central value in ensuring impartiality. Even-handedness and lack of bias are key to assuring the perceived authority and legitimacy of evidence in the eyes of the public and other stakeholders.

Knowledge co-production

Bradley and Nixon (2009: 430) argue for a new methodology of engagement built on establishing and sustaining 'long-term partnerships between police and academics' in which there is greater regard for 'diffusion and impact'. It is in this same vein that colleagues and I have been forging new forms of relations and deploying experimental methodologies with the aim of constructing the terrain for a new dialogue. The model of police–university collaboration that we have been building (through the ESRC and HEFCE projects) is founded on a philosophy of research co-production and knowledge mobilization, namely the systematic process of getting the best evidence to the appropriate decision-makers in an accessible and timely manner so as to influence decision-making (Bannister and Hardill, 2013). This model is closely related to, and builds on, traditions of participatory action research and co-operative inquiry (Heron, 1996). The idea of co-production was first articulated and developed by Elinor Ostrom and colleagues in a series of studies of the Chicago police in the 1970s (Ostrom and Baugh, 1973; Ostrom et al., 1978). They posited co-production as a means of increasing the effectiveness of local service delivery through increased 'consumer' involvement in service production:

> Coproduction involves a mixing of the productive efforts of regular and consumer producers. This mixing may occur directly, involving coordinated efforts in the same production process, or indirectly through independent, yet related efforts of regular producers and consumer producers.
>
> (Park et al., 1981: 1002)

Subsequently, co-production has acquired a foothold within policing, albeit primarily with regard to service production and community policing (Friedmann, 1992). Co-production has also gained considerable currency in debates on health and social care (Boyle et al., 2010; Realpe and Wallace, 2010).

Co-production contrasts with more traditional approaches to research, where the main involvement of nonacademics is as the subjects to be investigated or as commissioners and recipients of research findings. It departs from the more linear model of research engagement with policy set down in the Rothschild Report (1971) on *The Organisation and Management of Government Research and Development* which heralded a period of increased government research funding but did so in a framework of a customer–contractor principle, whereby the customer says what they want, the contractor does it (if they can), and the customer pays. Kogan and colleagues concluded that the Rothschild formula:

> failed to note how in those areas of policy where data are diffuse, and analyses [are] most likely to be strongly influenced by value preferences, problems must be identified collaboratively between policy-maker and scientist. It failed to acknowledge that policy makers have to work hard to identify problems, to specify research that might help solve them, and to receive and use the results of research.
>
> (2006: 15)

Despite such discerning observations, much the same assumptions inform the dominant 'donor–recipient' model of impact that underlies the UK assessment of academic research instituted by HEFCE in the form of the Research Excellence Framework (REF).[6] Implicit therein is an apparently benevolent knowledge producer (university/academic) whose research eventually effects change over an external community, organization, or policy domain. This presents a highly instrumental, mechanistic, and linear reading of impact as a causal chain by which one party does something to/for another party at a particular moment in time and space which is visible, concrete, and tangible in that it leaves traces. Such a 'mythology of impact' as an outcome is belied by the more complex, nonlinear, and nuanced multiple processes and relations through which impact ensues and develops. It ignores the very real dimension of serendipity, whereby impacts arise from opportunistic, unintended, or chance encounters.

By definition, co-production involves bringing together parties that may have markedly 'different priorities and preoccupations' (Martin, 2010: 212), with the aim of working together towards a mutually agreed 'production' (Brudney and England, 1983; see also Wood and Bradley, 2009). At the core of co-production is the idea of collaborative advantage, 'gained through collaboration when something is achieved that could not have been achieved by any organization acting alone' (Vangen and Huxham, 2003: S62). Hence, negotiating common purpose, forging shared priorities, and ensuring appreciation of the divergent contributions of differing partners are all cornerstones for mature partnerships in co-production. This notion of collaborative advantage when applied to knowledge generation, validation, diffusion, and application provides the framework for the approach to research co-production and knowledge mobilisation advanced here. As such, it is argued that co-production has greater potential than traditional approaches to provide practical and policy-relevant insights and impacts, as well as findings that advance intellectual understanding (Pohl et al., 2010): 'Co-production as a meta-methodology . . . may not just contribute to generating both academic insight and public benefit, but potentially also *different* (and *greater*) intellectual insights' (Campbell and Vanderhoven, 2016: 14–15, emphasis in original). Advantage derives not simply in the combination of perspectives but in framing and shaping questions, methodologies, and impacts differently. Co-production implies a reformed conception of what constitutes knowledge, how it is mobilised and used. In sum, our approach to co-production assumes mutual respect, a lack of a rigid hierarchy of knowledge forms, fluid and permeable disciplinary boundaries, a two-way flow of knowledge between researchers and nonacademics (not simply its 'transfer'), and a normative concern with usefulness and action.

A plurality of knowledge

Importantly, co-production challenges the notion of a distinct hierarchy of knowledge. By contrast, diverse forms of expertise – among academics, practitioners, businesses, and members of the public – are considered valuable and contribute to knowledge production and mobilisation. It is the interplay between different forms of knowledge in providing varied insights that matters. RCTs certainly have their place – in some cases an important place – but they do not and cannot stand alone. Moreover, there are many questions that RCTs are not well placed to answer or assist in constructing the evidence base and its utilisation. Co-production embraces plural sources of knowledge and mixed methodologies. Co-production also acknowledges the importance of police officer intuition, practical reasoning, situated knowledge, and, more generally, the role of 'police craft' (Bayley and Bittner, 1984). Whether recognised or not, 'policing "craft", or the culmination of knowledge based on hands-on experience, is a feature of police culture that poses a formidable obstacle to implementing new policies and practices' (Willis, 2013: 2). Rather than bemoan the lack of uptake of 'scientific evidence', as some EBP proponents do (Sherman, 2015), greater value would be derived from engaging with such sources of knowledge mobilisation. The argument here is not for the triumph of one over the other, but rather for a fuller appreciation of the qualities, merits, and insights provided by each in understanding and contextualising the other. There is no uncomplicated answer to the question of what counts as good (enough) evidence. In large part, it depends on what it is we seek to know, what purposes are sought, and in what contexts the evidence is to be used. Although it is wholly appropriate to debate and challenge the standards of evidence and rigours of methodologies, we also need to be realistic about the extent to which such standard setting will shape or influence the complex and highly politicised decision-making that policymakers, policing managers, and local practitioners engage in everyday (Nutley et al., 2013).

From this perspective, knowledge mobilisation is a collaborative process entailing critical reflection on social reality and possibilities for transformation in order to effect change. It underscores the value of ongoing lesson learning, reflexivity, and contingency in a way that radically departs from the fixity of the gold standard 'what works' that preoccupies some social scientists, the fear of failure that haunts police practitioners – aptly conveyed by one police officer in a focus group who described how 'policing initiatives are doomed to succeed' – and the quest for 'golden bullets' that fixates policymakers. It stands in stark contrast to the ingrained culture of institutional defensiveness which has marked much British policing, as evidenced all too clearly in the police response to the Hillsborough disaster over nearly three decades (Scraton, 2016). Co-production prompts a culture of learning, external engagement, and openness. Hence, for our purposes, co-production is a means to realising wider structural, organizational, and cultural change both among policing organisations and within universities.

The politics of evidence

Co-production also encourages not only a focus on the *supply* of evidence – to generate knowledge and to present it in a form that is accessible to policymakers and practitioners – but also to the *demand* for evidence. The approach to co-production advocated here is that those who are going to use research and apply the knowledge base should be involved in building it by actively co-producing the evidence. Policing professionals need to become knowledge producers as well as evidence users. Rather than research conceived as a distanced and linear process, it is an interactive, reciprocal, and iterative process. This means recognising the 'politics' of evidence-informed policymaking (Cairney, 2016) and the manifest centrality of emotions and affect to such questions. How people feel and their emotional sensibilities can be important dimensions in policies that centre on behaviour change (Hardill and Mills, 2013). This is particularly evident in relation to policing and punishment, where rational decision-making and evidence often take second place to deeply ingrained feelings, fears, and sentiments that are aroused by problems of crime and victimisation.

The political role of the PCC reinforces this dimension. In reality, the experiences of collaborative partnerships from the two projects between policing partners and universities highlighted that the relationship between the police force and PCC within an area is not a simple one. The relationship is embryonic, and many PCCs are still feeling their way as there remain evident questions and challenges over where the power lies and what delimits the full scope of the governance powers. The experience from the ESRC project highlighted that the two organisations should not be treated as undifferentiated or the same in priorities, values, and capabilities. Rather, their differing roles, contribution, and limitations need to be recognised. Furthermore, it should not be assumed that commitments made by the PCC can be relied upon with regard to the police force or that communication between the two is in any sense straightforward. The nature of the multilateral relationship made lines of communication and reporting more complex and even more important to get right. One of the recommendations of the ESRC project emphasised the value of police forces having a portfolio holder for promoting evidence-based policing and overseeing research relations via appropriate organisational structures that combine and straddle the Office of the PCC and police. It was felt that such a structure would ensure greater coordination, simpler lines of communication, and buy-in at the top. West Yorkshire Police have subsequently implemented such a model in the light of the ESRC project experiences with the establishment of the Joint Innovation Group (in early 2016).

The dissonances between police and PCC also raise questions about deliverability. It has long been recognised in policing that 'street level bureaucrats' (Lipsky, 1980) invariably subverted, transformed, and resisted policies in their implementation. Cultural obstacles to fostering change at the frontline are substantial and return us to the role of police 'craft' and intuition as impediments to the application of 'science'. A number of respondents voiced the concern that the 'culture' of the police organisation 'will trump whatever' the evidence says or even what the senior command team may seek to foster concerning the use of evidence. Once again, this demands a fuller appreciation of the qualities, merits, and insights provided by such practical reasoning in knowledge mobilisation and utilisation.

The challenges of co-production

This underscores the fact that co-production is neither easy nor uncomplicated. Co-production brings considerable challenges and raises tensions and differences that need to be managed. It blurs roles, relations, and boundaries. The boundaries between pure and applied research become less distinct as do disciplinary and professional boundaries. It implies greater flexibility and more fluid methodologies. Fundamental to co-production is an open and flexible research process and the relationships that are its backbone. Co-production challenges traditional research practices, working assumptions, and models of operation. Rooted in relationships, it demands flexibility in terms of methods. But flexibility is not only a product of relationships (which themselves shift and change over time), but also in recognition of the complexity of the social world and the challenges of *emergence*. People are active, reflexive subjects who exercise volition, and this often demands reflexivity built into modes of research and evaluation. Emergence highlights the potential effects, adaptations, societal changes, and unintended consequences that are associated with the introduction of new programmes or innovations (Pawson, 2013). Hence, co-production draws into sharp focus the nonlinear nature of the research process and of knowledge translation and impact. It also demands different skills and capabilities, notably with regard to leadership and the negotiation of relationships.

For some, it challenges conventional understandings of assessment and raises questions about rigour in research. As Pain and colleagues (2015) note, significant differences in time, openness, and relationships are required for co-production to reach its full potential and flourish. What is less often acknowledged is that co-production thrives in the right conditions and can be challenging to orchestrate without them. Serious barriers include funding, development time, institutional structures, priorities, and reward mechanisms. This presents problems for evaluating impact which arises as 'a process often involving a gradual, porous and diffuse series of changes undertaken collaboratively' (Pain and colleagues, 2015: 4). Whereas co-production is open, dynamic, and flexible, and hence, impact cannot be fully known in advance, this does not mean that it is left to chance or accident. Rather, this points to both requirements to foster the conditions that underpin and enable serendipity and the necessity to exploit and maximize the utility of serendipitous developments.

For some, co-production enables a democratisation of the research process. It conforms to an ethic of doing research *with* rather than *on* people. Notably in the context of participatory community studies, this translates into an ethical commitment to 'nothing about us, without us' (Pain et al., 2015: 8–9). Co-production has been described by Pain and colleagues (2015) as constituting a 'soup' made up of multifaceted knowledge that reflects lived experience and is stirred up and checked by many different people and diverse inspirations throughout the process. However, as this analogy suggests there are dangers that co-production is seen as blurring, effacing, and eroding professional differences and disciplinary foundations. Some celebrate this erosion and blending, arguing for 'embodied connection' as 'a state that is created when people are active together in a shared space with a common goal' (Pain et al., 2015: 8). Yet, particularly in the context of policing, there are a number of pitfalls with these rose-tinted visions of co-production.

First, the celebration of blurring is in danger of losing sight of distinctiveness, difference, and the diversity of contribution, expertise, and skills, as the varying different perspectives and priorities are commingled, melded, and (con)fused. In the 'soup' of co-production there are evident dangers that independence, autonomy, and the value of distinctive contributions are lost in a mixture of sameness. It is, after all, difference that constitutes the life-blood of collaborative advantage.

Second, there is an implicit assumption – particularly evident in research co-production work with voluntary sector and civil society organisations, as well as community groups – that co-production as a strategy is linked to empowering relatively powerless and disenfranchised groups. In the context of policing, this is far from the case. The police are a powerful, authoritative organisation that is well versed at articulating its own preferences and interests, as well as its narrative construction of events (as the police response to Hillsborough testifies). Additionally, PCCs have large budgets and are vested with wide powers and responsibilities. Research into various forms of policing partnerships invariably highlights the tendency of police to dominate agendas and to sideline dissenting voices (Crawford, 1997). Police officers themselves have recourse to significant legal powers, access to informational resources, and can deploy legitimate coercive force. The 'special competence' of the police is their capacity for decisive action; the authority to intervene where 'non-negotiable coercive force' may have to be used (Bittner, 1970: 46). This generic coercive authority, although relatively rarely used, differentiates the police from most other public servants.

In such a context, co-production is aligned less to the priority of empowerment but rather to engagement, reflection, and checking the legitimate use of power. The co-production process is not free of hierarchies, structural conflicts, and differential power relations, all of which require complex and subtle negotiation and management. Disagreements and tensions should not be sidelined, avoided, or subsumed in the rush for a 'goal of unity' (Crawford, 1997: 137–9) or quest for consensus. Rather, conflicts need to be recognised, addressed, and managed in appropriate open forums through deliberation. Shared understanding does not mean that all the partners necessarily agree on the problem/evidence or hold the same view of it (Crawford and Cunningham, 2015). This does not mean that the basis of a consensus cannot be constructed, but rather that to do so necessitates the acceptance of difference and the active negotiation of commonalities. Mutual recognition of difference represents a more secure premise for co-production relations than an assumed consensus or undifferentiated 'soup' of inspirations. Conflict may be the healthy expression of different interests which need to be negotiated in open and constructive ways that recognizes – and where possible seeks to compensate for – power differentials.

Critical reflection and 'independent interdependence'

All of this demands that knowledge creation and mobilization – co-produced or otherwise – should not become an extension of policing, driven purely by the needs and exigencies of the police organisations. Co-production is not a vehicle for the realization of research *for* the police (in place of research *on* or *by* the police), but rather the generation of knowledge that challenges policing assumptions and working practices and yet maintains a critical distance and autonomy. This also exposes deficiencies in the dominant model of EBP proponents who argue for the 'integration' of research with practice, whereby science and research are 'an organic part of the police mission' (Weisburd and Neyroud, 2011: 11). There are similar parallels here with Braga's (2013) vision of 'embedded researchers' working within police departments. If research becomes too closely tied to the organisational interests of the police, it will lose its vital critical distance and become an arm of, and justification for, prevailing practices (or dominant programmes of change) rather than an engine of critical improvement.

Hence, boundary crossing is both an essential and dynamic element of co-production that prompts continual reassessment of assumptions, critical self-reflection on values, and questioning of terminology. Boundary crossing affords considerable possibilities to challenge introspective organisational cultures and myopic managerial practices, as well as inappropriate attitudes and behaviours within organisations. Despite an inevitable blurring of boundaries, this does not mean that they disappear altogether. Research and researchers must retain their critical independence. To do otherwise would fall foul of the worse criticisms of some of the self-serving interests that blight some pharmaceutical research (Goldacre, 2012). 'Independent interdependence' becomes the standard for relations between organisations in co-production, constituting 'the weak force which binds' parties (Rock, 1990: 39). Partners need to have a shared understanding of mutual respect and appreciation for the divergent interests, values, and norms that hold the partnership together. However, for such partnerships to play an evident role in transforming organisational cultures, they also need to be embedded and sustained in frontline practices. The reality is that successful interorganisational partnerships need to be forged, nurtured, and supported at all levels by people committed to realising the benefits of collaborative working and exploiting the disruptive opportunities for innovation and cross-cultural learning that boundary crossing provides.

Trust

Co-production relies upon open and trusting interpersonal and interorganisational relations. Trust is a central coordinating mechanism of networks of co-production and is essential for cooperative behaviour (Tyler, 2010). A key ingredient in successful partnerships entails establishing and sustaining trust relations across agency boundaries (Crawford, 1997). This is not easy, particularly where there is a history of mistrust or misunderstanding. A crucial element in establishing trust relations is making different partners aware of the limitations and capabilities of their own and participating organisations' contribution, so that they neither try to 'do it all' (something that the police are particularly prone to do and often expected by others to do as a '24-hour' service), nor do they have unrealistic expectations of what others can deliver. Mutual respect and recognition of professional judgement, discretion, and differing organisational priorities help to foster open partnership relations built on trust. As one officer put it:

> There needs to be a common understanding of what collaboration means. It looks good on paper, but it means much more than ticking the box. It means sharing the challenges and the risks.

Another police respondent from the ESRC focus group categorically stated: 'I've learnt the benefits of collaboration and that *one plus one really is equal to greater than two!*'

The importance of the quality of partnership relations of building trust and mutual understanding, as well as ownership of and commitment to the relationship and its outcomes, has been a key finding from our experiences of co-production. Research is more likely to effect change if it is owned by the very people who have a capacity to effect change. Co-production, like models of participatory action research, can help overcome problems of knowledge mobilisation and deliverability, especially in contexts where there are high levels of mistrust of traditional sources of expertise, like policing and mental health services (Ungar et al., 2015). A key success of the ESRC project, according to one police focus group respondent, was felt to be that it 'provided an open platform for honest conversations'. Both researchers and police participants were surprised at the level of ownership that the police had in the ESRC initiative. From the academic focus group the research officer working on the project declared himself to be surprised at the level of police 'involvement in project design' and 'influence over' its direction. He had expected the academic team 'to be in the lead, with [the police] supporting implementation'. Similarly, police officers admitted to having initial scepticism that 'the academics might even have some sense of findings in advance of research'. This was dispelled by the nature of the partnership and the pivotal role accorded to co-production. The decision to shift the focus of one 'partnership' case study from the police–fire service relation to safeguarding children at the request of the steering group–heavily influenced by the persuasive arguments of the assistant chief constable – was frequently cited as an excellent example of how the focus of the research orientation changed as a product of genuine co-production. This translated into considerable buy-in from policing partners given the degree of ownership and stake they possessed in the partnership. Consequently, members of the academic team (with long-standing involvement in police research) remarked that they had not previously experienced the high levels of support provided by the policing partners via the steering group. This was both 'novel and helpful' according to one. However, developing sustained and good-quality interorganisational trust relations takes time. The longer a relationship develops, the greater the scope for the quality of trust relations based on shared experiences.

Conclusions

This chapter has sought to contribute to thinking about ways in which to fashion methodologies and collaborative infrastructures that are well suited to the tasks of fostering the use of evidence in practice and promoting cultures of organisational learning, innovation, and critical self-reflection in police and universities. This entails a better understanding of the complex interplay between evidence/knowledge, politics/values, and delivery/implementation in policing research and frontline practice. Ultimately, a key ambition of co-production is to transform the ways in which academic researchers engage with policing partners and ways in which policing practitioners utilise evidence that is rigorous and relevant. This chapter has sought to delineate and explore the contribution of co-production in identifying the most effective means of mobilising research-based knowledge and enhancing the role that social science research can make to policing policy and practice. This means moving away from top-down 'elitist' models of knowledge to an increasing recognition that the purposes for which knowledge is assembled, synthesized, and appropriated all matter. It demands that we contend with questions about the forms of knowledge that are appropriate in given contexts and how they might best be strengthened through use. Translating evidence into practice remains a central thorny problem, accentuating the importance of developing 'translational capabilities' among researchers and nonacademic partners (Campbell and Vanderhoven, 2016: 8). Given the significant cultural obstacles to the kinds of organisational transformation implicit in the aforementioned agenda, it is unlikely to be realised overnight. Such partnerships aspire to long-term goals and demand clear leadership and vision – creating and communicating a 'clear sense of what is at stake' – as to its direction, benefits, and realistic outcomes (Martin and Mazerolle, 2016). It necessitates planning for and creating 'short-term wins' which requires academics to think differently about the timeliness and accessibility of academic research and reporting, but also attend to the pitfalls of real-time reporting. Competing time horizons, therefore, need to be managed prudently in building and maintaining relationships of mutual trust and the appreciation of divergent contributions: the hallmark of *independent interdependence*. It requires forging coalitions to effect change, not only senior champions but various advocates at different levels of the organisation and, hence, anchoring change in the organisational culture (Kotter, 1995). Collaborative research partnerships built on relationships rather than one-off projects provide new spaces for both researchers and police professionals to engage with complex and vexed issues about shared norms and values and to challenge organisational assumptions and ways of working. Thus envisioned, co-production can help to 'do things differently' in ways that accord greater ownership over, understanding of, and regard to the value of research in building an evidence-informed knowledge base in policing.

Acknowledgments

I would like to thank Stuart Lister, Nick Malleson, Clifford Stott, and Xavier L'Hoiry for their work on the ESRC project and the various West Yorkshire Police colleagues and staff at the OPCC who collaborated on the study and the project steering group, notably Andy Battle, Fraser Sampson, Paul Money, and Andrew Staniforth. I would also like to thank Anna Barker, Jenny Fleming, Nick Tilley, Charlie Lloyd, and all the contributors to the Kongsvinger meeting, especially the editors, for comments on an earlier draft.

Notes

1 Summary reports from each are available along with further information from the project website, see: www.law.leeds.ac.uk/research/projects/an-exploratory-knowledge-platform-for-policing.
2 The focus groups included six researchers and five policing professionals from the OPCC and police. I would like to acknowledge the invaluable assistance of Claire Johnson, the project manager for the ESRC project, who conducted the focus group interviews.
3 For further information see: www.n8prp.org.uk.
4 The comparative role of NICE in health care is frequently lauded by proponents of EBP as an 'independent evidence assessment agency' (Sherman, 2009).
5 One of the core activity strands of the N8 PRP is dedicated to 'public engagement' to foster a public voice within debates about evidence and its role in public policy and delivery.
6 See: www.hefce.ac.uk/rsrch/REFimpact/.

References

Abeysinghe, S. and Parkhurst, J. (2013). *'Good' Evidence for Improved Policy Making: From Hierarchies to Appropriateness*, London: London School of Hygiene.
Bannister, J. and Hardill, I. (2013). 'Knowledge mobilisation and the social sciences', *Contemporary Social Sciences*, 8(3): 167–75.
Bastow, S., Dunleavy, P. and Tinkler, J. (2014). *The Impact of the Social Sciences*, London: Sage.
Bayley, D.H. and Bittner, E. (1984). 'Learning the skills of policing', *Law and Contemporary Problems*, 47: 35–59.
Bittner, E. (1970). *The Function of Police in Modern Society*, Washington: NIMH.
Boyle, D., Coote, A., Sherwood, C. and Slay, J. (2010). *Right Here, Right Now: Taking Co-Production into the Mainstream*, London: Nesta.
Bradley, D. and Nixon, C. (2009). 'Ending the "dialogue of the deaf": Evidence and policing policies and practices. An Australian case study', *Police Practice and Research*, 10(5/6): 423–35.
Braga, A. (2013). 'Embedded Criminologists in Police Departments', *Ideas in American Policing*, 13, Washington DC: Police Foundation. Retrieved from www.policefoundation.org/wp-content/uploads/2015/06/Ideas-17-final.pdf
Brudney, J.L. and England, R.E. (1983). 'Towards a definition of the coproduction concept', *Public Administration Review*, 43(1): 59–65.
Buerger, M.E. (2010). 'Policing and research: Two cultures separated by an almost common language', *Police Practice and Research*, 11(2): 135–43.
Cairney, P. (2016). *The Politics of Evidence-Based Policy Making*, London: Palgrave Macmillan.
Campbell, H. and Vanderhoven, D. (2016). *Knowledge that Matters: Realising the Potential of Co-Production*, Manchester: N8 Research Partnership.
College of Policing. (2014). *Five Year Strategy*, Retrieved from www.college.police.uk/About/Documents/Five-Year_Strategy.pdf
Crawford, A. (1997). *The Local Governance of Crime*, Oxford: Oxford University Press.
Crawford, A. (2016). 'The Implications of the English and Welsh Experiment in Democratic Governance of Policing through Police and Crime Commissioners', in J. Ross and T. Delpeuch (eds) *Comparing the Democratic Governance of Police Intelligence*, pp. 116–52, Cheltenham: Edward Elgar.
Crawford, A. and Cunningham, M. (2015). 'Working in Partnership', in J. Fleming (ed) *Police Leadership – Rising to the Top*, pp. 71–94, Oxford: Oxford University Press.

Eck, J.E. (2002). 'Learning from Experience in Problem Oriented Policing and Situational Prevention', in N. Tilley (ed) *Evaluation of Crime Prevention*, pp. 93–117, Monsey, BY: Criminal Justice Press.

Elliott, C. (2010). *White Coat, Black Hat: Adventures on the Dark Side of Medicine*, Boston, MA: Beacon Press.

Friedmann, R.R. (1992). *Community Policing: Comparative Perspectives and Prospects*, London: Harvester Wheatsheaf.

Goldacre, B. (2012). *Bad Pharma: How Medicine Is Broken and How We Can Fix It*, London: Fourth Estate.

Goode, J. and Lumsden, K. (2016). 'The McDonaldisation of police – academic partnerships', *Policing and Society*, online.

Greenhalgh, T., Howick, J. and Maskrey, N. (2014). 'Evidence-based medicine: A movement in crisis', *British Medical Journal*, 348: 3725, 1–7.

Hardill, I. and Mills, S. (2013). 'Enlivening evidence-based policy through embodiment and emotions', *Contemporary Social Sciences*, 8(3): 321–32.

Heron, J. (1996). *Co-operative Inquiry: Research into the Human Condition*, London: Sage.

Hope, T. (2009). 'The illusion of control: A response to Professor Sherman', *Criminology and Criminal Justice*, 9(2): 125–34.

Hough, M. (2010). 'Gold standard or fool's gold? The pursuit of certainty in experimental criminology', *Criminology and Criminal Justice*, 10(1): 11–22.

Kogan, M., Henkel, M. and Hanney, S. (2006). *Government and Research: Thirty Years of Evolution*, Dordrecht: Springer.

Kotter, J. (1995). 'Leading change: Why transformation efforts fail', *Harvard Business Review*, March/April, 59–67.

Lenzer, J. (2013). 'Why we can't trust clinical guidelines', *British Medical Journal*, 346: 3830.

Lipsky, M. (1980). *Street-Level Bureaucracy*, New York: Russell Sage Foundation.

Martin, P. and Mazerolle, L. (2016). 'Police leadership in fostering evidence-based agency Reform', *Policing*, 10(1): 34–43.

Martin, S. (2010). 'Co-production of social research: Strategies for engaged scholarship', *Public Money and Management*, 30(4): 211–18.

NICE. (2012). *Methods for the Development of NICE Public Health Guidance*, 3rd edition. Retrieved from www.nice.org.uk/aboutnice/howwework/developingnicepublichealth guidance/publichealthguidanceprocessandmethodguides/public_health_guidance_pro cess_and_method_guides.jsp

Nutley, S.M., Powell, A. and Davies, H.T.O. (2013). *What Counts as Good Evidence?* London: Alliance for Useful Evidence.

Nutley, S.M., Walter, I. and Davies, H.T.O. (2007). *Using Evidence: How Research Can Inform Public Services*, Bristol: The Policy Press.

Ocloo, J. and Matthews, R. (2016). 'From tokenism to empowerment: Progressing patient and public involvement in healthcare improvement', *British Medical Journal Quality and Safety*, online first.

Ostrom, E. and Baugh, W.H. (1973). *Community Organization and the Provision of Police Services*, Beverly Hills: Sage Publications.

Ostrom, E., Parks, R.B., Whitaker, G.P. and Percy, S.L. (1978). 'The public service production process: A framework for analyzing police services', *Policy Studies Journal*, 7(1): 381–9.

Pain, R., et al. (2015). *Mapping Alternative Impact: Alternative Approaches to Impact from Co-Produced Research*, Durham: Centre for Social Justice and Community Action. Retrieved from www.dur.ac.uk/beacon/socialjustice/prh/impact/

Parks, R.B., Baker, P.C., Kiser, L., Oakerson, R., Ostrom, E., Ostrom, V., Percy, S.L., Vandivort, M.B., Whitaker, G.P. and Wilson, R. (1981). 'Consumers as coproducers of public services: Some economic and institutional considerations', *Policy Studies Journal*, 9(7): 1001–11.

Pawson, R. (2013). *The Science of Evaluation: A Realist Manifesto*, London: Sage.

Pawson, R. and Tilley, N. (1997). *Realistic Evaluation*, London: Sage.

Pohl, C., Rist, S., Zimmernann, A., Fry, P., Gurung, G. S., Schneider, F., Speranza, C.I., Kiteme, B., Boillat, S., Serrano, E., Hirsch Hadron, G. and Wiesmann, U. (2010). 'Researchers' roles in knowledge co-production', *Science and Public Policy*, 37(4): 267–81.

Rawlins, M. (2014). 'Evidence, values and decision-making', *International Journal of Technology Assessment in Health Care*, 30(2): 233–8.

Realpe, A. and Wallace, L.M. (2010). *What Is Co-production?* London: The Health Foundation.

Reiner, R. (2010). *The Politics of the Police*, 4th edition, Oxford: Oxford University Press.

Rock, P. (1990). *Helping Victims of Crime*, Oxford: Oxford University Press.

Rothschild Lord. (1971). *The Organisation and Management of Government Research and Development*, Cmnd 4814, London: HMSO.

Scraton, P. (2016). *Hillsborough: The Truth*, London: Mainstream Publishing.

Sherman, L.W. (1998). 'Evidence-Based Policing', in *Ideas in American Policing*, Washington, DC: Police Foundation.

Sherman, L.W. (2009). 'Evidence and liberty: The promise of experimental criminology', *Criminology and Criminal Justice*, 9(1): 15–28.

Sherman, L.W. (2013). 'The rise of evidence-based policing: Targeting, testing, and tracking', *Crime and Justice*, 377–451.

Sherman, L.W. (2015). 'A tipping point for "totally evidenced policing"', *International Criminal Justice Review*, 25(1): 11–29.

Sparrow, M. (2016) *Handcuffed: What Holds Policing Back, and the Keys to Reform*, Washington, DC: Brookings Institution Press.

Thacher, D. (2001). 'Policing is not a treatment: Alternatives to the medical model of police research', *Journal of Research in Crime and Delinquency*, 38(4): 387–415.

Tilley, N. (2009). 'Sherman vs Sherman: Realism and rhetoric', *Criminology and Criminal Justice*, 9(2): 135–44.

Tyler, T. (2010). *Why People Cooperate*, Princeton, NJ: Princeton University Press.

Ungar, M., McGrath, P., Black, D., Sketris, I., Whitman, S. and Liebenberg, L. (2015). 'Contribution of participatory action research to knowledge mobilization in mental health services for children and families', *Qualitative Social Work*, Online first.

Vangen, S. and Huxham, C. (2003). 'Enacting leadership for collaborative advantage', *British Journal of Management*, 14: S61–76.

Weisburd, D. and Neyroud, P. (2011, January). 'Police Science: Toward a New Paradigm', in *New Perspectives in Policing*, Washington: NIJ.

Willis, J.J. (2013). 'Improving Police: What's Craft Got to Do with It?', in *Ideas in American Policing*, p. 16, Washington, DC: Police Foundation.

Wood, J. and Bradley, D. (2009). 'Embedding partnership policing: What we've learned from the Nexus policing project', *Police Practice and Research*, 10(2): 133–44.

13 Conclusion

A realistic agenda for evidence-based policing

Lisa Tompson and Johannes Knutsson

This chapter considers how evidence-based policing (EBP) might evolve to truly enhance policing. It draws heavily on the contributions to the book and concludes by outlining a roadmap towards an inclusive definition of evidence and EBP. First, we reflect on why we feel a recasting of EBP is needed.

Few would contest that the police role in the twenty-first century is both broad and complex. In addition to dealing with many routine tasks, as well as ongoing serious offending, contemporary police have to respond to crimes enabled by the Internet, such as online fraud and child sexual abuse; perform a counterterrorism role; and operate under even greater scrutiny than before. This comes at a time when resources are not increasing commensurately with public expectations of the police role; indeed in some countries, such as the UK, severe budget cuts have been imposed on the police.

One putative solution to the problem of police demand diversification is professionalisation. Among other things, the ambition of the professionalisation agenda is to equip police officers with greater knowledge and critical thinking skills so that they might perform their jobs more effectively and efficiently. In turn, this is believed to free up resources for the increasing demands on their service.

The evidence base espoused by EBP is specifically intended to draw upon research. The vision is that research findings should be taken into the heart of practitioner decision-making so that they inform and influence how decisions are made. In principle, this befits a range of decision-making, from 'top-down' decisions promulgated down the ranks by senior officers, to 'bottom-up' discretionary decisions made by officers at the frontline. Likewise, both strategic and tactical decisions might profit from the consideration of research findings. Ultimately, though, practitioners need to exercise judgement that is formed through their professional knowledge, to decide upon the relevance of research evidence and how to integrate it into decisions.

So what do the police need to know if they are to inform their judgements with research-based evidence? First, a good understanding of the situation about which they are making an operational (or strategic) decision is a helpful foundation. This may include, for example, the nature of a crime or disorder problem, public opinion on a policing matter, or relevant organisational structure and processes. A nuanced appreciation of the local context gives rise to accurate diagnosis of a problem, which in turn makes solutions to that problem more readily identifiable.

Second, police practitioners need to be able to assess whether an intervention will have a reasonable chance of success in achieving the intended outcome. This involves an appreciation of the reliability of the existing evidence base. It also involves ascertaining whether the setting, that is, the context and circumstances, and findings of a study are similarly applicable to a practitioner's specific circumstances (Cartwright and Hardie, 2012). In short, determining whether research evidence is relevant for informing operational decision-making requires a practitioner to judge whether 'what worked there, then, will work for my local issue here, now'.

One of the central arguments throughout this book is that one should not be seduced by the notion that randomised control trials (RCTs) can provide all the answers to the evidence needs of police practitioners. They can, typically, provide plausible evidence on the relationship between an intervention and an outcome. But the strong internal validity for which RCTs are known does not translate to external validity, which is the ability to generalise from the specific study to other settings (Hough, 2010; Eck, this volume). RCTs therefore fall short of helping police practitioners pragmatically decide whether something that has been tried and tested elsewhere will help to solve their local problems and/or satisfy their local stakeholders.

It is clear from a number of chapters in this book that RCTs cannot be universally applied to all research questions that address police evidence needs. To rehearse the points identified:

- The police are expected to act decisively in difficult and changeable situations. Their evidence needs are aligned to these fast-paced timescales. Emergent problems such as cybercrime and human trafficking pose great challenges to the police, and research is struggling to keep pace with the swiftness of these developments. This is particularly acute for RCTs, because well-conducted ones can take a long time to execute. Presently, then, there is a temporal mismatch between the evidence needs of the police and the timeliness with which those needs can be met by RCT studies.
- Social life is messy and convoluted, and interventions involving social actors are necessarily complex. To increase the reliability of findings, RCTs seek to control extraneous influences on the effect. This minimises or standardises the social processes that contribute to the intervention. Human factors, such as the operational discretion of the police, are potentially critical to the implementation and execution of an intervention. Ignoring their potential influence may prove counterproductive to producing useful evidence.
- The sets of circumstances that lend themselves to an RCT – that is, routinised programmes implemented in a standardised manner across multiple departments or jurisdictions – are not that common in policing (Sparrow, 2016). Instead, crime (or other) problems are often in flux, meaning that they change over the lifespan of an RCT, thereby compromising the reliability of the findings. On a related note, rare events, such as public disorder events or acts of terrorism, are not amenable to randomised sampling. There are hence many questions that RCTs are not well placed to answer.

The chapters in this book have shown, individually and collectively, that there is a deficit between the knowledge the police require to make better informed decisions and the types of evidence championed by the mainstream EBP community. Therefore, the central argument here is that the definition of EBP by some leading proponents to date does not holistically serve the evidence needs of the police. It is not fit-for-purpose. As we elaborate next, our conceptualisation of EBP is more inclusive and, we reason, comes closer to meeting the police requirement.

What evidence is needed to advance EBP?

Assessing whether a past intervention is transferable to another place, time, or situation requires deeper knowledge than just whether something 'worked'. Instead it entails answers to the questions concerning *why* it worked and whether that effect can be replicated. This hinges on a thorough understanding of the active ingredient – the *mechanism* – through which an intervention achieves its effects (see Bowers et al., this volume). Numerous factors may thwart a theoretically plausible mechanism from firing in an intervention. For instance, there may be contextual conditions that do not support the activation of the mechanism. Similarly, there might be barriers to implementing an intervention to prevent the contextual conditions interacting with the mechanism.

The EMMIE framework was devised to speak to the evidence needs of policymakers and practitioners. The acronym encapsulates five broad categories of evidence that are considered germane to decisions about crime prevention: the Effect of an intervention, the causal Mechanism(s) through which interventions are intended to work, the factors that Moderate intervention effectiveness, Implementation issues that may impede or facilitate the intervention, and the Economic costs of interventions (Johnson et al., 2015). In essence, the framework is built around factors that facilitate the firing of the mechanism to enable the intervention to 'work'.

The EMMIE framework is anchored in the principles of realist evaluation (Pawson and Tilley, 1997). At its heart, this perspective is concerned with an explicit focus on mechanisms and the contexts in which the mechanisms work. Few social interventions are context insensitive (Eck, 2002). Thus context is not just the backdrop of an intervention, but may well be an interactive component – the intervention can interact *with* the context to produce the effect. There is therefore a palpable danger in practitioners being encouraged to replicate interventions that have been shown to 'work' in different settings without due consideration of the level of context sensitivity attached to the results. What works in one location, under specific conditions, may not work elsewhere in different circumstances.

As Pawson and Tilley (1997) eloquently argue, implementing effective crime control practices requires far more wide-ranging knowledge than just 'what works'. To ascertain if a change in practice will result in favourable outcomes, a practitioner needs to have information on the context in which the intervention is likely to work and, simultaneously, information on the mechanism which led to the change: the 'how'. With both these pieces of information the practitioner is then able to make a judgment on the extent to which the initiative is likely to work in 'their' context (Johnson et al., 2015).

Contextual understanding is founded on solid analysis of the conditions that underpin local problems (Eck, 2002; Braga, 2008) and the operational policing environment (Braga, 2016). This is at the heart of problem-oriented policing endeavours, whereby understanding the problem is a critical step in being able to devise an effective solution. Historically, EBP has attached little weight to in-house analysis in police forces, though this is now changing. Sherman (2013) recently advocated an analytical approach when proposing his 'triple T' strategy. The triple T's refer to *targeting* (analysis), *testing* (experimenting), and *tracking* (the close monitoring of police activity). It could be argued that, using different terminology, Sherman (2015) is loosely describing the process of problem-oriented policing. As Scott (this volume) observes, there are certain areas of agreement across problem-oriented and evidence-based policing that would be worth exploring further.

In order for policing to evolve, we contend that greater emphasis needs to be given to the analytical competence within forces. To a large degree this pertains to the formal analytical function – the professional 'crime analysts' and 'embedded criminologists' (see Braga and Davis, 2014). Yet the insights provided by such analysis have been perennially underappreciated (Belur and Johnson, 2016). The professionalisation agenda seeks to challenge this by emphasising the importance of critical thinking and of being data led in practitioner understanding.

In extending the policing educational curriculum, police officers will be exposed to research methods, which will enable them to be intelligent customers of research or to become involved in conducting research and analysis themselves. This facilitates their involvement in generating 'practice-based evidence' (Boba, 2010), which relates to a 'bottom-up' approach to evidence generation, driven by the practitioner's experiential knowledge. This is in contrast to the 'top-down' approach, typically led by academics, that has characterised EBP to date.

Acknowledging the value that police experiential knowledge can bring to evidence generation is one means of increasing the relevance of the evidence base. Few would doubt that for the majority of police officers experience trumps research as their preferred source of evidence. Rather than seeing *craft* and *science* as competing forces in an evidence-based model, it seems to us that a true police profession requires an appreciation of both. Practice-based knowledge stemming from the police 'craft' can be systematically collected, analysed, and organised in such a way that it becomes scientific. Experiential police knowledge can usefully be turned into testable hypotheses or can guide the implementation of a new practice (Knutsson, this volume). The critical and rigorous use of experiential knowledge requires collaborative partnerships across police and academic communities. In these circumstances, the value that the fusion of craft and science can bring to the evidence-based policing model could be profound.

Another form of contextual understanding that should influence police decision-making is awareness of the broader implications of a new practice. This might pertain to (say) public perceptions, outcomes that affect wider stakeholders, or officer attitudes. As Maxfield et al. (this volume) illustrate with Lum et al.'s (2015) detailed analysis of the literature on body-worn cameras, evidence gaps on the impact of new practices are common. Lum and colleagues identify seven broad areas for research on body-worn cameras: 1) officer attitudes, 2) citizen and community attitudes, 3) impact of cameras on officer behaviour, 4) impact of cameras on citizen behaviour, 5) impact on criminal and internal police investigations, 6) impact on police organisations, and 7) national prevalence of use of body-worn cameras. Several of these areas cannot be studied with quantitative investigation, but require qualitative methods. A diversity of methodological approaches are hence required to broaden the current lens of EBP so that knowledge gaps can be authentically filled.

Qualitative methods have not historically been championed by EBP enthusiasts. Such methods are unconcerned with internal validity and thus do not feature on the Maryland Scientific Methods Scale (Sherman et al., 1997). This might be taken to imply that qualitative methods lack the 'quality' that is aspired to in evidence-based policing. The wide array of quality appraisal tools for quantitative and qualitative designs (e.g., see West et al., 2002), however, provide a different view. These expose that the *execution* of research has a noteworthy role to play in quality. The suitability of the research design for answering the research question, or hypothesis, is similarly important in deciding upon the quality of the research. Hence, the 'best available evidence', championed by EBP proponents, depends very much on the question being asked and the matching of this to an appropriate method.

Our vision of how EBP can advance

The role of research evidence in police decision-making is to reduce uncertainty. The history of science teaches us that confidence in evidence is fleeting, and its currency lasts until it is supplanted by a superior theory or observation. It is, as Tilley (2015) suggests, prudent to view evidence as falling on a continuum from 'inchy' to 'clinchy'. At one end, is evidence that 'inches' towards building confidence and at the other end is evidence that 'clinches' that confidence. In our open conceptualisation of EBP we propose that more efforts be directed towards research evidence that inches towards less uncertainty. This can be achieved with a plurality of evidence, coming from a variety of methodological quarters, with an emphasis on that which is carried out with rigour.

To date, the experiences from the research supporting the What Works Centre for Crime Reduction have been that the existing crime prevention research often fails to offer practitioners a full understanding of how to relate research findings to their own context (Hunter et al., 2016). Populating the EMMIE framework with evidence from systematic reviews has been challenging, because many reviews concerned with the effects of intervention are silent on the moderators or implementation factors that might activate the causal mechanism(s). This is partly attributable to the lack of this type of information in the primary studies on which these reviews are founded, and partly attributable to the reporting requirements of systematic reviews hitherto.

What can be done to improve this situation? There is growing support that attention should be directed to developing knowledge of mechanisms of interventions and the contexts in which they work best (Cartwright and Hardie, 2012). This has the potential to increase knowledge about the generalisability of an intervention, which is invaluable to the practitioner who wishes to know if it is likely to successfully address their local problem.

RCTs are good for testing the plausibility of causal mechanisms. However, the theory underpinning the understanding of a mechanism needs to be well developed before it can be subjected to rigorous testing. As Tilley (2015) notes, in medicine RCTs are preceded by a lot of 'heavy lifting' in terms of theory development and testing, using multiple methods. The policing field needs similar developmental work to underpin the design of RCTs.

The development of theory benefits from a smorgasbord of evidence, from a range of methodological perspectives, because each contributes different insights. The collective wisdom of many contributors to this book is that research that produces knowledge about police practice and processes – at the 'grassroots level' – has much to offer the development of theory. As elucidated in the earlier chapters, these could include evaluation studies of problem-oriented policing projects, knowledge that is co-produced by police–researcher partnerships and qualitative studies, or evaluation studies inspired by Bayesian methods. Such studies are the product of police–researcher collaborative partnerships, requiring both advanced research skills and access to, and knowledge of, the policing environment.

As internal validity is often an unrealistic aim in studies of fast-moving policing environments, such studies do not feature highly on the Maryland Scale, with the implicit assumption that they lack the methodological sophistication to provide worthwhile evidence. They do, however, offer rich information about the realities of conducting interventions in complex social and operational environments. They therefore have an important role to play in documenting contextual conditions that might moderate the effect of an intervention, or the implementation conditions that are necessary to support a positive outcome.

In medicine the distinction between 'efficacy' – that is, what works in laboratory conditions – and 'effectiveness', which is what happens in the real world, has provided clear guidance in translating evidence into policy or practice. We suggest this distinction is similarly relevant in policing. Studies documenting police practices and processes can contribute to revealing the distinctions between effectiveness and efficacy.

The accumulation over time of many diverse primary studies produces a knowledge base which can inform the design and implementation of RCTs. The EMMIE framework can be harnessed as a synthesis framework to consolidate findings into an *evidence* base. That is, with the aim of building stronger theories, studies can be synthesised according to whether they share a similar mechanism (theory of change), moderator (context), or implementation conditions. For example, some police practices invoke a mechanism of shaming the offender. These can be synthesised to generate fresh insight into the conditions under which this mechanism fires and, perhaps more importantly, backfires. Reflecting on the different circumstances in which a mechanism has been tested may give rise to fresh insight into the contextual conditions that support it working effectively. Synthesising knowledge in this way thus enables advances in theoretical understanding of the *processes* involved in successful police practice. Moreover, synthesis can increase the rigour of the evidence base by considering what the picture *as a whole* is telling us about police practice. For instance, a police practice that has been successfully observed over varied settings indicates that the underlying theory might be strong enough to generalise to other settings.

The synthesis of practice-based studies, absent from strict methodological principles, is not a new idea. Problem-oriented policing guides, produced by the U.S. POP Center, are produced in this spirit.[1] The documented responses to a crime problem are listed in an appendix with columns titled 'How they work' (mechanism), 'Work best if' (conditions under which they ought to be effective), and 'Considerations' (factors to consider before implementing). In this manner the guides' framework are similar to the EMMIE framework. They have a special place in the heart of many practitioners.

Towards an inclusive and open definition of EBP

One of the prominent critiques of progress to date is that 'evidence-based policing' has become closely associated with 'evidence-based crime prevention' (Telep, 2016), despite crime control being a small part of a police officer's role. The 'what works' agenda is primarily centred on *tactics* the police can use. It does not focus as intently on the myriad other tasks the police are expected to do or the organisational infrastructure that supports these. A focus on straightforward outcomes of police activity – like arrest – have been at the expense of understanding the *processes* and *people* who have been involved in producing the observed outcomes (Willis and Mastrofski, 2016). In the inclusive EBP model we are proposing, we echo others (e.g., see Greene, 2014; Telep, 2016) in arguing that evidence needs to infiltrate other areas of police business to support decision-making. Recruitment, training, communication, occupational health, and public satisfaction all seem areas that are ripe for building and consolidating an evidence base. It is our contention that it would be beneficial to the police if the full scope of policing responsibilities were to be integrated into the evidence-based practice movement.

A central message of this book is that at certain times and places RCTs can be very useful, but those times and places are rather limited. We believe that the evidence needs of police practitioners are difficult to meet with the existing evidence base that is reliant on experimental designs. The breadth of modern policing demands a breadth of knowledge accumulation. The chapters in this book propose alternative ways of thinking about evidence generation and about how we might integrate that evidence into improved police practice.

We believe that the EMMIE framework holds great value in advancing our theoretical understanding of police processes and practices. This framework can harmonise mainstream EBP and problem-oriented policing. It speaks to the knowledge requirements of practitioners and values their input in shaping evidence. It offers a framework for synthesising practice-based evidence (e.g., by mechanism or moderator) so that it becomes more robust and reliable. It is inclusive in recognising that a blend of research perspectives and a variety of knowledge are a fruitful means of advancing insight into issues related to policing (Tilley, 2016). Our suggested model of evidence generation is not intended to dislodge the conventional way of deriving knowledge about effectiveness in police practice. Instead, we hope that it complements thinking about evidence that provides actionable information to the police.

The evidence generated through an inclusive conceptualisation of EBP has the potential to feed directly into the 'bottom-up discretion' decision-making that Sherman (2009) and Tilley (2009) discuss. It speaks to the context-rich nuances that are prevalent in such discretionary situations. 'Top-down' guidance, in contrast, usually comes from governments or senior police officers and cannot account for context-sensitive elements of practice. Moreover, guidance needs to be reliable because significant resources are usually needed to deliver the associated policies. It could be argued that mainstream EBP evidence has been best suited for this latter form of decision-making. The inclusive EBP that we are proposing provides a better balance to the different types of decision-making in police work.

Lastly, we think EBP could best advance if we take an inclusive approach to the different epistemic communities, with differing ideas on what is useful knowledge, working within it. As Greene (2014) outlines, such communities often have the same goal. In our case this is the empowerment of police officers with knowledge rooted in evidence, so that they might individually, and collectively, make better decisions. Working competitively across communities impedes the speed at which we are able to achieve this goal. It would, instead, be preferable to maintain a dialogue about the direction of travel EBP should take through rigorous scientific communication. In this way dialogue can usefully challenge the underlying tenets of different epistemic approaches to evidence generation. Hopefully, this can be done within the overarching aim of pursuing stronger theories and improved insight about policing. If successful in realising our aims, we have the chance to make a tangible contribution to the evolution of policing into a true evidence-led profession.

Note

1 These are small handbooks – guides – which are written by researchers and informed by a thorough review of literature and police practice. To ensure quality and utility the guides are peer reviewed by both practitioners and researchers. The *problem-specific* guides summarise knowledge about how police can reduce harm caused by specific crime and disorder problems. They follow a format which encourages practitioners to assess whether their local problem is likely to be reduced by one (or more) of the documented responses. For the library of guides see www.popcenter.org.

References

Belur, J. and Johnson, S. (2016). 'Is crime analysis at the heart of policing practice? A case study', *Policing and Society*. 1–19, doi: 10.1080/10439463.2016.1262364.

Boba, R. (2010). 'A practice-based evidence approach in Florida', *Police Practice and Research*, 11: 122–8.

Braga, A.A. (2008). *Problem-Oriented Policing and Crime Prevention*, 2nd edition, Boulder, CO: Lynne Rienner Publishers.

Braga, A.A. (2016). 'The value of "pracademics" in enhancing crime analysis in police departments', *Policing*, 10(3): 1–7, doi: 10.1093/police/paw032

Braga, A.A. and Davis, E.F. (2014). 'Implementing science in police agencies: The embedded research model', *Policing*, 8(4): 294–306.

Cartwright, N. and Hardie, J. (2012). *Evidence-Based Policy: A Practical Guide to Doing It Better*, New York: Oxford University Press.

Eck, J.E. (2002). 'Learning from Experience in Problem-Oriented Policing: The Positive Functions of Weak Evaluations and the Negative Functions of Strong Ones', in N. Tilley (ed) *Evaluation for Crime Prevention*, pp. 93–117, Crime Prevention Studies, vol. 14, Monsey: Criminal Justice Press.

Greene, J.R. (2014). 'The upside and downside of the 'police science' epistemic community', *Policing*, (8)4: 379–92.

Hough, M. (2010). 'Gold standard or fool's gold: The pursuit of certainty in experimental criminology', *Criminology and Criminal Justice*, 10(1): 11–22.

Hunter, G., Wigzell, A., Bhardwa, B., May, T. and Hough, M. (2016). *An Evaluation of the What Works Centre for Crime Reduction Year 2: Progress*, London: ICPR.

Johnson, S.D., Tilley, N. and Bowers, K.J. (2015). 'Introducing EMMIE: An evidence rating scale to encourage mixed-method crime prevention synthesis reviews', *Journal of Experimental Criminology*, 11(3): 459–73.

Lum, C., Koper, C., Merola, L.M., Scherer, A. and Reioux, A. (2015). *Existing and Ongoing Body Worn Camera Research: Knowledge Gaps and Opportunities*, Report for the Laura and John Arnold Foundation, Fairfax, VA: Center for Evidence-Based Crime Policy, George Mason University.

Pawson, R. and Tilley, N. (1997). *Realistic Evaluation*, London: Sage.

Sherman, L. (2009). 'Evidence and liberty: The promise of experimental criminology', *Criminology and Criminal Justice*, 9(1): 5–28.

Sherman, L. (2013). 'The rise of evidence-based policing: Targeting, testing, and tracking', *Crime and Justice*, 42(1): 377–451.

Sherman, L. (2015). 'A tipping point for "totally evidenced policing"', *International Criminal Justice Review*, 25(1): 11–29.

Sherman, L., Gottfredson, D., MacKenzie, D., Eck, J., Reuter, P. and Bushway, S. (1997). *Preventing Crime: What Works, What Doesn't, What's Promising*, Washington, DC: U.S. Department of Justice, Office of Justice Programs.

Sparrow, M. (2016). *Handcuffed: What Holds Policing Back, and the Keys to Reform*, Washington, DC: Brookings Institution Press.

Telep, C.W. (2016). 'Expanding the scope of evidence-based policing', *Criminology & Public Policy*, 15(1): 1–10.

Tilley, N. (2009). 'Sherman v Sherman: Realism vs rhetoric', *Criminology and Criminal Justice*, 9(2): 135–44.

Tilley, N. (2015, 5 November). *The Big Debate: RCTs and Realist Evaluation, Presented at: The State of the Art of Realist Methodology*, Leeds, UK.

Tilley, N. (2016). 'EMMIE and engineering: What works as evidence to improve decisions?', *Evaluation*, 22(3): 304–22.

West, S., King, V. Carey, T.S., Lohr, K.N., McKoy, N., Sutton, S.F., Lux, L. (2002, April). *Systems to Rate the Strength of Scientific Evidence. Evidence Report/Technology Assessment No. 47*, Prepared by the Research Triangle Institute – University of North Carolina Evidence-based Practice Center under Contract No. 290–97–0011. AHRQ Publication No. 02-E016, Rockville, MD: Agency for Healthcare Research and Quality.

Willis, J.J. and Mastrofski, S.D. (2016). 'Improving policing by integrating craft and science: What can patrol officers teach us about good police work?', *Policing and Society*, doi: 10.1080/10439463.2015.1135921

Index